I0888839

Respectability and Reform

Irish Studies
James MacKillop, *Series Editor*

SELECT TITLES IN IRISH STUDIES

The Banshees: A Literary History of Irish American Women Writers
Sally Barr Ebest

Compassionate Stranger: Asenath Nicholson and the Great Irish Famine
Maureen O'Rourke Murphy

The Irish Bridget: Irish Immigrant Women in Domestic Service in America, 1840–1930
Margaret Lynch-Brennan

J. M. Synge and Travel Writing of the Irish Revival
Giulia Bruna

Kate O'Brien and Spanish Literary Culture
Jane Davison

Laying Out the Bones: Death and Dying in the Modern Irish Novel
Bridget English

"Other People's Diasporas": Negotiating Race in Contemporary Irish and Irish American Culture
Sinéad Moynihan

Relocated Memories: The Great Famine in Irish and Diaspora Fiction, 1846–1870
Marguérite Corporaal

Respectability and Reform

Irish American Women's Activism, 1880–1920

Tara M. McCarthy

Syracuse University Press

Copyright © 2018 by Syracuse University Press
Syracuse, New York 13244-5290

All Rights Reserved

First Edition 2018
18 19 20 21 22 23 6 5 4 3 2 1

∞ The paper used in this publication meets the minimum requirements of the American National Standard for Information Sciences—Permanence of Paper for Printed Library Materials, ANSI Z39.48—1992.

For a listing of books published and distributed by Syracuse University Press, visit www.SyracuseUniversityPress.syr.edu.

ISBN: 978-0-8156-3570-3 (hardcover) 978-0-8156-3588-8 (paperback)
978-0-8156-5436-0 (e-book)

Library of Congress Cataloging-in-Publication Data
Names: McCarthy, Tara M., author.
Title: Respectability and reform : Irish American women's activism, 1880–1920 / Tara M. McCarthy.
Other titles: Irish American women's activism, 1880–1920
Description: First edition. | Syracuse, New York : Syracuse University Press, [2018] | Series: Irish studies | Includes bibliographical references and index.
Identifiers: LCCN 2018000376 (print) | LCCN 2018000670 (ebook) | ISBN 9780815654360 (e-book) | ISBN 9780815635703 (hardcover : alk. paper) | ISBN 9780815635888 (pbk. : alk. paper)
Subjects: LCSH: Irish-American women—Political activity. | Women political activists—United States—History. | Irish question. | Ladies' Land League—History. | Labor movement—United States—History. | Women—Suffrage—United States—History. | Women social reformers—United States—History. | Irish-American women—History. | Irish Americans—Politics and government.
Classification: LCC E184.I6 (ebook) | LCC E184.I6 M116 2018 (print) | DDC 305.48/89162073—dc23
LC record available at https://lccn.loc.gov/2018000376

Manufactured in the United States of America

To Aidan and Ainsley

Contents

Illustrations

Acknowledgments

Finishing this book manuscript, which has been part of my life for so long, inspires quite a lot of reflection. I have been blessed by the support of mentors, family, and friends throughout the process. This project originated as a dissertation at the University of Rochester, where I first benefited from the vision, guidance, and patience of my adviser, Lynn D. Gordon, and second reader Dan Borus. Also while at the University of Rochester, I had the opportunity to participate in a conference focusing on the life and times of Susan B. Anthony, which resulted in an edited book project. Thank you to Christine Ridarsky and Mary Huth for including my chapter in *Susan B. Anthony and the Struggle for Equal Rights* (2012). The community of women's historians I met in western New York has helped me to develop as a scholar and as an educator.

A project like this one depends on the help of librarians, archivists, and interlibrary loan staff. I have benefited from their expertise and aid in making the research possible. With the help of friends who let me sleep on their couches, I made research trips to Boston, New York, and Philadelphia. I would particularly like to thank the staff at the American Irish Historical Society, New York Public Library, and Schlesinger Library, but I am also indebted to those archivists who sent me copies of sources when I could not visit. I also received a grant from the Irish American Cultural Institute–Irish Research Fund to help support my research.

My years at Central Michigan University have been productive, thanks in large part to generous support for research and conference presentations, including an early career grant and a sabbatical leave. I would also like to thank friends and colleagues here in Michigan for acting as a sounding board and providing support as I revised the manuscript. My editors at Syracuse University Press embraced this project. Thank you to Jennika Baines and Deborah Manion for their enthusiasm, guidance, and understanding and to the anonymous reviewers who sharpened the focus of this book. I hope I have been able to incorporate your suggestions.

Finally, I would like to remember those lost during the years that I have been working on this project: my parents, Eileen McCarthy and Francis McCarthy; my adviser Lynn Gordon; and my dissertation committee members, Harold Wechsler and Brenda Meehan. My life has been enriched by your passion, your knowledge, your guidance, and your generosity. This book is dedicated to my children—who teach, challenge, and inspire me every day.

Abbreviations

AARIR	American Association for the Recognition of the Irish Republic
AFL	American Federation of Labor
AOH	Ancient Order of Hibernians
APA	American Protective Association
CTF	Chicago Teachers' Federation
FOIF	Friends of Irish Freedom
INLA	Irish National League of America
IPL	Irish Progressive League
LAAOH	Ladies' Auxiliary of the Ancient Order of Hibernians
NAWSA	National American Woman Suffrage Association
NWP	National Woman's Party
UILA	United Irish League of America
WIEL	Women's Irish Education League
WTUL	Women's Trade Union League
WWS	Working Women's Society

Respectability and Reform

Introduction

In 1915, when former Fenian Jeremiah O'Donovan Rossa died, his body was returned to Ireland. Although he had been living in exile for many years, his funeral in Dublin became the biggest nationalist demonstration before the Easter Rising the following year. When Rossa's widow died in New York in 1916, an Irish immigrant named Marguerite Moore paid tribute to her old friend, describing her as "the brave, noble wife, who stood unfalteringly by his side and cheered him on in the thorny paths that must be trodden by the true Irish patriot." Moore, by then described in New York's *Irish World* as a "motherly looking woman, in the true sense of the word," and a "remarkable old lady," was a veteran of the Ladies' Land League of the 1880s, who helped fire up a new generation in America to fight for Irish freedom. At a memorial meeting in honor of Mrs. O'Donovan Rossa, Moore presented a message "from those about whom the sunset clouds are gathering to those of the younger generation, who are taking up the burden and who are not replacing the elders, but following them."[1] As the lives of both Mary Jane O'Donovan Rossa and Marguerite Moore tell us, Irish American women had been active nationalists for many years by then, but Moore did much more, actively supporting women's suffrage, educating crowds about the labor problem, and even campaigning for political candidates. For Irish American women, nationalist activities served as one catalyst for greater participation in community concerns. Although their causes, strategies, and motivations may have differed from middle-class Protestant women, Irish American women were part of a larger trend toward women's influence on public life.

Historians have traced the development of American women's influence outside the home through the study of women's voluntary organizations, reform movements, and debates over women's political participation—particularly suffrage. In the traditional narrative, middle-class Protestant women began to expand their influence early in the nineteenth century, a process that accelerated after the Civil War as women embraced expanded educational opportunities and entered reform organizations, particularly during the Progressive Era. As a group, Irish American women have a different narrative, one that begins with Irish nationalism and the labor movement in the late nineteenth century. These opportunities allowed a heterogeneous group of Irish American women to mobilize and become activists, while also launching widespread discussion among American Catholics about women's role in public matters.

In 2009 Janet Nolan praised the increased attention of historians toward women in Irish and Irish American history. Yet she also pointed out the need for more studies of nationalism and "the impact of politically active Irish American women."[2] Women in Ireland held a highly visible and relatively well-documented role in some phases of the nationalist movement, but the experiences of American women have received less attention until recently.[3] In his classic work on nineteenth-century nationalism, Thomas Brown found no inclination toward nationalist activism on the part of Irish American women, who, he suggested, were occupied with domestic concerns.[4] While this inaccuracy has partially been corrected by recent historians, particularly for the Land League era of the 1880s, a more comprehensive view of the period from 1880 to 1920 reveals that not only did some women remain active for many years, despite the ebbs and flows of various nationalist organizations and the conflicts between male leaders, but women's rhetoric and protest methods also evolved over time as women generally became more socially and politically active in American society as a whole.[5]

A transatlantic movement to reform the land system in Ireland in the 1880s ushered in a new era of women's visibility in the nationalist movement—for many Irish American women, this would be their first experience with public activism. When an agricultural depression in the late 1870s ignited fears of another widespread famine in Ireland, Irish leaders organized for land reform under the leadership of Charles Stewart Parnell. In August 1880, his sister Fanny Parnell published a letter in the Irish American press calling on women to organize in support of the Land League, an organization formed to aid peasant farmers, prevent evictions, and secure the passage of land-reform legislation. She expressed regret at the absence of women in the Irish nationalist movement, arguing, "Land League business is essentially women's business because it is essentially a work of philanthropy and humanity." Although not a "women's rights woman," Parnell explained that she believed that "every woman has the right to do good."[6] Thus, Irish American women actually organized before their counterparts in Ireland, but under very different circumstances.

Despite Parnell's cautiously worded appeal, over the next two years thousands of Irish American women (many of whom were Catholic) answered her call to aid the motherland, leading to a transnational discussion of the proper roles of Irish Catholic laywomen who had certainly been involved in charity and fund-raising before, but not in political matters. Therefore, the significance of the Ladies' Land League in America reaches far beyond the nationalist movement because Fanny Parnell's appeal led to a new trend toward Irish American women's organization, allowing for increased community activism as well. Debates about the proper role of women, which arose out of Land League activities and inspired women's devotion (and at times defiance), also provided a catalyst for women to organize in other reform areas such as industrial matters and even women's suffrage. Over the next forty years, women played a visible role in the debates concerning the preservation of Irish American identity, the drive for socioeconomic justice, and the relationship between the Irish American community and American educational and political institutions.

This study focuses on Irish American women's contributions and commitments to three movements: the nationalist movement, the labor movement, and the suffrage movement. Each movement has its own unique history, so the three are discussed separately, although they also overlap in terms of time period and sometimes in membership as well. Viewing the development of women's political roles for the period from 1880 to 1920 highlights three points: a commitment to Irish nationalism also opened doors to community and political activism for Irish American women; Irish American activists were a heterogeneous group; and women's rhetoric and protest styles evolved over time in the context of a broader women's movement in America. Significantly, the development of nationalist, ethnic, and labor organizations in the Irish American community coincided with expanded political mobilization for American women as a whole. Irish American women were able to carve out unique opportunities to serve the needs of their own communities. For some women this also meant a commitment to labor reform and suffrage, which led Irish American women (including many Catholics) into alliances with Protestant women reformers as well.

The experiences of Irish Americans were not monolithic, as interpretations of Irish American nationalists have come to reflect. In the 1960s, Thomas Brown argued that Irish Americans' devotion to nationalism derived not from a sense of duty to the motherland but rather from the rejection, alienation, and poverty that Irish immigrants experienced in the United States. Brown believed that a longing for respectability motivated Irish immigrants to push for the independence of their homeland. Through their nationalist activities, Irish immigrants expressed anxieties about their place in America.[7]

Although Brown's emphasis on respectability continues to provide a powerful explanation of the motives of middle-class nationalists, his thesis has been complicated by other studies of diaspora nationalism in America, particularly those of Eric Foner and Matthew Frye Jacobson, who have exposed the diversity of interests that coexisted in nationalist movements, specifically the tension between the middle-class goal of respectability and the presence of a more radical worker element. Yet these contributions have neglected the role of women until recently, when Ely Janis included a chapter on the Ladies' Land League in his 2015 book on the Irish National Land League of America.[8] Pushing the analysis beyond the Land League, and even the nationalist movement, shows a wide range of reform activities for women and supports the call for a more nuanced understanding of the Irish American community based on class, religious, regional, and political differences.[9] After years of heavy migration, the Irish American community of the late nineteenth century was diverse. This heterogeneity included the attitudes and experiences of women who shared a commitment to Irish nationalism but differed among themselves in terms of class outlook, political priorities, and gender ideology. There was no one way to be Irish American.

While studies of Irish nationalism in America have historically neglected the role of women until recently, studies of Irish American women have centered on their economic concerns and contributions but have not developed a portrait of their organizational activities and political activism. In *Erin's Daughters in America: Irish Immigrant Women in the Nineteenth Century* (1983), Hasia Diner offered several insights that continue to shape the discussion of Irish American women's experiences: she pointed to the high number of young single women among Irish immigrants, their tendency to postpone marriage, and their economic independence. Despite their economic assertiveness and labor activism, Diner found little activity for laywomen outside the Catholic Church. However, her study's focus on the nineteenth century leaves out some key developments at the end of the century, including the influence of Irish nationalism in America and the expansion of organizational activities among Irish American and Catholic women beginning in the late nineteenth century.[10]

The importance of domestic service for first-generation Irish women has also led scholars to investigate the relationship and influence between newly arrived Irish women and their American middle-class mistresses. For example, Diane Hotten-Somers asked how Irish women's domestic employers "shaped their immigrant experience." She concluded not only that Irish servants were expected to adopt a new "civilized" American manner but also that the Progressive Era brought more freedom to domestics, as they were able to live independently and reconnect with the Irish American community. Similarly focusing on first-generation immigrant women, Margaret Lynch-Brennan found that their work in American middle-class homes provided domestics with "their first inroads into acceptability" and that Irish women took what they learned in American homes back to their own families.[11]

However, the focus on questions about the influence of middle-class domesticity on Irish immigrant women has obscured the contributions that Irish American women made to their communities and to public debate. As Mary Kelly pointed out in a study of New York City, women "forged a key feature of the new Irish-American culture" and significantly influenced the formation of Irish American identity through participation in nationalist, literary, and social organizations.[12] This rings true for my current study, in which women are often second generation (or grew up in the United States), did not work in service, and in some cases remained single.

In addition to studies of the Irish in America, important scholarship has been done on the contributions of Catholic women (many of whom were of Irish descent) to the development of Catholic institutions and subculture. During the Progressive Era, middle-class Catholic reformers sought to limit the influence of Protestant organizations on the Catholic working class, while improving the reputation of Catholics in America.[13] Furthermore, as Paula Kane demonstrated in her study of Boston, Catholics developed a distinctive subculture in the era between the ethnic enclaves of the nineteenth century and the acculturated but separate Catholic America of the 1950s. Catholic institution building began in the nineteenth century and greatly benefited from the initiative and vision of Catholic women. Adding to a rich body of literature on Catholic women religious, Maureen Fitzgerald demonstrated how working-class Irish women embraced convent life, emigrated to America, and used their influence (and political connections) to develop an alternative system of social welfare institutions in New York City.[14]

In addition to the significant influence of Catholic women religious, Catholic laywomen also began building national organizations, particularly auxiliaries, in the late nineteenth century. Despite the pervasiveness of conservative gender rhetoric, and women's own use of such images, Kathleen Cummings has argued, "Many Catholics in the Progressive Era translated changing gender roles in the following manner: whereas the New Woman's unabashed assaults against the social order clearly augured disaster, the daughters of the Old Faith were simply bringing ancient wisdom to bear on modern culture."[15] Despite concerns about loss of faith and values in the modern age, Catholic women employed maternalist rhetoric to justify activities outside the home, pursued charitable efforts, and embraced reform causes to improve the status and reputation of fellow Catholics in the Progressive Era.[16]

This project focuses on a small group of lay Irish American women in the Gilded Age and Progressive Era who emerged as leaders, organizers, and activists between 1880 and 1920. I have focused on community and political activism, giving preference to national organizations and movements whenever possible. The book is organized into three parts, one for each movement. Some names (like Marguerite Moore) appear in more than one section, revealing the interconnectedness of many reform movements. A portrait of these women suggests not only that Irish American women had a political tradition dating back to the 1880s, but also that the heterogeneity of the Irish American community fostered different priorities and methods of activism. While some of these activists are already known in labor and women's history circles, they also need to be placed in the context of the long history of overlap between the labor movement and Irish nationalism that has been documented among Irish American men by Eric Foner and others, including David Montgomery, who wrote, "The closer one looks the more strands appear connecting the labor movement, land reform, and Irish nationalism."[17] Irish American women's commitment to social justice persisted not only during the more radical wing of the Land League movement, but until the World War I era as well. And finally, because of the largely Catholic composition of famine and postfamine Irish migrations, religion presents an important distinction to this portrait of women's activism. While some Irish American women (largely labor reformers) worked with middle-class Protestant women, others developed or contributed to separate Catholic organizations, particularly in the twentieth century. Therefore, these stories and choices help us understand the intersection with the larger context of American women's activism during the Progressive Era.

Finding sources for the study of Irish American women (particularly working-class women) remains challenging. The papers of a few labor leaders have been well mined. To create a portrait of these activists, I began my search in the Irish American press; these women were featured in the national or ethnic press or both. Despite the limitations of newspaper sources, this approach offered several advantages. Reading widely in the Irish American press allowed me to "discover" women who did not appear in other sources (even if information on them was limited). Some of the women in this study are virtually unknown. The research also revealed how ethnic newspapers portrayed women and their activities, exposing larger debates within the Irish American community. Finally, newspapers sometimes contain the voices of women who did not leave other documentation. Many of these women left few relevant letters but did write articles for publication. Therefore, the women in this study are those who emerged as leaders and spokespeople—women who made news and were well known in their communities and causes. The women of the Ancient Order of Hibernians provide the best example. The monthly newspaper of the AOH published articles by leading women on a regular basis in the early twentieth century, and these women also wrote about their activities in the Irish American press. Because most of these groups did not leave records, newspapers are still the best way to identify organizational activities and the women who led them.

There is no one "typical" Irish American experience, but opportunities for Irish American women expanded beginning in the late nineteenth century (as they also expanded for women in general) when women joined nationalist organizations, created new auxiliaries to religious and ethnic organizations, and supported labor and reform movements. This study begins in the 1880s not only because the unprecedented public agitation of Irish American women through the Ladies' Land League led to serious discussion of the roles and responsibilities of Catholic laywomen, a debate that did not end with the decline of the movement, but also because the labor movement of the 1880s inspired a new generation of women labor organizers as well.

Chapter 1 presents a general overview of life in the Irish American community, with particular attention to immigration trends, women's work patterns, women's role in the Catholic Church, and the development of women's ethnic organizations—specifically the Ladies' Auxiliary of the Ancient Order of Hibernians (LAAOH). This introductory chapter is followed by an in-depth discussion of Irish American women's role in the labor movement, beginning with the Knights of Labor in the 1880s. As the support of union men waned with the decline of the Knights of Labor, Irish American women needed new allies and new strategies. Therefore, beginning at the end of the nineteenth century, a small group of female labor activists forged their own reform outlook, often cooperating with middle-class Protestant reformers as they sought legal protections for working women, including protective laws for women and women's suffrage. Irish American women were pioneers in the labor movement, not only for industrial unionism but for teachers' unions as well. As Irish American women moved into teaching in significant numbers, particularly by the end of the nineteenth century, Irish American teachers became leaders in the effort to "secure professional status for teachers," including job security and professional autonomy.[18]

Chapter 3 argues that the Land League, a short-lived but popular agitation for land reform in Ireland, represents a watershed for Irish American women. The participation of women in this movement had important implications for gender roles. In the unique context of the Irish American community, nationalism provided a starting point for women to exercise political influence. It not only launched a dialogue on women's political roles, but also led women toward a greater level of organization and activism. Although, at the time, some supporters argued that women performed charitable works and therefore did not transgress traditional gender boundaries, others recognized their activities as a departure into the world of politics. A few high-ranking Catholics officials, on both sides of the Atlantic, publicly denounced the women's activities, but the American Irish generally supported women's participation, at least initially. As a unifying factor in the Irish American community and an expression of identity, nationalism allowed women to transcend traditional gender roles in the name of service, duty, and patriotism.

The Land League lasted only a few years. However, the temporary nature of the movement does not suggest that women receded from view after its decline. The anxieties that Irish Americans expressed through diaspora nationalism continued to fester after 1882, particularly through land and labor reform. In an age of tremendous economic instability, a radical faction within the Land League, inspired by the land theories of Henry George, continued to agitate for widescale reform of industrial capitalism during the 1880s. Irish Americans pointed out the parallels between injustice in Ireland and their own vulnerability in America, seeking political solutions to economic problems. Eric Foner has argued that the Land League "help[ed] to transform specifically Irish grievances and traditions into a broader critique of American society in the Gilded Age."[19] The Land League movement also served as a catalyst for women's organization and activism.

Although the radicalism of the 1880s soon waned, nationalism in the United States continued. The final push for the suffrage amendment coincided with another wave of Irish nationalism. In the wake of World War I, dramatic events in Ireland placed American foreign policy at the center of a strategy to win recognition for the recently declared Irish Republic. Thus, as chapter 4 demonstrates, newly enfranchised women played their most visible role in the nationalist movement since the Ladies' Land League. Although women continued to justify their nationalist activities in the familiar terms of charity, service, and patriotism, they also organized for propaganda purposes and political protest. As events in Ireland drew international attention, Irish American women began to seek a voice in politics, and they orchestrated the most militant nationalist protests of the period. Those with ties to organized labor sought to rally the power of consumers and laborers against the British Empire through strikes and boycotts, while also staging dramatic protest events to gain media attention and sympathy, such as the 1920 longshoremen's strike in New York City. Thus, women with experience in labor and suffrage campaigns were the most likely to initiate independent action, rejecting the leadership of male nationalists and advancing a class-based critique of international affairs.

The final part traces the history of Irish American women's involvement in the suffrage movement, from the first labor pioneers and nationalist crossovers through the final years of the state suffrage campaigns. Chapter 5 examines the relationship between suffragists, labor leaders, and nationalists in the nineteenth century, while the final chapter reveals the contributions of Irish American suffragists to the state suffrage campaigns of the early twentieth century. With the revival of the labor movement and the acceleration of suffrage campaigning in the early twentieth century, a small group of Irish American women played a more visible role in both movements. Although not without its complications, the cooperation between working-class women and middle-class reformers, which began in the late nineteenth century, continued in the early twentieth century. Suffragists understood that winning state referendum campaigns meant appealing to immigrant and ethnic voters, many of whom were Catholic, and Irish American suffragists adopted their own class-based arguments for suffrage. Working women sought political influence often as a means of self-protection; at the same time, some middle-class Irish Catholic women also endorsed suffrage, particularly as a way to elevate the Catholic working class.

The combination of Irish nationalism, the final push for suffrage, and the support for labor legislation made the early twentieth century a really active time for women activists. However, by the early 1920s, circumstances had changed dramatically for Irish Americans. In 1921 the creation of an Irish Free State resulted in a civil war. In America the decline of immigration, a backlash against the labor movement, and renewed anti-Catholic nativism led to changing priorities. Although many Irish Americans defended their right to be hyphenated before World War I, the formation of a distinctly Catholic subculture matured in the first half of the twentieth century.[20] This shift from the ethnic enclaves of the nineteenth century to what one historian has labeled "pan-ethnic militant American Catholicism" did not come without a struggle.[21] By focusing on how class and gender identities affected the political attitudes and behaviors of Irish American women, this study reveals the complex process of identity formation and persistence within the Irish American community, its diversity, and women's roles in shaping and defending it.

Although many Irish American activists did not see a contradiction between preserving their Irish heritage and proclaiming their loyalty to America before World War I, they disagreed on the priorities of the Irish American community. In *American Catholic Lay Groups and Transatlantic Social Reform in the Progressive Era* (2002), Deirdre Moloney concluded that middle-class Catholic activists generally rejected cooperation with Protestants, and women who appeared to pattern their behavior after, or seek the approval of, the non-Catholic establishment at the expense of their religious and ethnic heritage risked rebuff.[22] In contrast, because Irish Americans remained heavily clustered in the working class, labor reformers adopted a more Progressive agenda. Through the labor movement and reform organizations, they embraced a critique of industrial capitalism, advocating regulation and reform, particularly through alliances with middle-class Protestant reformers. Some Irish American women sought influence in political matters, supporting factory legislation and women's suffrage. Thus, these women became part of the women's movement in general but also sought social reform as a means of self-protection. Although diaspora nationalism presented new opportunities for women in the public sphere, Irish American women were drawn into other causes. They sought influence both through their own separate organizations (as defined by religious and ethnic priorities, but in conjunction with men) and as part of the movement of American women into Progressive Era politics and reform.

PART ONE

Life and Labor

1

Life in the Irish American Community

An Overview

In the fall of 1889, Alice Nolan, who was raised in County Kerry, departed from Liverpool aboard the *Floridian*, bound for New Orleans, where she would become Sister Columba. Nolan recorded her travels in a diary: "At 8:30 our vessel set sail and it slowly rent its way through the foaming waves we watched for the last glimpse of our dear and cherished fatherland which we hoped never again to see. Oh then what feelings of grief and emotion filled our breasts when the dim distance and darkness its green shores soon faded from our sight and left us to indulge in its view only in imagination."[1] Alice Nolan was one of many women to make the journey from Ireland to America in the nineteenth century. Between 1850 and 1914, four million people left Ireland, and the greatest number of these immigrants went to the United States. Waves of immigration began before the famine and lasted until well after. Three and a half million Irish came to the United States from the postfamine era through the 1920s, disembarking in cities such as Boston, New York, and Philadelphia. Because of the destruction and displacement resulting from the famine and its aftermath, by the turn of the twentieth century, Irish immigrants were predominantly young, single, and Catholic.[2] One of the most unique factors in Irish immigration history is the percentage of women among the immigrant waves. In comparison to other European immigrant groups, the number of women was high, particularly at the end of the nineteenth century, when women made up more than half of all

Irish emigrants.[3] Some, like Nolan, were part of a tradition of single Irish women who were recruited by Irish women religious living in the United States. Thousands of Irish women crossed the Atlantic in the nineteenth century to embrace religious life or become teachers in American parochial schools.[4] But most would work as domestic servants and in America's booming industrial sector.

Why Women? The Famine and Its Aftermath

The Irish were already leaving for the United States before the potato famine. Between 1780 and 1845, more than one million people left Ireland for North America. However, the famine would reveal some serious weaknesses in the structure of rural life, including an overdependence on the potato crop and the dangers of dividing land among multiple sons.[5] In 1845 the Great Famine began. In the first year of the blight, approximately 40 percent of the Irish potato crop was lost, but the following year that number rose to 90 percent. One million people died of disease and starvation, and three million were forced to depend on charity.[6] Such widespread suffering devastated the country. During the decade of the famine, one and a half million famine refugees left Ireland for the United States, but a recent analysis of Irish arrivals in New York City suggests that "the level of emigration in the famine years was significantly higher than scholars have previously understood."[7]

After the death and destruction of the famine years, circumstances changed in Ireland, particularly for the young. The practice of impartible inheritance (leaving the land to only one heir) became more widespread. As a result, parents who might previously have divided the land among their sons chose only one son (usually the oldest) to inherit. This also disrupted young people's ability to marry. While men might still be able to find work and remain single, women's chances for marriage were significantly altered after the famine. Unmarried women found work scarce in Ireland, but the importance of a dowry meant that many daughters would not be able to marry at all, since only one daughter received her "fortune." For those who did marry, parents arranged matches for the economic well-being of their daughters. By the late nineteenth century, the Irish married later in life and less often than other nationalities.[8] Since women in Ireland gained status through marriage and motherhood, single women faced a difficult future. They had little independence and held a "servile position" in the family.[9] With few job opportunities, young Irish women faced a life of dependence. In fact, unemployment among women was such a serious problem by the late nineteenth century that the government sponsored plans to aid women's employment.[10] This lack of options pushed many women to leave in search of work. In choosing to emigrate, they were following a common path, one that neighbors, friends, and family had also followed. Many women had relatives who helped to pay their passage and arrange for employment. By the end of the nineteenth century, the vast majority (90 percent) of Irish passengers had prepaid tickets for emigration, and many young women were paid for by sisters in the United States.[11]

Work

For those who chose to depart, American cities were the most common destination, and Irish populations became large in many urban areas, attracting more new arrivals. However, given that women emigrated young and single, these new arrivals needed work and housing. In the first generation, women went overwhelmingly into domestic service. By 1860 78 percent of foreign-born women worked as servants as compared to only one-third of native-born white women, who had a strong aversion to service. In fact, Helen Campbell, who investigated women's working conditions in the 1880s, accused American women of leaving middle-class homes dependent on "tenement house Irish."[12] A servant shortage meant that jobs were available for young Irish women to work and live in middle-class homes. For example, in 1850 almost 72 percent of Boston's domestic servants were born in Ireland. Likewise, in 1880 44 percent of domestic servants in New York City were natives of Ireland. Some women came with experience in service, but that number is unknown.[13] Data from New England and New York is also consistent with Patricia Kelleher's study of Irish immigrant women in Gilded Age Chicago, which found that more than four-fifths of young Irish women worked in "low manual" work, and 80 percent worked as servants in homes, hotels, and other similar jobs.[14]

Most new arrivals would have found the lifestyles of American middle-class homes unfamiliar, but middle-class women depended on Irish help. Frustration with the presumed inadequacies of Irish servants circulated widely in the American press, and in popular culture more broadly, but Irish women flocked to service despite the stigma and the scorn leveled at them. For example, newspapers entertained readers with brief anecdotes that were printed and reprinted in local and national media. Most of these were just a few lines—a joke, exposing the tension and frustration middle-class employers felt toward their hired help through a servant's (usually named Bridget) humorous response to some domestic situation. Some poked fun at newly arrived servants' lack of familiarity with American domestic life. The following dialogue appeared in an 1890 newspaper column labeled "Humor of the Hour." An employer said to a newly arrived immigrant, "You never saw a lobster before, did you Bridget?" In heavy brogue, the stubborn servant replied, "Shure, an Oi've see hundreds av the red things shwimmin' in the creeks av the old country." Informed that lobsters are green before they are cooked, Bridget responded, "Shure, an' there's boilin' springs roight in the creeks."[15] Another newly arrived immigrant story from 1902 described a servant who was told to iron some clothes and "hang them on the horse" (a drying rack). Unable to complete her task, she returned to the mistress with the clothes and explained that she tried, "but he kept movin' and they wouldn't stay."[16] These fictional Bridgets were presented as green, naive, and ignorant. Although many anti-Irish stories, jokes, and plays criticized Irish servant women for their lack of education, hygiene, cooking skills, and so forth, servants were in demand so Irish women could expect steady employment.

Although domestic workers were not protected by unions, Irish immigrant women also went into the factories, where some would become leaders in the fight for better wages and working conditions. Irish names stand out in the history of American unions. Between

1900 and 1920, although Irish men made up only one-thirteenth of the total male workforce, they held leadership positions in 50 of 110 American Federation of Labor (AFL) unions.[17] Likewise, the names of Irish American women stand out in the history of the labor movement. Hasia Diner explained that the "extremely active involvement" of Irish American women in the labor movement reflected a culture that measured the value of women in highly economic terms; they found assertiveness in the economic sphere culturally acceptable.[18] By the early twentieth century, as organizing women workers became a priority for middle-class reformers and women trade unionists, Irish American women took their place in a cross-class and multiethnic movement to improve the conditions of working women, an effort that led them to embrace the suffrage movement and to acknowledge the need for a permanent place for working women in politics.

This trend corresponded with a dramatic expansion of women in the labor force from 1870 to 1890, when the number of women working (outside of agriculture) doubled. In total, women made up one-sixth of the labor force. By 1920 the number of working women had reached eight million, and 25 percent of women worked.[19] Irish and Irish American women were the largest ethnic group in some areas and industries. For example, by the 1870s, Irish women made up almost 58 percent of textile workers in Lowell, Massachusetts, and in the state of Massachusetts Irish women represented 17 percent of all women in industry (the highest of any immigrant group) by 1889. Sewing and needlework were also common trades for Irish women. After the famine in 1855, 40 percent of Irish women in New York's Sixth Ward sewed for a living, while 50 percent worked in domestic service. By 1900 one-third of all seamstresses and dressmakers in the United States were Irish born.[20]

Although Irish immigration continued steadily into the twentieth century, by the late nineteenth century American-born Irish outnumbered the immigrant generation, and work choices also came to reflect this generational change. By 1900 US Census data shows that second-generation men and women outnumbered the Irish born in the workforce. Irish American women began moving into office work as secretaries, bookkeepers, and stenographers. But they also entered professions, particularly nursing and teaching.[21] In the early twentieth century, more than 8 percent of second-generation Irish American women workers had become teachers, and they made up one-quarter of the public teaching force in smaller cities such as Scranton, Lowell, and Buffalo. They were also one-third of the teachers in Boston and Chicago. By 1910 almost half of the grammar school teachers in San Francisco were also of Irish descent.[22]

This meant that Irish American women were earning an education. In fact, by the turn of the twentieth century, young Irish women were the largest ethnic group among graduates of urban high schools in Boston, Chicago, and San Francisco. Irish American girls also outnumbered Irish American boys in parochial and public schools. For example, at Pittsburgh Central High School, Irish American girls made up 37 percent of the student body between 1855 and 1865, while boys were only 20 percent. Likewise, in Waltham, Massachusetts, Catholic girls (likely many were Irish) graduated from high school at four times the rate of Catholic boys.[23] The significant presence of Irish American women in the teaching force has led Janet Nolan to argue that Irish American women led their communities' advance toward "respectability and prosperity" with a mass movement into public school teaching at the turn of the twentieth century. Although their salaries were low, teachers held "significant social and economic importance within families as well as in their home communities."[24]

Women and the Catholic Church

In terms of gaining an education and expanding their work options, women made important contributions to the Irish American community. Irish American women also constituted a key support within the Catholic Church at a time when the "woman question" was gaining new attention and creating new opportunities among American Catholics. Several important factors contributed to the dissemination of Catholic gender ideology at the end of the nineteenth century. The debate grew out of such internal factors as the development of a Catholic middle class and concerns over the loss of ethnic identity. In addition to internal divisions, Catholics reacted to external challenges such as the reemergence of nativism and the rise of the New Woman, who was educated, independent, and socially active.[25] By the late nineteenth century, priests and journalists counseled Catholic women to be pure and pious, domestic and submissive, celebrating the harmony of domestic life and endorsing motherhood as women's natural destiny.[26] In *The Christian Home in Victorian America, 1840–1900* (1986), Colleen McDannell suggested that Catholic gender ideology showed only "minor variation" from the Protestant ideal, which appeared earlier in the century, including a more traditional view of domesticity, with an emphasis on the hierarchical relationship between parent and child.[27] Like middle-class Protestant women, Catholic women began to employ maternalist rhetoric to justify activities outside the home, yet they generally used it more conservatively, embracing charitable efforts, while generally avoiding controversial issues like suffrage.[28]

Many Catholics rejected the New Woman, whom they identified with Protestant America.[29] In 1895 Cardinal Gibbons of Baltimore denounced modern women, insisting that the woman suffragist flattered herself with the label of New Woman; she was "very old—old as Eve, prompted by curiosity and lawlessness to gain information of the devil." Through the pages of the *Catholic World*, another Catholic critic of the New Woman expressed amusement at dire predictions of her destructiveness. He did not believe the "leaders of the present 'advancement' [were] at all representative of any considerable or important element in *our* community." They could not speak for "*our* mothers and sisters," who "still retain a great deal of their native good sense."[30] Yet despite such expressions of confidence in the submissive nature of Catholic women, and in contrast with women's own use of such rhetoric, Catholic women were indeed pushing for more responsibility in public life. Through advice literature and the press, American Catholics increasingly discussed the role of women, while Catholic women also became more active in charitable, fraternal, and educational organizations.

An expanding group with political connections and a large working class, Irish Americans faced the problems of nineteenth-century

American life in a number of ways. Irish immigrants played a significant role in the development of the American Catholic Church, and as a result of tensions between Protestants and Catholics in the nineteenth century, Catholics developed a preference for institutional charity.[31] These institutions, including orphanages, hospitals, and other services, were created and sustained largely by the efforts of women religious, many of whom were immigrants themselves, like the first Sisters of Mercy in New York, who came from Dublin in 1846. Between 1830 and 1900, 106 new foundations of women religious were established in the United States. These women founded, staffed, and secured funding for agencies and institutions that ministered to the heavily Catholic poor. As significant contributors to the growth of convents and their institutional activities, Irish American women expressed their "political agendas and social vision" through their religious vocation and their dedication to the needy.[32]

Women religious made significant contributions to the development of welfare programs; however, laywomen also sought a role in benevolence work. In the late nineteenth century, few male Catholic charities admitted women, and those that did organized separate women's auxiliaries. The leading Catholic philanthropic organization, the all-male St. Vincent de Paul Society, began allowing women as auxiliary members in 1902. Some laywomen also saw the contributions of Protestant settlement-house workers as examples of the potential for female leadership in the realm of benevolence.[33] After 1880, as parishes began expanding to incorporate social, recreational, charitable, and educational goals, women also seized the initiative in creating benevolent and fraternal organizations. For example, in Detroit two trends in the 1890s demonstrate that "an important minority" among Catholic women had begun to see their roles in more expansive ways—large numbers of women joined benefit societies, and laywomen organized various groups dedicated to adult education.[34] In addition, more Catholic activists were embracing the view that philanthropy must include social reform—that relief was not enough to tackle modern social concerns.[35] This presented opportunities for laywomen. An 1898 *Catholic World* article profiling the work of the Queen's

Daughters (first organized in St. Louis in 1889) noted the existence of "fields for cultivation by the laity awaiting the united efforts of the Catholic women," fields where women could apply "spiritual and corporal works of mercy . . . uplifting thousands of the unfortunate."[36]

In the first attempt to organize a national coalition of Catholic women, representatives of women's organizations met in Chicago, at the World's Columbian Exposition in 1893, to form the Catholic Woman's National League. The *Irish World* reported that Eliza Allen Starr (a Catholic convert from a prominent Boston family) "spoke eloquently of the mission of Catholic womanhood, and made a powerful plea for the organization of a national society of Catholic women." Drawing comparisons and concerns over the influence of Protestant women, Alice Timmons Toomy argued that Catholic women were beginning to realize their duty to help the needy and join "the W.C.T.U. [Woman's Christian Temperance Union] and other non-Catholic philanthropies because they find no organization in their own church."[37] The Chicago branch organized with 250 members, dividing its work into six departments: home, art and literature, education, kindergarten, temperance, and philanthropy. In 1901 the Chicago league responded to "calls for a National League of Catholic Women's Clubs for the purpose of mutual helpfulness, of widening the sphere of usefulness of our women, and at the same time of doing honor to our faith through our Catholic press." Among the chosen officers were some Irish American women who were prominent in other movements—Ellen Ford, formerly of the Ladies' Land League, and Leonora (Barry) Lake, an organizer for the Knights of Labor and a leader in the Catholic temperance movement. Despite some active local chapters, the league failed to support a national organization.[38]

In addition to an increase in Catholic benevolence activities for laywomen, ethnic and fraternal groups also developed to address the needs of particular groups. While Irish Americans played a prominent role in Catholic charities and in the American Catholic Church as a whole, in the nineteenth century Catholics came to the United States from throughout Europe. The desire to preserve distinctive ethnic traditions could be a source of friction, not only within the Catholic

Church but in American society as a whole. By the early twentieth century, Irish Americans became involved in renewed efforts to win Home Rule for Ireland, but they also sought to improve the reputation of the Irish American community and uplift their "race," insisting that hyphenated Americans were no less patriotic or valuable.

Ethnic and Fraternal Associations

Ethnic and nationalist organizations played a key role in the process of defining Irish American identity. Because in nineteenth-century Ireland many people defined their allegiances in local rather than national terms, immigrants' Irish ethnic identity developed in relation to their American context. Historians have argued that through nationalist and ethnic fraternal associations, Irish immigrants became Irish Americans. These nineteenth-century newcomers retained their Irish identity and developed separate institutions, while also promoting values associated with the dominant Protestant culture.[39]

Traditionally, these organizations were only for men, so the Ladies' Land League of the 1880s (discussed in part 2) marked a key development in the organization of Irish American women. Although the Ladies' Land League lasted only a few years, by the 1890s a number of heavily Irish organizations were adding women's auxiliaries, including the Catholic Order of Foresters and the Knights of Columbus. Furthermore, some organizations were limited to Irish immigrants and their children, like the Ancient Order of Hibernians. Ladies' county organizations, often restricted by place of birth, were also popular in New York. In 1910 there were twenty-six ladies' counties societies, which appealed to a largely single membership.[40] While members joined various groups for religious, economic, or social reasons, the development of auxiliaries for women, particularly the Ladies' Auxiliary of the Ancient Order of Hibernians, meant that women fought for a voice in the Irish American community. The rise of these ladies' auxiliaries provided a public outlet for moderate female aspirations, operating within a vision defined by conservative Catholic gender ideology, yet still creating new opportunities for women to organize in defense of religious and ethnic priorities. As the largest organization of Irish American women at the time, a portrait of the LAAOH also demonstrates the growing influence of women in grassroots public discourse and community organizing.

The Ancient Order of Hibernians was limited to Catholics of Irish birth or descent. In the United States, the AOH originated in New York City in 1836 with the motto "Friendship, Unity, and True Christian Charity." The organization provided sick benefits to members, assisted new immigrants, and offered opportunities for socializing. At the close of the nineteenth century, the men's organization reportedly boasted ninety-four thousand members.[41] Unfortunately, no comprehensive study of the American organization has been published. The available demographic information is based on male membership alone, which remained heavily Irish born until World War I and appealed largely to the working class. Although rank-and-file members of the AOH came from comparatively modest backgrounds, leaders of fraternal organizations in general often came from the middle class.[42] The AOH (with the support of its ladies' auxiliary) and other Irish societies sought to improve the reputation of the Irish American community by celebrating Irish history, censoring negative images of the Irish in popular culture, and constructing tributes to the role of Irish Americans in US history.

By the 1890s, the women of the Ancient Order of Hibernians were fighting to bring their local organizations together under the rubric of a national ladies' auxiliary. As their leaders' rhetoric suggests, they had to overcome obstacles, including the opposition of leading men within the AOH. The women's determination to form a national organization arose out of three significant trends in late-nineteenth-century America: the increased discussion of gender roles among American Catholics, the expansion of women's educational and public roles during the Progressive Era, and renewed nativism. Catholics were on the defensive at the end of the nineteenth century, as emotions ran high over the threat of nativist attacks. Founded in Clinton, Iowa, in 1887, the American Protective Association (APA) boasted a half-million members in the early 1890s.[43] More than one hundred nativist publications denounced immigrants during that decade, accusing them of threatening the American way of life. Often Irish immigrants appeared particularly ominous due to their reported affinity for alcohol and political corruption, devotion to the Catholic Church, and a perceived propensity for violence.[44] The women of the LAAOH organized to fight back.

Although very little information exists on the women who joined the auxiliary in its formative stage, and there was certainly variability on the local level, the national leaders of the LAAOH consistently employed traditional notions of women's domestic role and family influence, while also appealing to the politics of respectability. The earliest leaders of the LAAOH tended to be raised and educated in the United States, and some had a background in teaching. For example, the first national president, Anna Malia, was born in England of Irish parents and immigrated to the United States as a child. She taught in the Scranton public schools for many years. Malia appears to have remained single until her fifties, but she did marry Michael Ruddy, a contractor, in 1921.[45] The next president of the LAAOH, Ellen Ryan Jolly, was born in Boston of Irish immigrant parents. She served a three-year term on the school board in Pawtucket, Rhode Island, and ran a millinery business (which may have belonged to her mother). Her husband, John Jolly, was listed on the 1920 US Census as a cashier at a gas company. He was active in Democratic politics, and Jolly herself received several appointments from Rhode Island governors. Jolly became the first woman to receive an honorary doctorate (of law) from Notre Dame in 1918, and Pope Pius XI awarded her a papal medal in 1930 for her service to the church.[46] The third national president, Mary F. McWhorter, grew up in Ireland, where she was educated in the national schools. She recalled that her father, Michael Mulcahy, was a Fenian who died when she was very young. Newspaper accounts suggest that she immigrated to Chicago as a teen and married William H. McWhorter, a printer, in 1891. McWhorter founded Chicago's first division of the LAAOH in 1898.[47]

Two women also became national lecturers for the Ancient Order of Hibernians: Charlotte Holloway and Katharine O'Keefe O'Mahoney. Charlotte Holloway was born in Massachusetts. Well educated and successful, Holloway became a journalist and also wrote children's literature. In the early twentieth century, she moved into lecture work, both as a national lecturer for the Ancient Order of Hibernians and under the auspices of her own business. Unlike other prominent LAAOH women, Holloway was a suffragist in her home state of Connecticut.[48] And finally, Katharine O'Keefe O'Mahoney immigrated to Lawrence, Massachusetts, with her parents at a young age. She became the first Catholic teacher at Lawrence High School in 1875, where she taught history and speech. O'Mahoney first spoke publicly during Fanny Parnell's visit to Boston on behalf of the Ladies' Land League. She also served as a correspondent for the *Sacred Heart Review* and published the *Catholic Register*.[49] While biographies of these leaders present a small sample from the auxiliary's earliest years, and certainly do not represent the average or rank-and-file members' experiences, they were pioneers in organizing Irish American women, and they became highly visible in the Irish American community. The founding of the ladies' auxiliary allowed Irish American women to become active in campaigns designed to protect and promote the Irish in America—to help define, disseminate, and defend the values of the Irish American community.

These women were also concerned with political influence and economic security. As former teachers themselves, early leaders expressed concern about access to teaching jobs for women and felt threatened by the rise of nativism and its influence on policy for the public schools.[50] Women's experiences in the schools as well as their desire to serve and protect the Irish Catholic community motivated them to organize for political influence. The earliest efforts to form a national auxiliary clearly show the influence of these concerns. For example, when the women of Omaha, Nebraska, petitioned the national body of the Ancient Order of Hibernians for recognition of the ladies' auxiliary in 1894, they asserted their willingness and ability to work "shoulder to shoulder" with the men, expressing a need for "an organized effort . . . to suppress the encroachments on our rights as American citizens." Specifically, the women denounced efforts by the APA to "prevent Catholic ladies from teaching in our public schools," vowing to work with the AOH to protect women's jobs by "placing on our school boards, men who will not discriminate against our Catholic school teachers."[51] Such rhetoric suggests that women sought political influence, if indirectly, from the auxiliary's inception. Yet it also demonstrates that auxiliary leaders carefully placed limits on their ambitions: they wanted to work with men to advance mutually agreed-upon goals.

This proved difficult, and the women fought hard for the recognition of their organization while carefully defining their role and relationship to their brothers in the AOH. A few women attended the AOH national convention as nonvoting delegates in 1896 and addressed the crowd, calling for a national organization for women and a standardized constitution. As one speaker explained, "I fail to see how the ladies who are counted your equals can do their business other than through a national organization." However, she carefully qualified her demands. She made no claim as speechmaker or politician. She was not a "New Woman," but the daughter of a good Irish mother who taught her to put the care of husband and family first.[52] The leading women of the LAAOH celebrated their commitment to home and church but believed they could serve the community as well, thus pushing for the expansion of women's roles in the Irish American community. Women insisted on their value to the organization. For example, one speaker believed the auxiliary "accomplished a great work" in her state by uniting Irish women who "have rendered little assistance to the men of their race in the objects for which they labored" because they weren't in a position to do so. She relished the opportunity to demonstrate that women were as patriotic as men and could be a force for "the upbuilding of our people." A few months later, the same author scolded the national leadership for neglecting the ladies' auxiliary. She urged them to give their valuable aid and advice lest "we are given to understand that we are capable of managing our own affairs" and you awake to find us doing just that.[53] While women carefully explained their initiatives in terms that squared with Catholic gender ideology and traditional cultural roles, such remarks also reveal tension with male leaders who were perceived as unsupportive.

One newspaper account of the 1896 convention announced, "Ancient Order of Hibernians Having a Lively Fight with the Ladies Auxiliary Organization," explaining that the women were determined to form a national organization, but "a good many" of the leading men opposed it.[54] Mary McWhorter recalled of the early struggles of the auxiliary: "It is a strange feature in the usually social makeup of the average Irish American that, while having implicit confidence in the good judgment of the women folk of his household, he never, to use a common phrase 'warms' to the idea of their taking an active part in anything outside of their household or limited social circle." McWhorter attributed this attitude to the "Old Land" in the days before the Land League. She believed that "fresh blood and progressive ideas" in the AOH during the 1880s inspired by the Land League ultimately secured a place for women in building up the order.[55] Recalling the ladies' first initiative for organization, Anna C. Malia told delegates at the 1908 convention: "To some of the delegates no doubt, this request seemed ill advised, and they felt like saying, 'women have no business in Society affairs of this kind. Your place is in the home.'" Yet, she continued, "Every woman deserving the name loves her home . . . but how many lives are worn out with toil and care for home, as though there were nothing else to live for or think of!" In advocating women's organization, Malia called women's complete and exclusive devotion to the home "selfish."[56]

Despite the differences with the male leadership, women publicly rejected any rumors that they sought independence from the men of the AOH. Mary McWhorter wrote of the harmony of the organization and the dangers of independence. She hoped that no New Women "filled with a desire for a separate and distinct life apart from the AOH" would attend the national convention, but rather the "old-fashioned type, eager and willing to aid and assist the husband, the father, the son, the brother, and the friend." She claimed that the vast majority of female members opposed independence. In 1906 the

LAAOH obtained "home rule in a most liberal degree," as favored by the "general sentiment" among female state representatives. As a result, women gained the right to elect national officers and manage their own funds.[57] McWhorter rejected the idea that this measure of self-government made them an independent body and corrected the assumption that the women had "pulled away from the men." The auxiliary's first president, Anna C. Malia, also concluded that the women did not wish to be an independent body; they were proud to remain an auxiliary to the AOH.[58] The national LAAOH claimed fifty thousand members by 1907.[59] The women quickly found themselves playing important roles in several campaigns on behalf of the Irish American community, and the organization would also serve as a strong basis for women's entry into the nationalist movement (as discussed in part 2).

Ultimately, by the end of the nineteenth century, circumstances were changing in Irish America. The plight of Catholic workers, and their participation in agitation for reform in America and abroad, led Pope Leo XIII to begin working on an encyclical on the social question. Issued in May 1891, *Rerum novarum* addressed the conditions of labor and offered a program for social justice. The pope condemned the excesses of both capitalism and socialism, but supported labor unions and government regulation for the protection of workers. As one contemporary interpreter related the meaning of *Rerum novarum* in the American context, "[The pope] clearly lays down the inviolability of private property, especially in land." Yet he also shows "fatherly tenderness and sympathy" toward working people and encourages organization based on religious principles and motives.[60] According to Jay Dolan, *Rerum novarum* did initially inspire discussion of social questions, but the encyclical did not ignite a "Catholic crusade for social justice" in America, owing largely to internal division and growing conservatism in the church hierarchy.[61]

Irish American men and women still remained heavily working class, but women were beginning to make a visible impact in the teaching profession. Furthermore, women's opportunities to participate in clubs, charities, and other organizations were expanding. Whether through the nationalist movement, ethnic and fraternal associations, or the labor movement, Irish American women sought greater influence on public matters, but their experiences and motivations were as diverse as the community from which they came. The women of the LAAOH embraced a role as activists within the Irish American and Catholic communities. Despite their willingness to push for inclusion and independence, they defined their roles in terms of cooperation with men and service to their ethnic and religious communities. Sources on the LAAOH rarely mention suffrage or women's rights. However, as chapter 2 will demonstrate, the Irish also played a pivotal role in the development of the nineteenth-century labor movement. Irish American women were among the earliest leaders of industrial trade unions and also pioneered new strategies for teachers' organizations. They fought for legislation to protect working women, improve sanitation, create teachers' pensions, and advocate for equal pay, agendas that often brought them into contact and cooperation with middle-class Protestant reformers as well.

2

Radicals and Reformers

The Origins of Women's Labor Activism and Alliances

In 1898 Leonora O'Reilly expressed her great sadness at the death of utopian novelist Edward Bellamy. "Will I ever forget what an impression *Looking Backward* made on me and all the people with whom I associated in 1889," she wrote to a friend.[1] Bellamy's most famous novel offered a powerful critique of the effects of industrial capitalism and promised to solve America's widespread labor problems, presenting a futuristic model of a cooperative society where everyone worked and no job was considered menial. Many activists acknowledged their debt to Bellamy's work, but O'Reilly was not a typical reformer. Unlike most Protestant reformers, who attended college and came from middle- and upper-class backgrounds, O'Reilly left school at an early age to take up the same trade as her Irish American mother—sewing. Like many Irish American women who became activists, O'Reilly knew the perils of industrial capitalism firsthand. She, and her widowed mother, experienced the poverty and harsh working conditions that came with the boom-and-bust economy of the Gilded Age.

Historians have noted the effects of economic instability on the Irish in America during the 1870s and 1880s. After years of heavy migration to the United States—three million people between 1845 and 1889—many Irish-born workers still clustered in unskilled jobs. Despite the presence of middle-class merchants and professionals, the

Irish in America remained heavily working class, with movement from unskilled to skilled labor being the most common source of mobility among men. In 1900 only about 2 percent of Irish immigrant men were professionals, while just over 5 percent were merchants. Likewise, the majority of first-generation Irish immigrant women (54 percent) were in domestic service.[2] As late as 1910, 60 percent of male Irish immigrants remained in the ranks of unskilled or semiskilled workers. In the second generation, status did improve, but the most important shift for men in the second generation was toward skilled blue-collar jobs as machinists, printers, and other trades. The trend among women was more promising. Irish American women made up a significant portion of the working class—close to 21 percent of the Irish American workforce by 1880—as compared to almost 13 percent of the foreign-born workforce as a whole. But some historians argue that social mobility among women may have outpaced the men, as the second generation moved into skilled jobs, particularly teaching and nursing.[3]

For Irish Americans, the precarious nature of nineteenth-century industrial life and the Irish American community's place within it led to protest, organization, and advocacy. In relation to their representation in the labor market, workers of Irish extraction dominated leadership positions in the organized trades.[4] Like Irish American men, the names of Irish American women stand out in the history of the American labor movement because Irish American women found assertiveness in the economic sphere socially acceptable and therefore defied middle-class standards of proper female behavior to become leaders and organizers in the labor movement.[5] By the 1880s, the first generation of leading activists was beginning to emerge in the labor and nationalist movements. In her portrait of the Gilded Age, *New Spirits* (2006), Rebecca Edwards argues for an expanded understanding of the roots of reform that culminated in the Progressive Era, pointing out that once Americans felt the full impact of industrialization, they developed "national networks for reform and protest."[6] Many of the reform organizations that came to define Progressivism by the turn of the century were in fact inspired by Gilded Age reflection and revolt.

Beginning in the late nineteenth century, two very different groups of women were beginning to grapple with how to alleviate the worst excesses of industrial capitalism: female reformers and factory workers.

The Progressive Era marked a crucial period in the expansion of public and political roles for Protestant women, as they created settlement houses, joined the temperance movement, and formed women's clubs. Armed with a college education, many of these women chose to postpone marriage and devote themselves to ameliorating the effects of industrial capitalism. These reformers studied social conditions, championed reform legislation, and provided services and education to those in need. However, class and religious differences separated them from the immigrant and laboring communities that they served. Lay Catholic women also entered the world of social reform in the Progressive Era, although their experiences in Catholic temperance groups and settlement houses differed from those of Protestant women and started a bit later as well.[7]

While Irish American women were largely absent from the ranks of educated middle-class women's reform organizations in the nineteenth century, their role as leaders and organizers in the labor movement brought them into contact with women reformers and also led them into the halls of legislatures to push for labor reform. Women's participation in the labor movement provided the inspiration to embrace reform as a necessary means of aiding and protecting themselves and the most vulnerable in industrial America. This movement appealed to Irish American women, who also found that their need for allies drew them into reform organizations. Soon those women who endorsed the need to reform industrial capitalism in America, and protect its most exploited, also found it necessary to seek alliances outside the Irish-dominated labor movement. Without the necessary support from union men, by the close of the nineteenth century a small group of Irish American women began to explore other strategies to help "the working girl." This brought them beyond the Irish American community and the labor movement into the wider world of women's reform networks. Women's entry into the national labor movement through the Knights of Labor led to the emergence of a small cadre of

Irish American women labor leaders who would embrace several strategies to help working women: alliances with middle-class Protestant reformers, legislation to improve factory and working conditions, and entry into the suffrage movement. Despite the difficulty of such cross-class alliances, Irish American women were leaders in their communities in terms of embracing Progressive Era legislative reforms.

Women found themselves vulnerable and in need of allies, particularly when their alliances with working-class men were in question. They did not give up on the labor movement, but early leaders began seeking alliances outside of their unions by the late nineteenth century. In her book *Breadwinners: Working Women and Economic Independence, 1865–1920* (2009), Lara Vapnek uses the term *women's labor reformer* to identify those individuals who placed addressing the inequities of industrial capitalism for women at the heart of their activism. This group was a heterogeneous one; it included working women and middle-class Protestant reformers. However, middle-class and working-class women had different priorities within their alliances. Vapnek argues that while middle-class women saw themselves as the defenders and protectors of exploited women, working women sought economic independence and the recognition that, like working men, they too were "breadwinners." Furthermore, Vapnek asserts that by extending our view of women's activism in the Gilded Age beyond suffrage to include economic issues, historians can appreciate the urgent debates surrounding women's position in the labor force as well as the role of working-class women as activists.[8]

Women and the Knights of Labor

The Irish played a significant role in the Knights of Labor. Organized as a secret society in 1869, the Knights of Labor offered a new tactic to the American labor movement—a national organization of workers, regardless of race, sex, or skill level. In the words of Susan Levine, the Knights "extended trade unionism and a tradition of republican egalitarian reform to the growing mass of immigrant, unskilled industrial laborers." This population, of course, included a growing number of women.[9] After a series of successful strikes in the early

1880s, membership in the Knights soared. At its peak in 1886, the order had assemblies in every state and constituted 8 to 12 percent of the industrial labor force.[10] However, its quick rise was followed by an even more rapid decline, leaving a large vacuum in the labor movement for unskilled workers, particularly women, by the end of the nineteenth century.

The Knights of Labor also had close connections with the Irish National Land League. According to Eric Foner, "The labor consciousness that flowered in the 1880s . . . owed a great deal to the Ford-George wing of the Land League." Irish Americans merged social radicalism and Irish nationalism in the Knights of Labor, as they had done in the league. However, the Knights of Labor also gave voice to uniquely American concerns arising out of the tumultuousness of industrial life and the precarious position of the Irish in American society.[11] The Knights of Labor promoted a social reform agenda that included temperance, land reform, education, and workers' cooperatives. The Knights provided opportunities for women to organize, envisioning a community of producers that came to include women's work in the home and the factory. Women's early experiences with land and labor reform ultimately increased activities in the public sphere, as the Knights "holistic reform vision" encouraged women to take an active part in social reforms, including temperance and suffrage, and women sought political solutions to social and economic problems.[12]

In 1880 the General Assembly of the Knights of Labor authorized Grandmaster Workman Terence Powderly (an Irish Catholic and ardent Irish nationalist) to prepare regulations for the admission of women, and in early 1881 a local Knights organizer inducted the first women into the order; the number of women's assemblies grew steadily. An estimated sixty-five thousand women belonged to the Knights at its peak in 1886, about 10 percent of the overall membership. During the 1880s, the Knights boasted more than four hundred local assemblies that included women; most were single sex, but about one-third were mixed-sex assemblies. The Knights also had an expansive understanding of women's work, including domestic services, where many women workers (including large numbers of Irish immigrants) were clustered. Twenty-five percent of women's locals were associated with domestic work, and another 25 percent were textile workers.[13]

In addition to this inclusive attitude toward women as workers, the Knights of Labor endorsed egalitarian principles, especially equal pay for equal work and women's suffrage. Powderly told members, "The rights of the sexes are co-equal. . . . The working women of America ask for the cooperation of men . . . as a right to which they are entitled by reason of the nobility of toil no matter by whom performed."[14] Some women rose to leadership positions, including several Irish Americans. Elizabeth Rodgers emigrated from Ireland with her mother as a young child. She helped organize the first Working Women's Union in Chicago and led the Eighth Ward Irish National Land League before emerging as a leading female Knight. As a master workman in Chicago, Rodgers represented her local in the city's district assembly, and in 1886 she became the organization's first female district master workman. Other future labor leaders like Leonora O'Reilly and Mother (Mary Harris) Jones also acknowledged the important influence of the Knights in their early careers.[15] One of the most visible Irish American women reformers during the nineteenth century, Mary Elizabeth Lease, also began her reform career with the Irish nationalist movement and the Knights of Labor.[16]

Despite the egalitarian rhetoric of the Knights, women who did assume leadership roles faced an uphill battle. Some men continued to resist the participation of women in the order. At the 1885 General Assembly, the first women delegates organized a national committee to investigate women's work. This Committee on Women's Work surveyed women's locals and pushed for a permanent investigator to be appointed at the 1886 convention. Sixteen female delegates chose Leonora Barry as general investigator for the Department of Woman's Work.[17] Born in Ireland and raised in upstate New York, Barry obtained a modest education and taught school before her marriage. When disease took her husband and daughter, Barry entered the factory to support her family. She quickly rose through the order, becoming a master workman and then assuming the job of general investigator.[18] Leaving her two sons behind, Barry traveled, lectured, and organized for four years, but not without encountering opposition. Although the Knights officially supported egalitarian principles in the workplace, the Knights also generally glorified the role of women in the home in their speeches and publications. There was resistance to women in the organization. Some men worried about competition from female workers, while others rejected any public role for women. One member expressed his disapproval to Powderly, arguing that the presence of women at meetings struck him as inappropriate and unseemly.[19]

Although a nondenominational organization, the Knights of Labor attracted many Catholic workers (perhaps as many as half).[20] Because of the Knights' secrecy, and a perceived association with violence and socialism, the order encountered controversy within the Catholic Church. Fearing that a papal condemnation of the organization in the United States would alienate many Catholic workers, Cardinal Gibbons of Baltimore interceded on behalf of the Knights in 1887, arguing that many of the officers, including Powderly, remained devout Catholics.[21] The issue of women's participation in the order also raised some concern among Catholics. One priest denounced Barry as a "lady tramp" and branded the Knights as vulgar for encouraging a woman to act as an organizer, but Barry defended her right as "an Irishwoman, a Catholic and an honest woman" to promote the workers' cause.[22]

Through her travels, Barry identified two major obstacles to women's status and success in the organization: male hostility and women's reluctance to unionize.[23] Barry embraced what she considered a realistic rather than an idealistic vision of women's proper roles. Although she agreed that women belonged at home "when she has one," she also explained, "I do not speak to create a sensation, but because I am a workingwoman, who has learned . . . the need of organization among the workers, especially female laborers." She insisted that women who were forced from their homes by economic circumstances must protect themselves.[24] As she reportedly told an audience in 1889, "I do not believe in charities much—not the kind that gives you a tract and a bowl of soup and says 'be content in the station in life in which God put you.'"[25] That year she also offered her final report to the Knights' General Assembly, supporting women's political rights and urging men to support legislation against sexual harassment. By 1890 the Knights had declined to only one hundred thousand members. As of 1889 only fifteen women's assemblies remained. Barry resigned amid factionalism, financial problems, and hostility to her role as women's organizer.[26] She married a printer named Obediah Lake but also continued to champion social reform, becoming the most prominent woman in the Catholic Total Abstinence Union (CTAU) and a supporter of women's suffrage.

New Alliances in an Age of Reform

Rebecca Edwards's view of a long Progressive Era—beginning with the awakening of reform activity in the Gilded Age—is particularly illuminating when it comes to a discussion of the Irish American community.[27] Through the Knights of Labor, Irish American workers adopted a class-based reform agenda that went beyond the narrow circles of nationalist and ethnic organizations, while provoking discussion of women's roles as Irish American women entered public activities and embraced political strategies to ameliorate social problems. Although prospects for women workers diminished along with the Knights of Labor in the late 1880s, some Irish American women continued to work within the American reform tradition, emerging as spokespeople for the rights of women, particularly working women. One young Knight, Leonora O'Reilly, quickly moved beyond the labor movement to cooperate more broadly with middle-class reformers. Her reform career demonstrates the possibility of alliances across class lines, as well as the unique perspective of reformers who became activists because of their experiences with labor exploitation. She is a leading example of the agency of working-class women who pioneered new strategies and efforts to improve the lives of factory workers and tenement dwellers. The decline of the Knights of Labor in the late 1880s, and the American Federation of Labor's neglect of working women, led those individuals seeking to improve the conditions of women wage earners to seek alliances with middle-class reformers. Throughout her career, O'Reilly moved in both labor and reform circles, working for improved working conditions through settlement houses, industrial education, union organization, and the suffrage movement.

Leonora O'Reilly was the only child of John and Winifred O'Reilly, both of Irish descent. Her parents ran a grocery store in New York, but the store failed, and John O'Reilly died when Leonora was very young. Winifred O'Reilly raised her daughter alone, keeping her in school as long as she could. At age eleven, Leonora entered the factory to help support them. While still in her teens, O'Reilly attended her first Knights of Labor meeting, sponsored by her godfather, Jean-Baptiste Hubert, a survivor of the Paris Commune.[28] During the 1880s, the young O'Reilly had mentors in the labor movement, including another Paris Commune radical named Victor Drury and the leader of New York's Central Labor Union, Edward King, but she would later form close relationships with middle- and upper-class women reformers as well.[29]

While still in her teens, O'Reilly joined the Working Women's Society (WWS) in New York, which began holding weekly meetings in 1886. The group, founded by working women, sought to organize unions, advocate for shorter hours and higher wages, and press for enforcement of existing labor laws.[30] By 1890 the Working Women's Society supported strikes, investigated working conditions, and supported legislation to improve the lives of laboring women.[31] Although the WWS was initially a group of working women, O'Reilly and her coworkers began to find allies outside the labor movement, most notably Josephine Shaw Lowell, the head of the New York State Board of Charities, who attended meetings at O'Reilly's request. Lowell help organize the group's first mass meeting in 1888, where they outlined a platform, including equal pay for equal work and the need for protective legislation.[32]

The cross-class experiment begun under the WWS did not survive, but O'Reilly continued to navigate the difficult terrain of cross-class cooperation. In 1894 she joined the Social Reform Club, organized by Felix Adler (founder of the New York Society for Ethical Culture). The group was intended to promote practical reform, limiting plans to ones with "a fair hope of early success." Other members included Josephine Shaw Lowell and Samuel Gompers (head of the American Federation of Labor). The club attracted twice as many non–wage earners as laborers, but all members were expected to have an active interest in the elevation of society, particularly in improving the condition of wage earners.[33] O'Reilly found her role to be somewhat awkward. As the only woman factory worker, O'Reilly held a unique place in the club, and she found herself called upon to explain the needs of working women. She confided to a friend that the other women "keep telling me all the time that I am the only real representative working-woman in other words I am the only factory girl."[34] Despite the difficulties of working with middle-class reformers, who often had different strategies and priorities, Leonora O'Reilly devoted her life to the causes of women and workers. By the turn of the twentieth century, a new organization developed to formalize the relationship between women labor leaders and middle-class reformers: the Women's Trade Union League (WTUL).

The early twentieth century saw a revival in labor activism. Between 1897 and 1904, trade union membership grew remarkably—more than quadrupling. The American Federation of Labor was founded in the 1880s as the Knights of Labor went into steep decline. The AFL would grow to account for 81 percent of all union members but focused primarily on gaining better wages for skilled male workers, thus neglecting the needs of working women.[35] Without the aid of trade union men, working women sought new allies at the same time that middle-class Protestant women moved most dramatically into social reform. The Progressive Era also marked a crucial period in the expansion of public and political roles for Protestant women, as they created settlement houses, joined the temperance movement, and formed women's clubs. Inspired by widespread immigration, rapid industrialization, economic instability, and labor strife, by the late nineteenth century women found an outlet for their talents and a rationale for their desire to serve the public good. For example,

Jane Addams founded Hull House in an immigrant neighborhood in Chicago in 1889. By 1910 there were four hundred settlement houses in all the major US cities, and the majority of residents were educated women.[36] The association between women's reform activities and politics also led to support for women's suffrage within third-party movements (from the Populists through the Progressives) and attracted new allies, including the Woman's Christian Temperance Union.

Working women found valuable allies in Progressive Era women's organizations, as the following story illustrates. In 1900 Hannah O'Day and Maggie Condon (both Irish American Catholics) led a walkout of about seventy-five women from a canning department in Chicago's meatpacking district to protest the third wage cut in a year. Unorganized and without financial support, the strike failed, and the leaders lost their jobs. Despite unemployment and blacklisting, a group of women began to meet as the "Maud Gonne Club," named after the famous beauty and Irish nationalist who had just toured the United States in opposition to Irish soldiers serving in the British army during the Boer War (1899–1902). With help from the women of University Settlement, the Maud Gonne Club became Local 183 of the Amalgamated Meat Cutters and Butcher Workmen of North America, growing to five hundred strong and attracting women across ethnic lines.[37]

Although Local 183 faltered in 1904, alliances between women across class, ethnic, and religious lines became more frequent in the early twentieth century, particularly through the Women's Trade Union League, modeled after the Women's Trade Union League in Britain, which had been founded in the 1870s. The WTUL in the United States was founded at the 1903 American Federation of Labor Convention in Boston after settlement worker William English Walling presented his idea to Mary Kenney O'Sullivan.[38] Mary Kenney was born in Missouri to Irish immigrant parents. She had a fourth grade education when she went out to work. With the death of her father, Kenney supported herself and her mother in the bookbinding trade. Moving to Chicago in search of work, she became interested in organizing the bookbinders. This brought her to the attention of

Hull House, and Jane Addams gave them a place to meet. In 1892 Samuel Gompers appointed Kenney to be the first female organizer for the American Federation of Labor, a post she held for only five months before the executive council of the AFL decided not to renew her contract.[39] In 1894 she married John O'Sullivan, a labor organizer who also wrote for the *Boston Globe.* The family lived in Boston, where Mary and John had four children. But a tragic accident left Mary a widow in 1902 when John stepped off the wrong side of a train and was killed.[40] The following year, Mary Kenney O'Sullivan helped found the Women's Trade Union League.

The mission of the WTUL was to organize working women and cooperate with the American Federation of Labor. The new national organization had an executive board composed of women trade unionists and middle-class sympathizers called allies. The WTUL's constitution required that the national board have a majority of trade union members. Mary Kenney O'Sullivan and Leonora O'Reilly both served on the first executive board.[41] However, the first national officers were wealthy club women, including Mary Morton Kehew (former president of the General Federation of Women's Clubs) and Jane Addams. The three largest branches of the WTUL were in Boston, New York, and Chicago, all associated with settlement houses there.[42] Through the WTUL, Irish American women joined a cross-class and multiethnic movement to improve the conditions of working women, an effort that also led to their increasing presence in politics, including the suffrage movement.

Irish American women played foundational roles in a number of branches, including Leonora O'Reilly, who helped found the New York branch of the WTUL; Mary Kenney O'Sullivan, who worked to form the national WTUL and served as its first secretary; and a garment worker named Hannah Hennessey, who started an active branch in St. Louis. While the WTUL was a cross-class and multiethnic organization, these women present an opportunity to study conceptions of political activity among Irish American women in the labor movement. Through the study of labor leaders, we can see the possibilities and pitfalls of political activities for working-class women, but also some of the first Irish American women to lobby in the state legislatures, endorse political roles for women, and embrace suffrage.

The goal of the WTUL was primarily organizational—to join women together into unions and to cooperate with the American Federation of Labor. The task was a daunting one, needing the skills of union organizers but also the cooperation of middle-class allies who could bring their connections, funds, and time to the cause of working women. Although they sought women's integration into the labor movement, WTUL leaders became disillusioned with attempts to cooperate with the AFL. Margaret Dreier Robins, a wealthy ally and president of the national WTUL from 1907 to 1922, confided her frustration to Leonora O'Reilly in 1914. She wrote that she wanted to "bombard" the American Federation of Labor's convention with women delegates to force them to recognize the cause of laboring women. She accused them of arrogance and contempt for working women.[43] This tension was not new, and WTUL leaders recognized the difficulty of advocating for women within the labor movement. But union organization was not the only goal of the WTUL, which expressed interest in supporting legislation to improve the conditions of working women from its founding. Even at its inception in 1903, the league committed itself to securing "new legislation to protect women workers and to obtain better enforcement of existing laws." At the league's first national convention in 1907, their platform included equal pay for equal work and an eight-hour day.[44]

Factory Inspection Laws and Protective Labor Legislation

Before the first laws restricting working women's hours, the first female factory inspectors were hired as a result of cooperation between middle-class reformers and union activists, beginning in the late nineteenth century. While still a Knight, Leonora Barry reached out to reformer Florence Kelley to cooperate on a Pennsylvania law regulating the work of women and children and providing for state factory inspectors.[45] Barry defended the need for the law in the pages of the *Irish World*, which published her article in June 1888. She told her "brother workingmen of Pennsylvania, you are to blame for existing conditions," until they used their ballots and insisted on enforcement of the laws of their state. She further called for a state factory inspector law, "for the sake of our women and children."[46] Barry worked with Florence Kelley (who grew up in Philadelphia) to bring together a coalition of elite and working-class women to form the Philadelphia Working Women's Society with the purpose of helping women to "form organizations for self-protection . . . and for obtaining and enforcing legislation in the interests of the working class." In 1889 this alliance resulted in a law that not only regulated the employment of women and children but also led to the hiring of the first female factory inspectors in the United States.[47]

Similar legislation had some success in New York as well. For example, the Working Women's Society in New York also supported an eight-hour-day bill for women workers and advocated a factory inspection law, which passed in 1890.[48] In a letter to Leonora O'Reilly, her old friend Margaret Finn (ethnicity unknown) reminisced about the WWS. Finn pointed out that "our society was most active" in working for a factory-law amendment to appoint women inspectors. She recalled lobbying politicians and working "day and night for its passage." As a result of its passage, Finn became one of the first appointees.[49] The bill, known as the Van Etten Bill, after WWS founder Ida Van Etten, created eight positions for women factory inspectors. As Finn explained, the hope was that women workers would be able to "confide to women inspectors grievances relating to matters of propriety, that they would not tell to inspectors who are men."[50]

In addition to supporting female factory inspectors, advocates for labor reform were also pursuing legislation to protect women wage earners, particularly through a shorter working day. The first laws designed to restrict women's work were advocated in the 1870s, but these laws were largely unenforceable.[51] Massachusetts passed a law limiting the workweeks of women and children to sixty hours in 1874, but the first eight-hour-day law for women was crafted by reformer Florence Kelley. The bill, which passed the Illinois Legislature in 1893, had a built-in measure for enforcement and created positions for female factory inspectors.[52] By the time Kelley moved to Chicago, she already had experience working for factory legislation in Pennsylvania and New York. Kelley grew up in a wealthy and politically progressive family. Her father, William Kelley, was a judge who also served many years as a Republican in Congress, where he supported civil and voting rights for former slaves and woman suffrage. Florence Kelley earned a bachelor's degree from Cornell, had a strong interest in social science, and pursued graduate work in Zurich, where she also embraced socialism.[53]

In the 1890s Kelley relocated to Chicago and joined Jane Addams at Hull House. The Illinois Bureau of Labor Statistics also hired her to investigate the sweatshop system in the garment industry. In Chicago she found a community of like-minded women. With the support of Hull House, Kelley spearheaded the drafting of a bill to limit women's hours, prohibit child labor, and establish factor inspection. Members of the Hull House community supported the legislation at union meetings, social clubs, and church organizations.[54] Under the new law, Kelley became chief factory inspector for the state of Illinois, with Mary Kenney as one of her assistants.

Two years later, the limit on women's hours would be overturned by the Illinois Supreme Court. Despite the setback, advocates of labor reform continued to sponsor bills to protect women workers, including minimum-wage laws and shorter workdays for women. By the early twentieth century, most states passed some form of regulation on women's employment. Women's groups, including the General Federation of Women's Clubs, the WTUL, and the National Consumers' League (under the leadership of Florence Kelley), led the drive for protective legislation, and their efforts were successful. In 1908 the US Supreme Court heard the case of *Muller v. Oregon*, based on a 1903 Oregon law that restricted women's factory work to ten hours a day.[55] The Court upheld Oregon's law and established a precedent for protecting women workers, arguing, "The two sexes differ in structure of body, in the functions to be performed by each, in the amount of physical strength." Therefore, the Court believed that owing to "the influence of vigorous health upon the future well-being of the race, the self-reliance which enables one to assert full rights, and in the capacity to maintain the struggle for subsistence," women could be treated differently when legislation "is designed to compensate for some of the burdens which rest upon [them]."[56]

The contributions of club women and female reformers are unquestionable to the history of progressive labor legislation, but working women and trade union women also weighed in on these measures. One such law, while written with the aid of the WTUL and its lawyers, was passed due to the lobbying efforts of working women, including Agnes Nestor. Nestor was born in Grand Rapids, Michigan. Her father, Thomas Nestor, came to the United States from Galway as a child. During the depression in the 1890s, the family moved to Chicago, where Agnes went to work as a glove maker. At the age of eighteen, she led her first strike in 1898. She became president of her local, and in 1902 Nestor served as a delegate to the founding convention of the International Glove Workers' Union.[57] A sympathetic article in the *Chicago Tribune* described Nestor as the "clever little president" (she was only five feet tall) of a well-organized union of four hundred "clear-headed girls."[58]

Her union leadership brought her to the attention of Illinois club women. In 1905 Nestor was asked to speak to the convention of the Illinois Federation of Women's Clubs. Under the headline "Clubdom Extends Hand to Toilers," the *Chicago Tribune* described Nestor as a "toiling girl," but also reported her discussion of the demand for a nine-hour day and better working conditions. Although the headline suggested that elite women were extending a benevolent hand to working women, Nestor was also fostering an important relationship across class lines. The newspaper also quoted her mother as saying, "My daughter is doing all she can to advance the interests of the working girls and I am glad that the club women have given their sympathy." Nestor later recalled that trade union women did not usually appear on the programs of club women at that time, but she credited the efforts of Jane Addams and Mary McDowell for paving the way for a relationship between the two groups.[59] Nestor's union leadership eventually took her out of the factory when she accepted a paid position with the International Glove Workers' Union. She also devoted her life to working women. Nestor attended her first WTUL meeting at Hull House in 1904, and she quickly applied for membership. The next time she appeared in the *Tribune*, it was not as a little toiler but as a skilled lobbyist who "ran the legislature" after shepherding a women's ten-hour-day bill through the Illinois Legislature in 1909.[60]

The successful defense of protective labor legislation in *Muller v. Oregon* inspired a renewed effort for factory legislation in Illinois. The Chicago Women's Trade Union League, and their attorney, drafted a bill for an eight-hour day, and four working women, including two Irish Americans (Nestor and a waitress named Elizabeth Maloney), took the lead in supporting it.[61] The women spent months lobbying the bill through the legislature, and although the original bill did not pass, a compromise ten-hour bill did. Two years later, Nestor and Maloney returned to Springfield to champion a bill for a shorter workweek. Although originally aiming for fifty-four hours, the final bill extended the ten-hour day to all women except agricultural and domestic workers and limited the workweek to sixty hours. Nestor went on to serve as president of the Chicago WTUL from 1913 to 1948, where she would finally see an eight-hour-day bill passed in 1937.[62]

Teachers' Pensions and Teachers' Rights

As studies of Irish women in America have shown, first-generation women worked overwhelmingly in domestic service, but their daughters began to move into female-dominated professions such as teaching and nursing. Teaching offered young women and single women a stable career and source of income. Furthermore, the teaching profession was "held in high esteem" by Irish servants, whose daughters later "flocked into public school teaching."[63]

Before stricter preparatory standards were put in place for teachers around the turn of the century, teachers needed the equivalent of a high school education. For example, in 1880 almost half of Chicago teachers came from working-class backgrounds, and more than half of Chicago's elementary school teachers did not have four years of high school education.[64] Efforts to reform education and increase standards in the profession would hurt the daughters of immigrants and the working class. Still, by the turn of the twentieth century, Irish American teachers were a significant presence in urban school districts. They made up one-quarter of the public teaching force in smaller cities like Scranton, Lowell, and Buffalo, but also one-third of the teachers in Boston and Chicago. By 1910 almost half of the grammar school teachers in San Francisco were also of Irish descent.[65]

By the early twentieth century, a transition was under way from the teachers' organizations of the nineteenth century, which focused on professional issues but not economic ones, toward more political activism among teachers. Early teachers' associations were dominated by men, focused on administrators and school leadership, and were divorced from the financial concerns of the rank-and-file teachers. The National Education Association (1857) was an organization of administrators (and mostly male). Even in the 1890s, 50 percent of active NEA members were school administrators, while only 11 percent of members were classroom teachers.[66] Instead of NEA membership, women formed associations at the local level. From the 1870s until the turn of the century, women teachers formed clubs in many cities, including Boston, Chicago, Minneapolis, and Buffalo. One such association, the Lady Teachers' Association of Boston, focused on self-improvement, mutual aid, and sociability, often downplaying members' political views and keeping their suffrage sympathies separate from their professional activities.[67] By the end of the nineteenth century, concern about teacher security, unequal pay, and teachers' rights led to the formation of teachers' organizations that were focused on economic issues and necessarily political, a process that began with two Irish American schoolteachers: Catherine Goggin and Margaret Haley.

The movement for teachers' pensions was a response to legislation expanding the availability of military pensions under the Dependent Pension Act of 1890. Supporters of teachers' pensions argued that pensions would encourage loyalty and service. According to Karen Leroux, "Teachers portrayed themselves as self-sacrificing soldiers in the underpaid work of education, stressing their contributions to building a strong, independent citizenry."[68] But the issue of pensions was a gendered one. At the beginning of the pension movement in 1890, women teachers earned an average of $52–65 a month, as compared to the average male teacher's salary of $132–65 a month. However, most of the teachers were women. In 1900 women made up 70 percent of the teaching force, and 95 percent of female teachers were single (widowed, divorced, or never married).[69] Therefore, single women were vulnerable to economic problems as they aged. The movement for teachers' pensions had widespread success, with ten states passing legislation in the 1890s. Twenty-two states had some form of teachers' pension by the early twentieth century, and by 1916 thirty-three states had some form of funding for teachers' pensions.[70]

In Chicago the pension movement was led by Catherine Goggin, who came to be described in the press as "the little general." Goggin was born in upstate New York of Irish immigrant parents. She graduated from high school in Chicago, where she immediately went into teaching.[71] She lost both her parents (and a sister) in the 1870s, while still in her twenties. Goggin never married and was struck by a car and killed in 1916.[72] She became a founding member of the Irish Women's Club of '98, a group intended to unite women of Irish birth and descent, while also studying Irish history and folklore.[73] However, her most visible impact was on the fight for teachers' pensions and the organization of the Chicago Teachers' Federation. In her autobiography, Margaret Haley recalled, "The legislation of 1895, granting a pension to teachers, had been the direct result of Catherine Goggin's interest in other teachers and foresight for them."[74]

The success of teachers' pension laws was not without controversy and challenge. There was opposition from male teachers and administrators. Under most plans, teachers voluntarily deferred a percentage of their salaries (usually 1 percent) in exchange for a pension after a certain number of years of service (twenty for women, twenty-five for men). These pensions were not transferable to dependents, and because male salaries were larger they contributed more of their income, leading to the concern that male earnings were being used to subsidize women's pensions. In 1897, because of legal challenges to the system, two thousand Chicago teachers rallied behind the pension plan and formed the Chicago Teachers' Federation to protect their interests.[75]

Although not the first president of the CTF, Goggin challenged the incumbent within the first year (and lost), but the following year she teamed up with Margaret Haley and won a bitter campaign. As the president of the CTF, Goggin promised to focus on economic issues: pensions and salary increases.[76]

Goggin's chief ally was Margaret Haley. Haley was born in Joliet, Illinois. Her paternal grandparents had emigrated from Ireland to Canada, and her mother was Irish born. Haley described her mother as valuing "education as only the Irish, who had been denied the full measure of education they desired, could value it." The family leased a farm when Margaret was young, but her father was also involved in quarrying. Financial problems would ultimately force a young Haley out of school and into the classroom. When her father lost the quarry, she recalled, "I knew it meant I must begin to dig for myself and for the rest of the family. . . . It meant for me the end of school and I had to prepare to do something else."[77] That fall, at the age of sixteen, she began teaching in a rural school near Dresden Heights, Illinois. She continued her normal school education and moved a few times, entering the Chicago area in 1881.[78] Haley was an astute politician and a feisty opponent. She called her career advocating for teachers' rights her "battleground." These two Irish American teachers, Haley and Goggin, led the discussion on teacher pay.

One of the biggest victories during the early partnership of Haley and Goggin was in a tax fight that would ultimately secure more funds for the city schools. Although Chicago teachers were due to get a raise in 1899, the board of education maintained that they did not have the funds to pay it. Haley wrote in her autobiography about the day she conceived of the tax strategy. A teacher at the CTF office was describing a newspaper article about large corporations that were not paying property taxes, which gave her the idea. She recalled, "I don't know why I should have seized upon the information with avidity. . . . It looked as simple to me in the moment as it does now after thirty-five years of sight and range. If the great corporations paid their legal taxes, there would be plenty of money to operate the schools."[79] In 1900 Haley took a leave from teaching to devote herself to a full-time investigation of corporate taxes, researching taxes and tax law for ten months. As a result, the CTF hired a tax attorney and sued five utility companies. In May 1901, Haley and the federation won their case: the judge ruled that the tax assessments were illegal. Although the companies owed much more, the board of education received six hundred thousand dollars. When the board still failed to pay the teachers' raises, Haley sued again. In 1904 the teachers were finally awarded back salary.[80]

After the tax fight, Goggin sent Haley on the road, where she conducted a national speaking tour of teachers' organizations.[81] In addition to her success in closing corporate loopholes, Haley promoted other strategies to help teachers: she was a suffragist, and she advocated for cooperation with organized labor. She once told the NEA, "To bring the teaching profession from 'below the bread line,'" there must be equal suffrage. She further supported the inclusion of teachers in labor reforms, telling the convention, "Minimum wage commissioners never investigate the wages of teachers, because they do not class teachers as working-women, and teachers themselves do not wished to be classed as workingwomen."[82]

In 1902 the Chicago Teachers' Federation and its five thousand members affiliated with the Chicago Federation of Labor (CFL), creating a new type of teachers' organization—one that not only brought economic issues to the fore but also cooperated with organized labor. Between 1902 and 1910, eleven teachers' organizations affiliated with the American Federation of Labor.[83] The CTF also affiliated with the WTUL, which had an active branch in Chicago. Not all teachers' organizations affiliated with trade unions during this time period, but Haley and Goggin both advocated for this relationship. In 1908 Goggin told a group of Catholic women in Detroit, "Teachers need the unions and the unions need the teachers. . . . Let Standard Oil get hold of your public schools and where is your American republic." She assured Detroit teachers that organizing with the American Federation of Labor would improve their conditions.[84]

Chicago teachers led the way on affiliating with organized labor, but this strategy was only a temporary success. The board of education in Chicago attacked this alliance in 1915, passing a resolution (also known as the Loeb rule) declaring that teachers could not belong to organizations affiliated with trade unions.[85] Despite the protests of the CTF and the Chicago Federation of Labor, in 1916 sixty-eight teachers were denied reappointment, including the leadership of the CTF. Furthermore, in 1917 the Illinois Supreme Court ruled that the "board has the absolute right to decline to employ or re-employ any applicant for any reason," which led Jacob Loeb (president of the board) to declare a complete victory over unions in the public schools. The Chicago Teacher's Federation of Labor backed off from its alliances with both the CFL and the WTUL, at which point the fired teachers were reinstated, but the CTF had suffered great losses in membership and funds.[86]

While most of the historical scholarship on teacher activists before the founding of the American Federation of Teachers in 1916 focuses on Chicago, other political efforts (although not trade union affiliated) developed out of teachers' organizations in early-twentieth-century cities. Women had become influential in city organizations in Chicago, Cincinnati, Boston, New York, and San Francisco. By 1910 half of US cities had organizations of women teachers.[87] More research needs to be done on the role of Irish American teachers in these organizations. Certainly, many rank-and-file members in cities such as Boston, New York, and Chicago were likely of Irish descent by this time period. A preliminary look at the leadership also identifies the involvement of Irish American women.

In New York, the principle of equal pay for equal work was gaining support among teachers when women teachers organized across the boroughs, first as the Women's Teachers Organization and then with the name Interborough Association of Women Teachers (1906). The group's first president, Kate Hogan, was a classroom teacher, but she also told the group that the movement for equal pay had been extended "so as to include all women in the system from Principal down to class teacher."[88] Both teachers and administrators were active in the organization. Hogan, who was likely Irish American, was a lawyer by training. In 1893 the *Albany Law Journal* described Hogan as an attractive thirty-five-year-old who had been teaching for fifteen years. If accurate, that means she was a veteran teacher of more than twenty-five years by the early twentieth century. She led the drive for an equal pay law after failing to get assurances from the board of education, but she did not survive to see the campaign through. She died of pneumonia within the first year.[89] Her successor was an administrator named Grace Strachan. Strachan was a graduate of the Buffalo Normal School. Her parents were Irish (mother) and Scottish (father) immigrants, and she was a practicing Catholic.[90]

Like Haley, Strachan was also a suffragist (although unlike Haley she minimized her suffrage support until after the equal-pay fight was over).[91] Under her leadership, the bill for equal pay made its way through the New York Legislature more than once. According to an NEA survey in 1905, women high school teachers made 69 percent of their male colleagues' salaries. In New York City, entry-level women teachers made 66 percent compared to their male counterparts. By 1905 cities such as Chicago, Pittsburgh, and Buffalo altered their pay scales to provide the same maximum salary to men and women at the top of the pay scale.[92] The New York City equal-pay bill, sponsored by Senator Horace White of Syracuse, passed the legislature easily, only to be vetoed by Governor Charles Evans Hughes, who argued that the principle of equal pay should not be passed on a city-by-city basis. The teachers never gave up on the bill, but it took four attempts to get the bill through under a new governor in 1911. The provision for equal pay would not be extended to the rest of the state until the 1920s.[93]

The same year that New York teachers founded the Interborough Association of Women Teachers, teachers in San Francisco founded the City Federation of Teachers under the leadership of Margaret Mahoney, a medical doctor (and daughter of Irish immigrants) who also taught night school. Influenced by the tax fight in Chicago, the City Federation of Teachers focused their criticism on the distribution of public lands by the board of education, arguing that those properties represented a source of revenue for schools.[94] Mahoney specifically objected to the leasing of school board–owned land for noneducational purposed at low or no rates. Her exposure and criticism of the practice ultimately led to a legal battle with the school department in 1907, which intended to try her for insubordination and conduct unbecoming a teacher. Although Mahoney lost her legal battle to prevent the trial, no mention of it exists in the *San Francisco Call*. However, she did not disappear from the teachers' federation.[95] In advocating for an expanded base of funding, Mahoney learned from the Chicago example, but teachers in San Francisco also had a history with advocating for teacher pay. Kate Kennedy, who emigrated from Ireland with two siblings during the famine, fought for an equal-pay law in 1874—the first of its kind. Kennedy also won tenure and pension plans for San Francisco teachers; however, many of these victories would later be repealed. Kennedy died in the 1890s, but she was not forgotten. In 1911 the Kate Kennedy School Women's Club began meeting and also advocated to name a school after her.[96]

A Radical Tradition among Irish American Women

Research on Irish American men in New York suggests that between the Civil War and World War I, Irish Americans in the labor movement organized to become militant and radical opponents of industrial capitalism, but eventually came to dominate a more conservative labor union bureaucracy.[97] As we have seen, women followed a different pattern, largely by necessity seeking out middle-class reformers and alliances outside the labor movement. But some Irish American women rejected the influence of reformers, taking a more radical approach.

Leonora O'Reilly is a good example of someone who moved between the worlds of women reformers, trade unionism, and socialism. Her earliest mentors were survivors of the Paris Commune, and she maintained a relationship with socialist activists. However, these loyalties could also clash with the world of women's reform. For example, when she disagreed with suffrage-parade organizer Harriot Stanton Blatch about the date of the New York march in 1912, O'Reilly determined to march with the suffragists and the socialists. The conflict began when Blatch insisted on holding the parade during the day, when she believed most women could come. She wrote to O'Reilly, "The parade must not be for this class of women only, or for that, it must aim to draw out the largest number of women of all sorts and conditions." In reply, O'Reilly expressed concern over its conflicting with the Socialist's Labor Day Parade. Since O'Reilly sympathized with both causes, she wrote, "If I'm in the city I'll be in both—For I'm just enough Irish to be always on a parade or a fight—That's [how?] The world thinks of us at least—."[98]

O'Reilly also became close friends with an Irish American surgeon named Gertrude B. Kelly. Born in Ireland around 1862, Kelly immigrated to the United States with her parents and eleven brothers and sisters.[99] Her father became a public school principal in Hoboken, New Jersey. Both parents appear to have been active in the Land League, and her mother has also been described as sympathetic to the cause of labor. Gertrude Kelly taught school before graduating from medical school in 1884.[100] Although very little evidence exists for her early career, she (and her brother, John F. Kelly) wrote for three anarchist publications in the 1880s. Benjamin Tucker published *Liberty*, an individualist anarchist publication and a voice of American radical thought, from 1881 until a fire put him out of business in 1908, but Kelly wrote for him for only two years.[101]

Kelly is sometimes mentioned by historians of Irish nationalism (in the twentieth century), but she became a radical voice for social change much earlier. In 1889 the *New York Evening Post* reported on a meeting of the Women's Conference of the City of New York, held to discuss the idea of providing a few hours of nonsectarian entertainment for children who did not go to Sunday school. Dr. Gertrude Kelly read a paper "describing the tenement-house life of hard-working people," and "Miss [Leonora] O'Reilly spoke from the point of view of those who live in tenement-houses."[102] Although it is unclear when the two women first met, in 1920 Leonora O'Reilly wrote of Dr. Kelly, "I've known her for thirty-five years—When I was just a song of the shirt little woman she was a brilliant young doctor—she helped me to good reading and clean thinking."[103]

O'Reilly's diary clearly shows that the two women consulted on O'Reilly's social reform work. In 1905 O'Reilly temporarily resigned from the WTUL over a sensational book titled *The Long Day: The Story of a New York Working Girl as Told by Herself* (1905) by Dorothy

Richardson. O'Reilly objected to what she considered Richardson's exploitation of the working girl and the WTUL's plan to publish it. In her diary, she recorded her reaction to the article and her plans to write her own rebuttal, a plan she shared with Gertrude Kelly. O'Reilly thought the "poor trash hardly worth reading let alone writing about," but she "saw Dr Kelly about it." And when she finished writing the article, "Dr Kelly calls unexpectedly" and "advises me to send it just as it is without any additions or corrections." A few weeks later, O'Reilly confided her frustration in her diary; her article would not be published: "Home only a few minutes when Dr Kelly comes—No hope for Nora's voice being heard—'The dear girl' trash [is] what will be published."[104]

Unfortunately, Kelly left no personal papers and her life is very hard to trace, but her published articles do tell the story of a committed reformer who saw labor and class exploitation as an urgent calling. Through her writing, Kelly urged reform rather than charitable work, criticizing efforts to ameliorate the suffering brought about by industrial capitalism without addressing its causes. In an article from the 1880s titled "Bourgeois Charity," Kelly asserted that charity efforts assumed "that these burdens are the result of individual misfortune, laziness, drunkenness, etc., and that they are therefore to be relieved by individual efforts." She offered a scathing review of a meeting of the Newark Bureau of Associated Charities, where the "cultured classes" proposed to provide some insight about the causes and cures of poverty. According to Kelly, "The society, which has four paid superintendents who devote their whole time and energy to the work, and an executive committee of forty ladies who have nothing else to do, after four years investigation has not yet discovered that monopoly has any share in the production of poverty."[105] These "philanthropic ladies" attracted her derision because Kelly viewed their efforts to aid working women as patronizing and humiliating. But worse than looking down on working girls, she believed, these women gave lessons on the evils of trade unionism. Therefore, the best and brightest working girls (who were most likely to join such societies) were taught not to question their condition and the reasons for it.[106]

Kelly also argued that any chance for lasting reform required the education of women. In this article she takes aim not at wealthy women but at radical men. In "A Woman's Warning to Reformers," Kelly pleaded with male anarchists to take an interest in the Woman Question because the success of the revolution depended on educating and emancipating women. She turned traditional notions of women's influences around to argue that women served as important factors in stalling social progress. Mothers' influence kept children from social reform because women had been conditioned not to think independently or risk defying public opinion. She told her readers, "Unless you convert the women . . . what is gained in one generation will be lost in the next, and all because women are supposed to have no intelligence to which you can appeal. You do not know whether they have intelligence or not, for you have never tried to find out."[107]

In the wake of the Haymarket affair in 1886, Kelly defended anarchists as true revolutionaries, the successors of abolitionists and the patriots of 1776. She described anarchism as a product of "American soil, the fruit of American liberty," and "the heritage of a free people." As abolitionists had demanded that the government withdraw its support for the institution of slavery, anarchists called for the government to stop aiding the power of capital over labor. Kelly reminded her readers that they lived "in the midst of a tremendous revolution." She assured would-be reformers that their age did not lack in opportunities for heroic action, but instead offered "excellent opportunities for the continuation of the abolition movement . . . the abolition of ownership of man by man—which can only be accomplished by the abolition of usury in all its forms."[108] Unfortunately, Kelly's views on social questions are impossible to gauge once she stopped publishing. However, she became visible and controversial in New York Irish nationalist circles in the twentieth century.

Other Irish American women, like the "Rebel Girl," Elizabeth Gurley Flynn, also emerged as labor radicals, particularly by the early twentieth century. The Flynn family's socialism was closely connected to the influence of Irish nationalist and socialist James Connolly, who died for his leading role in the Easter Rising of 1916. Connolly, founder of the Irish Socialist Republican Party and an organizer for the Socialist Party of Ireland, spent several years in the United States. He believed in a link between socialism and nationalism, asserting that a socialist revolution in Ireland also meant the formation of a separate Irish government; Ireland had to be independent first.[109] James Connolly led a brief push to establish a relationship between socialism in Ireland and the socialist movement in the United States; he lived in the United States for several years and tried to organize Irish American socialists for educational work. Connolly proposed a socialist federation in the United States, affiliated with the Socialist Party of Ireland. In 1907 a meeting was held to form the Irish Socialist Federation (ISF) with the purpose of educating Irish Americans about socialism and supporting the Irish working-class movement. The federation sought to prepare Irish American workers to become part of the American proletariat's struggle and to help the movement in Ireland. Through the *Harp*, organ of the Irish Socialist Federation, Connolly encouraged Irish American socialists to maintain ties with the Irish community and to translate socialist teachings into "terms of Irish thought" rather than raising barriers between socialists and other Irish men and women.[110] He defended the needs for a separate effort among Irish Americans because, he claimed, Irish American capitalists and politicians tricked workers and took their time and money in the name of Irish nationalism.[111]

Elizabeth Gurley Flynn and her father were both members of the Irish Socialist Federation. Elizabeth Gurley Flynn was born in 1890. Her mother, Annie Gurley, was an Irish immigrant, while her father was born in the United States of Irish parents. Tom Flynn became a devoted socialist by the early twentieth century, bringing his children along to socialist events in New York. Although she recalled that her father "had a tendency to overdo it" and "tried to turn everything into socialist propaganda," Elizabeth Gurley Flynn gave her first public speech as a teen in 1906 at the Harlem Socialist Club, where she discussed women's oppression under capitalism.[112]

Flynn met Connolly in 1907, and the two families became close: his children played with her younger siblings. In her autobiography, she recalled, "The Federation [ISF] was born one Sunday afternoon at our house in the Bronx." Initially, the ISF organized street meetings, while Connolly prepared a statement of purpose and published the *Harp*. But she also recalled of Connolly, "It was a pathetic sight to see him poorly clad, at the door of Cooper Union or some other East Side Hall, selling his little paper. None of the prosperous professional Irish, who shouted their admiration for him after his death, lent him a helping hand at that time."[113] By 1909, as Connolly contemplated a return to Ireland, he confided, "I am, as ever, or more than ever, convinced that the propaganda of Socialism amongst the Irish in this country will wait upon Socialist success in Ireland." Connolly transferred the *Harp* to Dublin and returned to Ireland in 1910.[114]

Meanwhile, Elizabeth Gurley Flynn had begun to speak at open-air meetings, and as she recalled, she "took to it like a duck in water." Flynn did not remain in New York for long, however. Soon after beginning her speaking career, she joined the Industrial Workers of the World in 1906 and helped organize her first strike in Bridgeport, Connecticut, in 1907.[115] The IWW was formed in 1905 by a small group of radical labor organizers, including Mother (Mary Harris) Jones (who did not become active in the organization).[116] Flynn described Jones as "the Greatest woman agitator of our time." And the newspapers described her as the daughter of "an Irish agitator" who still had "a caustic tongue, a martial spirit, and a philosophical mind" in her eighties.[117] Jones was an Irish immigrant from County Cork who lost her family in a yellow-fever epidemic in Memphis, Tennessee. In the 1870s she worked with the Knights of Labor and remained friends with Terence Powderly, but found her niche with the United Mine Workers beginning in the 1890s.[118] These radical women were activists and reformers, although not necessarily suffragists like the other women in this chapter. Mother Jones in particular was quoted as saying that "women are out of place in political work," and she was "in no sense . . . in sympathy with woman's suffrage."[119]

Despite such differences, these reformers have one thing in common: they were all leaders and pioneers in the labor movement and often for the rights of working women as well. Between 1880 and

1920, many Irish American women experienced American industrial capitalism from the bottom: as industrial wage earners. Yet their experiences with the workforce also moved them to become leaders in the effort to unionize women and to push for legislation to improve the lives of working women. While unionized men tended to seek shorter hours through collective bargaining, women turned to alliances with middle-class reformers who helped to seek protective legislation and women's suffrage. By the early twentieth century, these alliances were formalized in the development of the Women's Trade Union League.

By the early twentieth century, the role of Irish American women in the workforce was also changing, as many moved into teaching. Low wages and unequal pay also led women teachers into politics to advocate for teachers' pensions, raises, and equal pay for equal work. Many of these early laws were initiated by or lobbied for by Irish American women in conjunction with their middle-class allies. In both cases, for teachers and factory workers, economic matters and working conditions led Irish American women toward political engagement, particularly by the turn of the twentieth century.

PART TWO

Irish Nationalism

3

Charitable Colleens or Voracious Viragoes?

The Influence of the Ladies' Land League and Its Legacy

In the spring of 1881, the East Boston Branch of the Ladies' Land League issued a call for organization, declaring, "The hour has come when England should be made to understand that never will the expatriated children of Erin allow her to be the beggar of nations." Americans of Irish decent had the means to prevent this, but, more important, it was considered their "duty."[1] The insistence that Irish Americans should support the poor and suffering of Ireland certainly would not have raised much opposition, but what obligation did women have to the movement? Could their "duty" lead them into activities previously considered unwomanly, or was the Ladies' Land League simply a charitable endeavor—a logical extension of women's role in the family and the church? The activities of the Ladies' Land League sparked this debate on both sides of the Atlantic. This chapter argues that the formation of Ladies' Land Leagues throughout the United States in the early 1880s made two significant contributions to the development of political participation for Irish American women.

This chapter is derived in part from a chapter originally published in *Susan B. Anthony and the Struggle for Equal Rights*, edited by Christine L. Ridarsky and Mary M. Huth.

In its brief existence, the Ladies' Land League brought women into a national movement years before any national organizations of Irish or Catholic laywomen existed, mobilizing women in the name of service, duty, and patriotism and thus giving them opportunities to participate in public affairs previously forbidden them.[2] The Land League movement also overlapped with the labor movement and introduced many Irish American women to reform rhetoric and activity for the first time. Thus, the Ladies' Land League marks a watershed for Irish American women's participation in public life. Women's role in the nationalist movement, although originally conceived narrowly, led to a more permanent trend toward women's organization and activism. In other words, the history of the Ladies' Land League demonstrates two key points: Irish nationalism created a role for women in the public sphere, and women's activities also exposed them to larger debates about land reform, labor issues, and women's rights—issues that mattered dearly to the Irish in America but also drew them into a wider American reform tradition.

Irish Americans remained passionately committed to the motherland during the Gilded Age and Progressive Era. Immigrants continued to arrive, ethnic newspapers circulated news from home, young people sent money to their families in Ireland, and the cause of Irish nationalism found eager audiences. Between 1820 and 1920, more than four and a half million Irish men and women settled in America, and many of them arrived young and single. As discussed in chapter 1, the Great Famine left lasting scars on Irish society and severely limited young people's opportunities. Because rural peasants depended heavily on potatoes to feed their families, when blight began to destroy their crops, widespread devastation spread throughout Ireland. One million people died of disease and starvation, and another two million people left during the famine period. This tragedy led to permanent changes in marriage patterns, with couples postponing marriage and having fewer children. Those Irish who would not inherit property or could not offer a dowry had few options, and many chose to leave. Thus, Irish immigration to the United States continued long after the famine had subsided. Approximately three and a half million Irish immigrants arrived in America between 1851 and 1921.[3]

The Irish in America have a long tradition of supporting nationalist agitation in Ireland. In fact, the American Irish supported nationalism with a fervor not seen in other Irish immigrant communities in Australia or Canada.[4] American support for nationalist movements in Ireland resurfaced regularly throughout the nineteenth century. In the 1820s, Daniel O'Connell's appeal for Catholic Emancipation found support in the United States, and by the 1840s Irish Americans organized to raise money for O'Connell's efforts to repeal the Act of Union (1801) that dissolved Ireland's parliament and made Ireland a part of the United Kingdom.[5] Six months after O'Connell founded the Repeal Association in Ireland, Boston organizers launched the first branch, which spread quickly throughout New England and beyond. As Irish Americans organized to raise funds for parliamentary reform, this opened up opportunities for women. In 1841 the Young Men's Repeal Association of New York organized a committee to solicit support from women, and Philadelphia's Repeal Association admitted sixteen women to full membership. By 1843 a Philadelphia newspaper reported an estimated three to four hundred women at one repeal meeting. Women from Boston and Providence were also taking on important fund-raising responsibilities.[6] Although the repeal movement was short-lived in the United States, collapsing in 1845, Irish American women continued to support nationalist movements in Ireland.

After the famine and the revolutions of 1848 in Europe, Irish nationalists turned to a physical-force strategy. The Fenian movement began in the late 1850s, with organizations in Ireland and the United States, which were in regular contact. The American Fenians had an estimated fifty thousand members by 1865, but the number of supporters was much greater, making it the first mass movement of Irish nationalists in the United States. Although the Fenians identified themselves with an ancient warrior tradition and constructed a highly masculine image, women were visible in fund-raising efforts.[7] In 1865 the Fenian Sisterhood, women's auxiliary of the Fenian Brotherhood, sent Ellen Mahoney to raise money in New York. Although the *New York Times* denounced Mahoney for taking money from hardworking domestic servants, Mahoney urged women to support the Fenian movement, purchase bonds, and advertise the campaign to friends and neighbors. In New York, women not only donated money to the cause but were also visible at public meetings. Women organized committees and laid a base of support for Irish nationalism in the 1860s.[8]

The New Departure

The tradition of physical-force nationalism had a dedicated following in the United States, first through the Fenians and then continuing under the leadership of Clan na Gael, which was founded in New York in 1867. However, the physical-force wing of the nationalist movement was badly divided, and the parliamentary strategies of land reform and Home Rule would take center stage after the decline of Fenianism. The Land League began with an alliance of nationalist leaders that stretched across the Atlantic. When, in the 1870s, an agricultural depression ignited fear of another famine in Ireland, nationalists formulated a new strategy to mobilize the Irish countryside to reform the land system in Ireland, particularly the predominance of absentee landlords. Michael Davitt, a former Fenian and organizing secretary of the Irish Republican Brotherhood, traveled to the United States after his release from prison, where he had served a sentence on arms charges. Davitt met with another Irish revolutionary, by then exiled to New York, John Devoy. Devoy spent five years in prison, before being exiled by the British government for his activities in the Irish Republican Brotherhood.[9] Arriving in New York in 1871, Devoy would play a central, if tumultuous, role in Irish American nationalism for the next half century. The two men planned an alliance known as the New Departure, bringing physical force and parliamentary nationalists together under the leadership of Charles Stewart Parnell (1846–91).[10] A young parliamentarian who advocated Home Rule for Ireland, Parnell attempted to steer a moderate course, harnessing popular support for Irish nationalism while avoiding its history of violence. Although Devoy still believed in armed rebellion for an independent Ireland, Parnell and his parliamentary allies wanted an Irish parliament within the British Empire (Home Rule). This alliance gave nationalism a broader base of support. Divorced from its history of rebellion, martyrdom, and violence, nationalism became more appealing to three groups in particular: the Irish American middle class, the Catholic Church, and women.[11] Parnell assumed leadership of the Irish National Land League in 1879 and quickly turned to America for support. In January 1880 Parnell arrived in New York to rally American support for the Land League and raise funds. His tour would culminate in an address to Congress and preceded the founding of the Irish National Land League of America.[12]

Like its Irish counterpart, the Irish National Land League of America consisted of several factions in an unlikely alliance. Under the influence of John Devoy, Clan na Gael, described by one historian as "the most formidable exponent of Irish physical-force nationalism to be found in the world," joined moderate nationalists to found the American league in May 1880. However, internal division on the Clan's executive committee prevented its domination of the new organization in the first year. Moderates retained control until Buffalo clansman James Moody became president in 1882.[13]

Meanwhile, through the pages of the *Irish World and Industrial Liberator*, Patrick Ford collected funds for the Land League and encouraged the organization of branches, making himself a powerful and independent voice in the movement. Patrick Ford was born in Galway and came to Boston with his parents when he was eight. As a teenager, he worked as a printer's devil for William Lloyd Garrison at the *Liberator* (an abolitionist paper) and eventually published his own, short-lived, antislavery journal. He founded the *Irish World* in New York in 1870, which became one of the most important papers of the Irish American press. Ford dedicated his paper to the concerns of the Irish American working class.[14] As a convert to the land theories of Henry George, Ford used his newspaper, and the funds it raised, to support his own reform vision. The American movement thus had three components: moderates, physical-force nationalists, and land and labor reformers with a broader social reform agenda. In addition to the political alliances among the men, the Land League offered a second new approach to Irish nationalism—the formal and visible organization of women.

The Role of Irish Nationalism in America

Despite their short lives (1880–83), the Irish National Land League of America and the Ladies' Land League initiated a mass movement of Irish nationalism in America and changes in the public activities of Irish American women. Although women had participated in fund-raising before, the Ladies' Land League evolved into a movement whereby women engaged in political debates, advocated reform principles, and laid the groundwork for other kinds of political and social activism. Although the story of Anna Parnell and Irish women's contributions to the land war have been told, until very recently historians of the Irish in America have only briefly acknowledged the contributions of American women. In his classic work on Irish nationalism in the nineteenth century, Thomas Brown argued that Irish Americans' devotion to nationalism derived not from nostalgia or a sense of duty to the motherland but from the rejection Irish immigrants experienced in America and "the realities of loneliness and alienation, and of poverty and prejudice." Brown characterized Irish American nationalism as containing a "pervasive sense of inferiority" and an "intense longing for acceptance and respectability." Brown maintained that although the Irish attacked privilege, in reality they aspired to be middle class.[15] Through nationalist aspirations, Irish immigrants responded to their communities' needs and vulnerabilities in America.

Although Brown's thesis accurately described the motives of some nationalists, more recent scholarship has complicated our understanding of diaspora nationalism. In his study of nationalism among Irish, Polish, and Jewish communities in the United States, Matthew Frye Jacobson has pointed out that the pervasiveness of ethnic nationalism does not suggest "a real or perceived identity of interests or a unanimity of opinion among diverse individuals." Although nationalism might obscure differences within ethnic communities, it could not "conceal such diversity entirely." Nationalist movements embodied the concerns of immigrant communities, but class differences remained. Laborers "were wary of the hegemonic potential couched in the ideal of national unity; and middle-class nationalists worried over each movement's demeanor and respectability."[16] Far from homogeneous in intent or outlook, a radical faction led by Patrick Ford existed within the Land League, but this unique working-class culture inspired Irish Americans to adopt a broader vision of industrial capitalism. Thus, one significant aspect of the Land League lay in its incorporation of the working-class Irish into an American reform tradition. In the words of Eric Foner, the militants of the Land League "help[ed] to transform specifically Irish grievances and traditions into a broader critique of American society in the Gilded Age."[17] For women, this transformation would ultimately mean creating women's organizations and forming alliances outside the Irish American community.

Formation of the Ladies' Land League

Thomas Brown found no inclination toward nationalism on the part of Irish American women, who, he suggested, were occupied with domestic concerns.[18] However, as David Brundage has pointed out in his study of labor radicalism in Denver, the Ladies' Land League "provided a kind of political baptism for a generation of Irish women activists."[19] More recent scholarship suggests that the close relationship between Ireland and the Irish in America created a vibrant nationalist movement during the Land League era, one that allowed for the voices and influence of workers, radicals, and women. Yet the demise of the Land League and the reassertion of conservative control within the nationalist movement effectively sidelined these alternative visions for many years.[20] Within the nationalist movement in America (and more so in Ireland), women did play a less visible role in the Home Rule movement. However, when we take a broader view of social activism in the nineteenth century, the activities of the Ladies' Land League do take on significance beyond nationalist circles, as women who were mobilized by the land war also moved into ethnic and fraternal associations, labor leadership, Populism, and even the suffrage movement.

Although Irish American women were experienced fund-raisers through the Catholic Church and also in previous waves of nationalism, the Land League years launched a crucial debate about gender roles, inspired many women to defy narrow constructions of womanhood, and led some into connections with various other reform movements. Thousands of women responded to Fanny Parnell's call to aid Ireland, and her initiative to form the Ladies' Land League in America actually preceded the organization of women in Ireland. At the time, Charles Stewart Parnell's American-born mother, Delia, and his sisters, Anna and Fanny, were living in the United States, organizing famine relief efforts and raising money for the league. In August 1880, Fanny Parnell published a letter in the Irish American press calling on women to organize. The idea did not stem from a desire to expand women's traditional sphere. In fact, Fanny Parnell capitalized on Irish gender roles, which promoted rigid sex segregation and fostered competition between men and women.[21] The growth of the men's organization had slowed after the initial burst of activity surrounding its organization. It boasted 292 branches by January 1881. So after consulting with Michael Davitt, Fanny Parnell founded the Ladies' Land League to stimulate the growth of the overall movement and raise more funds.[22]

A few months after Fanny Parnell's appeal, the Irish ethnic press reported on the formation of a Ladies' Land League at a meeting in New York. The *Irish World* claimed the presence of one hundred prominent women, although Fanny Parnell's later account of the founding placed the number at forty. The assembly elected Delia Parnell president and Ellen Ford (sister of Patrick Ford) vice president. The Ladies' Land League's first public meeting offered listeners speeches by Michael Davitt, then touring America in support of the Land League, and Henry George, an American journalist, self-taught economist, and land reformer. After the formation of the New York branch, Fanny Parnell recalled being "overwhelmed with applications for copies of our constitution . . . for advice how to organize, etc." Parnell and Ford traveled extensively, holding meetings and organizing branches. By January 1881, Ellen Ford reported the formation of about twenty-five branches, with a membership reaching five thousand. Although no membership numbers exist, the *Irish World* reported 150 ladies' branches by the end of 1881, and Ely Janis estimates the national membership at at least seventeen thousand.[23]

Frustration with the slow growth of the men's leagues and approval of the women's actions soon became apparent in the pages of the *Irish World.* One man urged "our Irish and Irish-American ladies not to belie the reputation of their sex, but commence the good work which has long been their duty" and to assist the men in the struggle. Another writer, Mrs. Ellen Hagarty of Chicago, asked, "Why it is that you women of our race have not been up and doing?" She exhorted women, "Let the memories of childhood come back once more, and under their quickening though sad influence, resolve to do your part in stimulating the manhood of our nation, and *force* them to advance boldly against the enemy of Ireland and mankind, the brutal Irish and English aristocracy."[24] The women found plenty of support in the pages of the *Irish World.* Both letter writers urged women to get involved, invoking memories of Ireland and the virtues of Irish womanhood, while Hagarty also expressed disappointment in the efforts of the men.[25]

Lady Land Leaguers appealed to sisterhood and solidarity, expressing the hope that women's organizations would inspire the men. One columnist wished that the Ladies' Land League would "by its example incite the men of the parish into an earnest organization likewise." Ellen Ford praised women for "accepting the doctrines of the Land League much quicker than the men everywhere that we have been." At the same gathering, Mrs. Parnell asked women to encourage their friends, fathers, brothers, and beaux to enroll.[26] She also anticipated that the women's movement would remain separate from the men, although still in harmony with them. Most of the ladies' branches, she pointed out, had been formed without any assistance from the men, and she expected they would continue to work independently.[27] Patrick Ford also offered his support of women's efforts, praising the ladies of Worcester, Massachusetts, whom he called the life of the movement there. The *Irish World* repeated President Maria Dougherty's attack on the indifference among leading Irish men there and also reported that the women of St. Louis "have shamed the men into action."[28]

In addition to creating a rivalry to spur growth, the ladies' presence in the movement also offered the potential to avoid the violence associated with nationalism in the past, an issue of concern in Ireland that would affect public opinion in the United States as well. As Delia Parnell explained in an interview, "I know that revolution is very distasteful to the American people, and we want to prevent it."[29] Another author anticipated that the organization of women in Ireland would act as a moderating influence on the men, operating outside the "rough-and-tumble of Irish politics" and helping to "put a check upon those acts of lawlessness" that might drive off moderate men.[30] Despite these assurances, agrarian violence did increase, as frustration in Ireland grew over evictions, although Anna Parnell denounced it.[31] With the increase of agrarian violence in Ireland, Delia Parnell reminded supporters in 1881, "There is no need for violence in contending for principle." She continued, "I have read that a fringe of ruffianism hanging on noble movements embarrasses and destroys them. . . . Let us leave such weak acts . . . to the Government that is now, more than ever, showing its weakness and narrowness."[32]

Although the presence of the women offered advantages in terms of spurring on the men, while also lending an air of respectability and nonviolence, Land League leaders usually justified the participation of women in other ways. The main controversy surrounding women's involvement concerned the nature of their activities: Were they performing a charitable role, or did the league cross the line into politics? Early leaders proceeded cautiously, encouraging women to participate and defending their right to do so, in terms of women's traditional roles. One speaker, Patrick Meledy, told a Boston audience that the movement was "purely charitable, and in all charitable movements woman is supreme." He applauded women for joining this "great moral war."[33] Fanny Parnell also urged men and women to accept this new role as an extension of women's proper sphere. She regretted that "Irish women in America have been very supine." However, she argued, "Land League business is essentially women's business because it is essentially a work of philanthropy and humanity." Assuring her readers that she was not a "women's rights woman," Parnell insisted that "every woman has the right to do good." The women's work fell outside the realm of politics, providing aid for the poor and downtrodden of Ireland. Thus, Parnell not only called on women to organize but also reassured men that these activities would not be unwomanly, urging men to support the organization of their wives, sisters, and daughters.[34]

The *Irish World* also emphasized continuity rather than change in women's roles, pointing out, "No one thinks it wrong for women to beg for church fairs, sell tickets for lotteries. . . . [W]hy should they not form clubs or societies to-day for the relief of the wives, mothers, and sisters in Ireland?"[35] A few months later, another article in the *Irish World* explained, "One of the remarkable and distinguishing features of the present era is the prominence assumed by women in leading humane and progressive movements." Emphasizing the complementary nature of the sexes, the article continued, "The heart of woman is an auxiliary of the brain and strength of man that can make any righteous movement irresistible."[36] Thus, women lent credibility and humanity to the cause.

Leaders tried to overcome the appearance that women's involvement brought them beyond their proper sphere, but clearly women's behavior stood out as exceptional. As one supporter acknowledged, the women were "about making themselves heard in public," but "the occasion certainly justifies departure from that privacy which is woman's legitimate sphere." These women sacrificed their individual priorities and concerns for the success of the cause. As the writer concluded, "When ladies of position and influence give up their domesticity to be the public appellant for such sympathy, we can have but one expectation, as we have but one hope, of the results."[37] The *Irish World* also contributed to upholding the reputation of lady Land Leaguers, assuring readers of their gentle refinement. For example, when honored in her hometown for service to Ireland, Maria Dougherty of Worcester, Massachusetts, was described as "a self-sacrificing lady" who had done more than any other to promote the Land League in her state. An editorial note was added, calling Dougherty modest, devoted to duty, and unconscious of self, while also a zealous worker for the cause.[38]

Although the *Irish World* described her as a respectable lady, Dougherty also led her branch of the Ladies' Land League in a radical direction, squarely behind the efforts of Patrick Ford, which also explains the laudatory coverage in his paper. Although membership lists do not exist for the Ladies' Land League, research on particular local branches suggests that women's occupations did not necessarily correlate with the tendency to support the moderate or radical factions of the Land League. For example, in Worcester, Dougherty (who ran her own millinery shop) found close allies in professional women and teachers. Although professional women dominated leadership of the Worcester branch, a branch of three hundred women in Woonsocket, Rhode Island, was composed largely of young single industrial workers—many of whom were likely to be second generation.[39] Despite class and ideological variations, the nature of the Land League invoked questions about women's participation in politics.

A popular movement, which managed to pull together a coalition of various groups within the Irish American community, the Land League also benefited from clerical support. Despite the discussion that their participation provoked, women found aid from nationalist clergy. Many local leagues grew with the aid of parish priests like Father O'Beirne, who "generously offered the ladies [of Brooklyn] the use of [the] school hall" to meet and form a permanent organization. In another branch, Father O'Loughlin, described as a "good old Irish priest" with a largely Irish American congregation, chaired the organizational meeting of a branch of the Ladies' Land League with two other parish priests. The "good bishop of Kentucky" attended as well.[40] The ladies of Jersey City also met in the basement of a Catholic church, and Father Corcoran, of South Boston, even rescheduled "important ceremonies" to allow the ladies of his parish to attend a reception for Fanny Parnell—a Protestant.[41] Thus, on the local level, Land League branches benefited from the support of local parish networks and priests, although in some cases it also meant that the branch was run under clerical control, as was the case in Worcester, where Father Thomas Conaty chaired the ladies' meetings.[42]

Despite the support of many Catholic officials, critics on both sides of the Atlantic insisted on the political nature of the Ladies' Land League and condemned it. One Catholic newspaper columnist declared his hope that if Catholic women marched in the streets, God would make it rain.[43] Bishop Thomas Grace of St. Paul, Minnesota, delivered a public address on St. Patrick's Day 1881, in which he described the Land League as "repulsive" for encouraging Catholic women to investigate political issues "foreign to their minds, their training, and their duties." Blaming the men for drawing women into this inappropriate role, the bishop considered it an "infringement upon the sacredness of the home life."[44] In response, the organizer of the St. Paul Ladies' Land League, William Markoe, defended his and their actions. In a letter to the press, Markoe offered three arguments: he had the aid and supervision of a Catholic priest in organizing the women, he found no Catholic teaching against the Ladies' Land League, and he considered the condemnation of a "charitable association for the relief of heartrending social distress" as a political organization to be inaccurate.[45] In other words, Markoe was not defending women's right to be involved in politics; he was characterizing their activism as charitable.

By the time Bishop Grace condemned the Ladies' Land League, a transatlantic discussion of the issue had commenced. At the urging of Michael Davitt, the Irish parliamentary men reluctantly endorsed the creation of a Ladies' League in Ireland. Irish women's interest in the league had grown after the Irish press reprinted Fanny Parnell's letter to American women. Anna Parnell returned to Dublin and agreed to lead the Ladies' Land League in January 1881. Anticipating a government crackdown on the male leadership, Irish women fulfilled a very different function than the women of America. They organized with the intention of taking over the movement, which became necessary when Parliament passed the Coercion Act (March 2, 1881), suspending habeas corpus and allowing for the imprisonment of the men.[46]

The Ladies' Land League in Ireland grew to five hundred branches within a year. A small group of full-time organizers, mainly from the Catholic middle and strong farmer classes, risked arrest to coordinate activities, hold mass meetings, confront landlords' agents, and supply relief for evicted tenants.[47] A few American women also traveled to Ireland, after Anna Parnell requested women of "intelligence, physical strength, reliability, and refinement" to help the cause.[48] One American, Jennie Byrne of the New York Central Land League, reported being dragged by two members of the Royal Irish Constabulary, but American women had more protection from the police. Thirteen Irish members of the Ladies' Land League served time in jail, including Marguerite Moore.[49] While authorities arrested men under the Coercion Act and treated them as political prisoners, women were arrested under an ancient statute designed to remove women of ill repute from the streets—prostitutes. The men had the right to relatively free communication and remained isolated from other prisoners, but women could not communicate with each other. When member of Parliament T. P. O'Connor visited his sister Mary in prison, he found her in solitary confinement.[50]

The Ladies' Land League in Ireland performed a dramatically different function from the one in the United Sates, but the arguments over gender roles remained similar: Were women's actions political or charitable? Although the *Nation*, a nationalist newspaper, praised the Ladies' Land League as a charitable organization, Anna Parnell saw the purpose of the league as falling somewhere between solely charitable and explicitly political, and the women who joined the movement recognized the departure into the political sphere that it represented.[51] These developments led to a dispute between two Irish archbishops—one denounced the women's activities, while the other supported them.

In a pastoral letter read aloud in all the parishes of his dioceses, Archbishop Edward McCabe of Dublin expressed concern for the modesty of Irish women, "summoned under the flimsy pretext of charity to take their stand in the noisy arena of public life." The archbishop denounced the means being employed by the Land League, which he argued could not receive the "sanction of religion," urging parish priests to "set your faces" against women who forget their modesty and bring shame on their families.[52] As Archbishop McCabe's concerns suggest, he did not accept the argument that women were providing aid to poor women and children and therefore acting in a role consistent with their place as guardians of the family.

The archbishop's condemnation quickly drew a public response from A. M. Sullivan, an Irish member of Parliament and a devout Catholic, who defended the charitable and patriotic activities of the Ladies' Land Leaguers, including his own wife. Archbishop Thomas Croke of Cashel then published a letter applauding Sullivan's defense and adding his endorsement of the women's activities. Defending the "character of good Irish ladies who have become Land Leaguers," Archbishop Croke called Archbishop McCabe's allegations "monstrous imputations."[53] Both letters gained notice in the United States as well. As the discussion became transnational, the *Irish World* also came to the women's defense, maintaining that Irish wives, mothers, and daughters had a "duty" to the cause and calling the movement a "holy war."[54]

Since both letters circulated in the Irish American press, Land Leagues in the United States reacted to the exchange, rising to the defense of Anna Parnell and the other women. Ellen Ford recommended that lady Land Leaguers resist the urge to condemn Archbishop McCabe but instead pass a vote of thanks to Archbishop Croke for his "noble vindication" of their Irish sisters across the Atlantic.[55] The criticism of Catholic leaders also put Irish American women on the defensive. For example, Philadelphia's Ironsides Ladies' Land League resolved: "We deny in advocating the cause of Irish liberty we are doing what is immodest or unwomanly but on the contrary we are engaged in holy work." They vowed not to rest until they achieved the total extinction of landlordism in Ireland, inviting the assistance of "all women, lovers of liberty, without regard to color, creed, or nationality."[56]

While the women defended their womanly conduct and their right to serve the cause, men, like Sullivan, insisted on their duty as men to defend the respectability of Irish women nationalists. Likewise, Patrick Meledy addressed the Ladies' Land League of Lowell, Massachusetts, calling it "the business of every man to defend the character of the women of his country" and "the duty of every Irishman to refute the imputations hurled against his race." He expressed alarm that a priest or prelate would take to a political platform to denounce "heroic and charitable women." The women of Ireland, he maintained, had been the guardians of the home, but now they had extended their family circle to include every child of the race. Insisting that the movement reinforced rather than challenged traditional family roles, he urged all Irish ladies to follow their lead and join the league.[57]

Political Aspects of the League and the Influence of Land Nationalization

These debates over women's participation in the Land League, on both sides of the Atlantic, centered on the nature of their work. Although the activities of women in Ireland and America differed, the arguments were the same—those individuals who defended women's participation claimed that league work did not represent a departure from women's proper sphere, while critics disagreed. Some individual branches clearly engaged in political activities. For example, a Philadelphia branch with 230 members passed a resolution to boycott all English goods, declaring, "We here pledge ourselves not to buy, sell, nor wear any good of British manufacture." The women of Central Falls, Rhode Island, announced plans to hold public demonstrations every month. The ladies of Worcester forwarded resolutions to Massachusetts senator George Hoar, appealing for State Department intervention in the case of an American citizen and Civil War veteran imprisoned by the British.[58] Irish American women also spoke at public meetings for the first time. For example (as previously noted), Katherine O'Keefe O'Mahoney, of Lawrence, Massachusetts, who later became a national lecturer for the Ancient Order of Hibernians, began her speaking career with the Ladies' Land League.[59]

In addition to political behaviors, the ideas being discussed and championed by some branches of the Land League were both political and potentially revolutionary. Opponents like Bishop Grace called the matters under discussion at league meetings foreign to women's minds, but Delia Parnell told a Boston journalist that one object of the Ladies' Land League was to improve women's knowledge of industrial and financial matters in Ireland and the United States. She also promised increased "capacities for talking and debate."[60] Parnell urged members, "Go to lectures on religion, education, and industrial matters," suggesting, "There is nothing more interesting in the world than the industrial matter of this enormous country." Likewise, Mrs. John Kelly of Hoboken, New Jersey (likely the sister-in-law of Gertrude Kelly), told her audience to "think, read, and talk on this great question, which was a movement not for Ireland alone but for humanity."[61]

In addition to fund-raising and education, some lady Land Leaguers openly declared their solidarity with labor. As an organizer, Alice May Quinn of Chicago expected "rousing accession to the League" in coal regions, because "miners are still aware of the meaning of the word coercion and tyranny when applied to legalized robbers and plunderers." Mrs. Elizabeth Rodgers, who would become one of the most prominent women in the Knights of Labor, also served as president of Chicago's Eighth Ward Irish National Land League.[62] Some Land League men also declared their support of women workers. In 1882 Boston's Trans-Atlantic Branch passed a resolution of sympathy with strikers in Lawrence, Massachusetts, when five thousand Irish and native-born women walked off their jobs. The branch declared that "the cut-down in wages . . . is only one more of countless instances of the grinding injustice of the present industrial system" and called for "the producers" to recover "their rightful inheritance of the soil, and their equally rightful title to surplus products."[63]

Irish Americans played a leading role in the development of the labor movement, and the ties between the labor movement and the nationalist movement have been acknowledged by several historians. In the words of David Montgomery, "The closer one looks the more strands appear connecting the labor movement, land reform, and Irish nationalism."[64] Many Irish Americans became interested in economic theories through the Influence of the *Irish World*, which championed the land and tax theories of Henry George. A powerful voice in Irish America, Patrick Ford embraced a variety of reforms to ease the hardship of the Irish American working class.[65] His opposition to land monopoly found a new face and voice when he discovered the work of Henry George. Land League women, like Land League men, represented a wide spectrum of the Irish American community, and some supported Ford's more radical social agenda. As one speaker told her New Jersey listeners, every working man and working woman ought to read Henry George's *Progress and Poverty*: "If it does not give you any new ideas there is one thing it will do—that is, cause you to get rid of your old ones." She praised the *Irish World* as the voice of labor and insisted that the "fruits of toil belong to the toiler."[66]

The New Departure, as agreed upon by Davitt, Devoy, and Parnell, called for "vigorous agitation of the land question on the basis of peasant proprietary," a plan to allow peasants to purchase the lands that they farmed. A more radical plan of land nationalization took shape through the Ford-George faction of the Land League movement.[67] Henry George had been an important figure in the movement since publishing *Progress and Poverty* (1879) and an article titled "The Irish Land Question," republished in the *Irish World* in 1880. Patrick Ford endorsed George's ideas on land reform and hired him as a correspondent to Ireland during the land war. George spent a year in Ireland, promoting his theories, and was even arrested briefly by British authorities.

Although George was active in the land war, his work had implications far beyond Ireland, and he sought to win converts among the American working class. At its core, *Progress and Poverty* tackled the causes of poverty and inequality in the United States, asking why such poverty existed amid such wealth. George argued that the inequitable distribution of wealth left the majority without access to the bounty of progress. A deeply religious man, George insisted that man, not God, created the system that deprived so many of their basic necessities. He pointed to landownership and rent as the cause of this disparity, condemning land monopoly and land speculation. George argued that private property was unnatural. His solution, not only to the plight of tenant farmers in Ireland but also for the exploited workers of industrial society, called for a tax on the "unearned increment of land." The government would determine taxes based on the rental value of the land, and therefore landowners could no longer profit from their property.[68]

As a result of his theories, George amassed a following among laborers and reformers, and his role in the Irish land question also endeared him to the radical wing of the nationalist movement. Under the leadership of Ford and George, many Land Leaguers adopted a more radical social agenda than the one originally envisioned under the New Departure. Like her brother, Ellen Ford championed George's land theories and promoted a radical view of economic reform for Ireland and America. She told one Boston audience that she had little faith in a parliamentary solution to the land crisis as advocated by Charles Stewart Parnell: "The Irish Question must be settled outside that body."[69] This position, of course, put her in conflict with not only Charles Stewart Parnell but also his sister Fanny.

From its founding, the Land League in the United States was rife with factionalism. Patrick Ford held a powerful position because he raised so much money, but his ideas were unpopular with moderates and the Clan na Gael alike. This ideological dispute affected the women as well. As early as February 1881, Fanny Parnell had reservations about the influence of Patrick and Ellen Ford. She considered their land-nationalization theories communistic and anathema to the Catholic clergy, whose support the Land League sought. By October, after a confrontation with Ellen Ford at an executive meeting, Parnell resolved to challenge Ford and her supporter Mrs. Kelly. At the first anniversary meeting of the Ladies' Land League of New York, she had them expelled for "not having paid their dues and for having violated the rules of our constitution." Parnell considered the expulsion of Ellen Ford a small victory over the *Irish World*.[70]

Privately, she pointed out that among the Ladies' Leagues, only one-third contributed funds under the auspices of the *Irish World*, which she considered evidence of the women's good sense. In 1882, when Parnell recounted the events of the founding of the Ladies'

Land League, in an article written by another prominent Lady Land Leaguer, Margaret Sullivan, she neglected to mention the role of Ellen Ford at all.[71] Despite Fanny Parnell's small victory, Ellen Ford continued to speak and raise funds for the Ladies' Land League of Ireland after her expulsion from the New York branch. She and Sabina Davitt (sister of Michael) also occupied important committee assignments at the second annual convention of the Irish National Land League of America in 1882.[72]

Like many moderate Irish nationalists, Fanny Parnell rejected the idea of land nationalization for Ireland, endorsing peasant proprietorship over the agenda envisioned by Henry George and promoted by the Fords. She considered an open rupture with the *Irish World* inevitable and thought the American Irish too discerning to follow Ford in the event of a split.[73] Parnell's last article, before her death in the summer of 1882, refuted George's land theories, which she argued would be "nothing short of disastrous" if implemented in Ireland. Parnell rejected what she considered efforts to emancipate one class, while the country remained in political bondage. How could land be nationalized without an Irish nation? Although Henry George was not a socialist, she insisted that "the Irish mind, to its honor be it said, has always recoiled from the idea of injustice, of dishonesty, involved in the plans of the Socialists."[74]

The division between moderates and supporters of land nationalization became most pronounced after Charles Stewart Parnell's arrest in October 1881. He decided to issue the "No-Rent Manifesto" from Kilmainham jail, calling on tenant farmers to withhold rent payments.[75] Although the manifesto was offered as a strategy to put pressure on Prime Minister William Gladstone and the British government, land-reform advocates like Patrick Ford and Henry George celebrated Parnell's actions, expecting further commitment to radical land reform. However, in America, the "No-Rent Manifesto" accelerated debates among the various factions of the movement, ultimately leading to the fractioning of fragile alliances.[76] An Irish Race Convention in Chicago in December 1881 gave a tepid endorsement of the no-rent policy, but only as a politically expedient move on Parnell's part. Both moderates and ardent nationalists also criticized Ford at the annual convention of the Land League in the spring of 1882. Although a significant player in the movement, Ford and his radical agenda were blocked as the other two wings of the movement united against him.[77]

Some of the most political aspects of the Land League, the "No-Rent Manifesto" and land nationalization, did win support among some ladies' branches. The eight ladies' branches of Philadelphia (including one named after Archbishop Croke) sent Sabina Davitt as their delegate to endorse the "No-Rent Manifesto," declaring, "We think a Davitt great enough to represent us all." Ellen Ford assured the Manhattan Land League, "We are not going to have any patching with Landlordism, but abolish it, and its death sentence has been issued from Kilmainham Jail." Some compared the manifesto to the Declaration of Independence. For example, one speaker insisted, "The No-Rent Manifesto of the Irish people is equivalent to that issued by the American people in 1776." The women of Worcester, Massachusetts, exclaimed, "Thousands for independence, not one penny for rent!" And Mary Malone of Kentucky wrote the *Irish World*, "God bless Dr. McGlynn, Davitt, Ford, and all who are in favor of the nationalization of the land."[78] Clearly, some women continued to support the radical wing of the movement.

Despite the enthusiasm of some in the Ford-George camp, the "No-Rent Manifesto" did lead to more conflict, not only within the league but also with the clergy. Individual members of the Catholic hierarchy in Ireland and America condemned the manifesto and even prohibited priests from attending Land League events. One Irish American priest called the policy "not a Christian, nor a Catholic" cry, and Bishop Bernard McQuaid of Rochester, New York, withdrew his support from the league because of it.[79] The most serious disputes between Catholic women and the clergy in the United States also occurred in 1882 after the Land League took this radical turn. In addition to earlier exchanges on the political nature of Land League activities, the specter of perceived socialistic principles aroused renewed opposition to the Ladies' Land League.

In January 1882 a dispute occurred between a branch of the Ladies' Land League and the local Catholic newspaper in Baltimore. Annie Maguire of the West End Ladies' Land League wrote to the *Irish World* about their successful ball. Nothing marred their delight, she reported, until a "scurrilous article" appeared in a paper "styling itself" to be the official organ of the Catholic Church. The women were "grossly insulted" by criticism in the *Catholic Mirror*, accusing them of overstepping the bounds of propriety and breaching public decency with their actions. Warning of the dire consequences of the women's role, the *Catholic Mirror*'s editorial writer regretted that such steps "had been taken by Catholic ladies who pride themselves upon their faith and upon their respectability." The article counseled, "It is not for women to agitate publicly a political question: leave this to the men." Instead, the ladies could aid male leaders "by your prayers," and if women chose to contribute their "pin-money" to the cause, they were advised to do so "unostentatiously." The writer insisted that by organizing a ball and generating publicity, the women risked bringing reproach on the Catholic Church and exposing themselves to "malicious criticism from a heartless world."[80] As with the earlier comments from Archbishop McCabe, the women defended their right to serve the cause, while critics condemned their behavior as unwomanly and inappropriate for respectable Catholic ladies.

The most serious conflict occurred a few months later in Cleveland, Ohio, when Bishop Richard Gilmour forbade the women of his dioceses from attending Land League meetings. The controversy quickly gained national exposure and showed a willingness among Catholic women to disregard the dictates of the clergy in the name of nationalism. The dispute began when the Parnell League organized a ladies' branch. The bishop condemned this move, advising the women of his dioceses not to join and warning against the threat it posed to their modesty. As the exchange of words began, two points became clear: Gilmour opposed the "No-Rent Manifesto," and the bishop had long been opposed to the Ladies' Land League.[81] In a letter to the parishes of his diocese, and also published in the press, the bishop denounced the men of the Land League for advocating communistic principles and dragging women into politics. Charging them with unmanly behavior, the bishop declared that if he merely had differences of opinion with Land League men, they could "differ and act it out as men." However, since the men attempted to unsex the women of his flock and destroy female modesty in the name of "pretended" patriotism, Gilmour felt compelled to say, "The Catholic woman must live within the modesty of the home. She must be the ornament of the family circle, and her womanly delicacy and gentle nature shall not be tainted with the noisy brawl of the virago."[82] Gilmour insisted that women who sought to become "brawling politicians" would not be Catholic women, revealing his intention to excommunicate any Cleveland women who attended Ladies' Land League meetings or joined the organization after his order of excommunication.

A week later, the *New York Times* reported that the ladies met as usual, most members attended, and five new members joined.[83] League president Mary Rowland declared the righteousness of their cause, which she called a grand and holy duty. Refusing to accept the indictment of their behavior as unwomanly, she accused the bishop of an "ungallant, unmanly, and bitter attack" and defended the women's conduct, maintaining that their "pure, high motives would be worthy of imitation by any lady outside the Parnell Ladies' Land League." Rowland congratulated the women for their brave stand. Conscious that this standoff had larger meaning, she told her audience that their actions had been watched by the press and every Land League in the country: "Had we remained quiet and been submissive under the severe blow leveled at our organization, our noble work, we should have been hounded as cowards, losing the respect of all." Instead, expressions of admiration and sympathy poured in, like a resolution from St. Louis urging them to "stand firm by their country and their God, regardless of any vulgar tirades, even when uttered in the robes of an abused religion."[84]

Although initial arguments were framed in terms of manliness and womanliness, the use of the term *abused religion* is significant. Like the incident in Maryland, this controversy raised concerns about potential damage to the image of the Catholic Church in America.

As the story hit the national press, questions emerged as to whether the bishop had in fact overstepped his position as a spiritual leader and entered the political sphere. A Buffalo, New York, branch passed resolutions supporting the women, and one speaker insisted that by entering the political arena, Bishop Gilmour had left the "sanctity of his office" and thus should be treated as any other individual.[85] The *Boston Pilot* commented that the actions of the bishop had "naturally excited intense feeling of regret and astonishment." The newspaper warned that the actions of the bishop had far-reaching repercussions because "there are many thousands of the most respectable Catholic ladies of America enrolled in the Land League."[86]

John F. Finerty, a leading nationalist and Chicago newspaperman, also questioned the bishop's actions. He argued that although Catholics recognize and submit to the authority of the clergy in spiritual matters, they retain independence in political matters, and they would not let the actions of one member of the clergy steer them from their loyalty to the Catholic Church. Finerty expressed his doubt that the bishop had the power to excommunicate the women.[87] In the midst of the controversy, Father Edward McGlynn of New York, a disciple of Henry George, spoke in Cleveland. Despite an appeal from the vicar-general of the Cleveland diocese, McGlynn addressed four thousand people at a Land League picnic. When asked about the Ladies' Land League, he reportedly refused to "curse" any of them.[88]

However, the open rebellion of Catholic women against their bishop also caused concern and raised opposition to the women's insubordination (but not their participation in the league). Although always supportive of the Ladies' Land League, and the leading advocate of land nationalization, the *Irish World* reacted critically to the women's position. Describing the bishop's action as unwise, unjust, and undignified, an article on the Cleveland ladies also expressed regret that the women had not "preserve[d] their temper and kept out of print." The *Irish World* charged that the women's public defense had been indiscreet, exposing themselves and the church to criticism. Patriotic ladies should, instead, make respectable protests "against the imputations cast upon their womanly character" but bow in submission to their bishop, humiliating as it might be. Such Christian and womanly heroism would lead to a moral victory, doing "substantial service to the Land League and the Irish cause."[89] In other words, women must submit to clerical authority or risk damaging the image of the Catholic Church. This notion can only partially be explained by Patrick Ford's views on the Catholic Church. By the latter half of the 1880s, Ford repudiated his radical views and became a staunch defender of the church.[90] However, criticism of the women's stance was more widespread. Archbishop Lynch of Toronto also criticized the women of Cleveland, whom he suggested "had always more or less been a hindrance to the proper carrying out of the rules of the church in that city."[91]

A number of Cleveland's Irish organizations also criticized the women. The Hibernian Rifles, a military drilling corps of the Ancient Order of Hibernians, refused to parade at the "so-called" Ladies' Land League picnic, and twelve other branches of the AOH, representing more than one thousand men, condemned "as unpatriotic and un-Irish" the women's opposition to clerical authority, denouncing them as "uncatholic and out of harmony with the whole history of our country." They also challenged Land League men as well, describing them as "a few unscrupulous malcontents . . . [who] have pushed the ladies forward to brave the authority of their bishop." The women reacted by calling the AOH men "cowardly" and afraid of the bishop. In response to all this controversy, one article in the *Chicago Daily Tribune* ended on an ominous note, warning of a "big split in the Catholic Church."[92]

At question was the authority of the Catholic Church in political matters. In the earlier debates on women, critics condemned the participation of women as political, and thus inappropriate, while defenders argued that the work was in fact charitable. However, in this later debate, many defenders of the women dismissed the bishop's authority because it was a political matter. The focus shifted to the respectability of the women and the legitimacy of the bishop's attack on them. While some Irish American men continued to support women's right to be a part of the Land League movement, those men who criticized the women did so largely in terms of their failure to submit to clerical authority. Regardless of their sympathy with the women's goals, some cringed at the spectacle of Catholic women openly defying church authority, fearing damage to the reputation of the Catholic Church. These controversies over the behavior of Irish American women are part of a much larger dialogue occurring in American Catholic circles at the end of the nineteenth century; they foreshadow a far more serious rebellion within the American Catholic Church that occurred a few years later in response to Father McGlynn's support of Henry George.

The Decline of the Land League

In 1881 Parliament passed a land act that guaranteed rights for tenants by offering the Irish tenant fair rent, fixity of tenure, and the freedom to sell "his right to occupancy at market value."[93] In 1882, with much of the male leadership in jail, a compromise between Charles Stewart Parnell and Prime Minister Gladstone led to Parnell's release from prison and an amendment to the Land Act, offering protection to tenants who had fallen behind on their rent. Although far short of the land nationalization advocated by a few radicals, these reforms addressed the concerns of many Irish farmers and effectively brought the land agitation to a close. As leader of the Irish Parliamentary Party (IPP), Parnell promised cooperation with Gladstone and the Liberal Party, but his ultimate goal had always been Home Rule for Ireland. The brutal slaying of Lord Frederick Cavendish and his undersecretary, Thomas Henry Burke, in Phoenix Park, Dublin, horrified the leaders of the Land League, and the reaction against extremism soon strengthened a more moderate agenda—the switch from land reform to parliamentary agitation for Home Rule.[94]

The return of the male leadership also led to conflict with the ladies, who were asked to disband their organization, while continuing to provide relief to evicted tenants under the direction of the men.[95] The women had operated autonomously once the men's organization was suppressed by the British, formulating policy and dispensing aid in a manner that departed significantly from the original operation.[96] According to Henry George, then a correspondent for the *Irish World* in Ireland, the women felt "bitter toward the parliamentary men. They have been treated badly and their obligations have not been kept, and on several occasions the men got a very frank piece of their minds."[97] Anna Parnell's account of the Land League suggests that the women wanted to step aside because of their disagreements with the men but stayed on until a settlement could be reached and their debts paid.[98]

After the women negotiated an agreement to disband, in August 1882, several women organizers, including Marguerite Moore, left Ireland. Anna Parnell, who later described the Land League movement as a "great sham," never forgave her brother for his role in orchestrating the league's demise. She largely disappeared from public life and was living in Britain under a fake name at the time of her death. Significantly, women would be excluded from nationalist activities in Ireland for decades. Founded in Dublin, in October 1882, the Irish National League succeeded the Land League. Focusing on securing a Home Rule bill, a clearly political focus, the new organization declared itself "an open organization in which the ladies will not take part."[99] Despite Gladstone's support of Home Rule for Ireland, attempts to pass a bill failed. Then news of Parnell's affair with a married woman rocked the movement. Parnell attempted to salvage his reputation and the movement, but infighting continued, even after Parnell's death in 1891, leading to the decline of the Irish National League.

American women had a different experience. After months of conflict, declining membership, and dwindling contributions, the Irish National Land League of America officially disbanded in 1883, but the newly established Irish National League of America did not bar women. Although members of a much smaller organization, forty women delegates attended the organizational meeting, and Delia Parnell took a leading role in organizing women's branches. Marguerite Moore, who had served time in prison for her role in the Ladies' Land League in Ireland, immigrated to the United States and became active in the Parnell Branch of the INLA.

The INLA allowed any Irish societies (literary, fraternal, and charitable) to affiliate with the national organization, but since its goal of Home Rule gave it a definitively political mission, suffragists began to take notice. In an article entitled "Woman Suffrage to Help Ireland," the *Woman's Journal* (a suffrage paper published in Boston) applauded the North End Branch of the Irish National League for electing five women to the executive committee, describing its "exceptional liberality of enlisting women in politics."[100] Connections between suffragists and nationalists are discussed in part 3.

So why is a short-lived and controversial movement for land reform in Ireland a significant watershed for Irish American women? While the Ladies' Land League in America brought thousands of Irish American women into a political mass movement for the first time, unleashing debates about the proper behavior of women and the appropriateness of their influence on political matters, such debates did not end with the organization's demise. Irish American women, many of whom were Catholic, would continue to push for greater roles and responsibilities in public matters, even as the rise of conservative gender rhetoric celebrated Catholic women's contributions to home and family. Although these changes occurred slowly, beginning in the late nineteenth century, Irish American women became active in the labor movement, ethnic and fraternal associations, and charitable organizations, but Irish American women are not a monolithic category. Their experiences varied, just as the factions and loyalties differed within the Land League. Some women moved into the fairly moderate circles of Catholic literary and benevolent associations. For example, Katharine O'Keefe O'Mahoney was remembered as "a loyal, outspoken Catholic: honoring her faith as teacher, lecturer, writer, and in the privacy of her home: giving freely of her time and her gifts to the service of her religion."[101] After her service to the Ladies' Land League, O'Mahoney founded the first local Ladies' Auxiliary of the Ancient Order of Hibernians in Lawrence, Massachusetts; served as a national lecturer for the AOH; and later oversaw the use of ritual for the national LAAOH. O'Mahoney also worked as a journalist, serving as correspondent for the *Sacred Heart Review* (a popular Catholic family paper), contributing to the *Boston Pilot*, and publishing her own Sunday paper, the *Catholic Register*. While we can see that O' Mahoney had a long and influential public life, she represents only one path to activism after the decline of the Ladies' Land League.

Other Land League women became active in labor and social justice organizations. Maria Dougherty of Worcester, Massachusetts, a nationalist leader in her community, embraced a more militant stance. Dougherty, an unmarried milliner who ran her own shop, became president of the Worcester Ladies' Land League in November 1880. Under her leadership, the ladies' branch grew to four hundred members, allied itself with the more radical faction of the Land League (those persons advocating land nationalization), and raised far more money than the moderates of the men's branch. After the decline of the league, Dougherty also joined the Ladies' Auxiliary of the Ancient Order of Hibernians. When Father Edward McGlynn died in 1900, Dougherty led the local effort to build a memorial to him.[102] Like O'Mahoney, Dougherty first became active in the Ladies' Land League and later joined the Ladies' Auxiliary of the Ancient Order of Hibernians; however, the women's views clearly differed.

Another significant Irish American women reformer, Mary Elizabeth Lease, also began her reform career with the Irish nationalist movement. Remembered as the Populist orator from Kansas who reportedly fired up her audiences by telling them to "raise less corn and more hell," Lease took her first steps into public life in 1885 when she toured in support of the Irish National League—the successor to the Land League. Describing her father as an Irish exile who fled British authorities and lost his land, Lease saw her rebelliousness as part of her family heritage. Lease's first widely attended public lecture compared the oppression of Irish tenant farmers and the plight of American farmers, calling for agrarian reforms for both groups. Her speech endorsed Home Rule for Ireland, and other Kansas organizations invited her to repeat it, culminating in a statewide fund-raising effort.[103]

Father McGlynn and the Anti-Poverty Society

Women's participation in the labor movement, and their support of land nationalization through the Land League, made Irish American women more visible in reform circles. Despite the decline of the Land

League, the social agenda championed by Ford and George lived on, and some women emerged as active supporters of this vision, demonstrating the transition from nationalist activities to the wider tradition of social reform, which began to percolate during the Gilded Age. As the Knights of Labor peaked in strength and numbers in the mid-1880s, a local controversy—centered on New York City—also took on national and international importance as supporters of Henry George entered the political fray, leading many Irish Americans to question the boundaries between religious authority and secular reform.

In addition to the precarious socioeconomic position of many in the Irish American community, the Gilded Age was also characterized by deepening ideological differences within the American Catholic Church. By the time Henry George returned to New York in the fall of 1882, after serving as a correspondent to Ireland for the *Irish World*, Father Edward McGlynn, the Irish American pastor of one of New York's largest parishes, had become an ardent supporter of George's work. As early as the 1860s, a small group of liberal priests in New York, including a young McGlynn, began holding private discussions about the doctrine of papal infallibility, clerical celibacy, and other controversial topics. McGlynn also became a critic of the high cost of maintaining parochial schools, and he supported Catholic involvement in the Fenian movement.[104] By the 1880s, this outspokenness, and his support for Henry George, led to a conflict with Archbishop Michael Corrigan, a leader among conservatives in the American Catholic hierarchy. McGlynn's views became the center of an international controversy that reflected growing tension in the church as a whole.

This tension, known as the Americanist Crisis, peaked in the 1890s, but the ideological divides began much earlier. A group of liberal Catholic clergy became known as "Americanists" because of the vision they espoused for reconciling Catholic teachings with American institutions and ideology. The leading proponent of Americanism, Archbishop John Ireland, sought to bring the Catholic Church into harmony with the spirit of the modern age. As he explained, "The Church of America must be, of course, as Catholic as ever in

Jerusalem or Rome; but so far as her garments assume color from the local atmosphere she must be American." Ireland believed that the Catholic Church needed to adapt to the "new order" by changing its "method of action," including supporting the separation of church and state, integrating Catholics into the public schools, and abandoning hostility toward Protestants. Americanists also promoted assimilation for Catholic immigrants, desiring a larger role for lay Catholics in American public life.[105] This vision, however, was contested by others in the American hierarchy and ultimately condemned by Rome.

While Ireland, McGlynn, and others embraced American values and institutions, promoting a vision of the compatibility of American and Catholic life, conservatives sought to construct a bulwark against the dangers of modernity and irreligion. In an era of hostility toward Catholics, many bishops, priests, and nuns supported the creation of separate Catholic institutions. For example, the Third Plenary Council of Baltimore (1884) called on each parish to establish a parochial school. Generally, conservatives in the American Catholic hierarchy encouraged the development of separate Catholic institutions, retained close ties to Rome, and encouraged the maintenance of ethnic traditions.[106] The conservative faction, most closely associated with Archbishop Michael Corrigan and Bishop Bernard McQuaid (of Rochester, New York), was generally wary of government intervention, saw Protestantism as a threat to the Catholic Church, and eschewed interfaith cooperation. For example, when Bishop Ireland and other leading Americanists participated in the International Parliament of Religions in Chicago in 1893, the outcry led the Vatican to instruct against such gatherings. A few years later, in 1899, the pope issued an apostolic letter, *Testem benevolentiae*, challenging some of the core beliefs of the Americanists.[107]

Despite the growing emphasis on building separate Catholic institutions and organizations, some Catholics joined with non-Catholics to promote a new vision of economic justice. A prime example is the partnership of Father Edward McGlynn and Henry George. Father McGlynn first came into conflict with his superiors for speaking on behalf of the Land League and refusing to build a parochial school in Saint Stephen's Parish. He would later assert that the leadership of the Catholic Church in New York (which he called the machine) endangered "the liberties and integrity of the American citizen." He opposed the emphasis on parochial education, reportedly accusing the hierarchy of usurping "control over the education of the young, until a premium is placed at letting a child run wild in the streets rather than that it should go to the accursed public school."[108] This criticism led to open conflict with the Catholic hierarchy, but McGlynn's ideas also endeared him to many lay Catholics.

In the years before the Vatican began to articulate its vision for social justice, McGlynn and his supporters championed their own plan to support the working class, bridging his own interpretation of Catholic teaching with the needs of Catholic laborers in the United States. Beginning in the late nineteenth century, Protestant leaders formed the core of a movement known as the social gospel—the application of Christian teaching to the social and economic problems brought on by the rapid industrialization of America. The social gospel was led by Protestants, but historians have also sought to expand the understanding of social gospel advocates to reach beyond a small cadre of Protestant ministers who formed the intellectual heart of the movement and examine the experiences of the men and women who sought to implement its principles.[109] As architects and organizers of an early social gospel program, George and McGlynn fitted this expanded definition. Across denominational lines, and in the spirit of divine law, they shared a commitment to the equitable distribution of wealth and use of the land, linking the oppression of peasants by landlords in Ireland with the subjugation of workers by capitalists in America and calling for social justice through land reform. Their message appealed to the Irish American working class, particularly after the Land League movement popularized George's ideas and workers began to organize for political influence.[110]

This acceptance can be seen most dramatically in Henry George's political campaigns. In 1882 the labor unions of New York City centralized to form a new body called the Central Labor Union, with the intention of asserting workers' concerns in the political arena.

After a couple of poor electoral showings, delegates from 165 local labor unions voted overwhelmingly to establish an Independent Labor Party and asked Henry George to run for mayor.[111] Although he initially expressed doubts, George came to see the mayoral race as a campaign to "bring the land question into practical politics."[112] George did not win, but his mayoral campaign of 1886 represented a pinnacle of reform agitation in New York City, mounting a serious challenge to Tammany Hall's candidate and drawing Irish American votes away from the Democratic Party. With the support of McGlynn and many Irish American Catholics, Henry George mounted an impressive campaign. He carried 30 percent of the vote, including a strong showing among German, Jewish, and second-generation Irish voters.[113]

As radical reform rhetoric entered the political arena, there could be no doubt that women's participation represented a declaration for political influence. One of the clearest examples of the link between Irish nationalism and American politics was the participation of Marguerite Moore. George and Moore first became acquainted while he was in Ireland. A Ladies' Land League organizer in Ireland, Moore refused bail and served six months in jail for inciting discontent and establishing a branch of the league. Readers of the *Irish World* had also been introduced to Moore as an "active, fearless, and most eloquent exponent of Land League principles" even before her arrival in the United States.[114] Moore left Ireland with her children two years after the dissolution of the Land League and quickly "gained a reputation as a speaker on social matters, woman suffrage, [the] labor question and land reform."[115] She supported George, the Anti-Poverty Society, and single-tax principles as well as women's suffrage.

Her ethnic background became an important part of her activism, in terms of both her public image and her rhetorical strategy. According to one newspaper, Moore appealed to audiences with her "genuine Irish wit," but she also connected her experiences in Ireland to the plight of the Irish in America.[116] She told a labor audience that she had seen ten thousand times as much persecution in America as in Ireland: "'Keep your eyes on Ireland' they say and while your eyes are turned that way pluck your pockets empty." She warned another audience,

"Don't look at Ireland, look to your land theories at home. . . . Labor in America is being crushed by landlordism just as it is in Ireland.[117] Moore took a deep interest in American politics, supported Henry George's land-reform agenda, and played an active role in George's political campaigns, speaking at two or three meetings a night.[118]

Moore represented a group of Irish Americans who saw Henry George as an advocate of social and economic justice, fusing a burst of Irish nationalism with the larger goal of economic reform. However, as a woman, she also demonstrates the entry of Irish American women into partisan politics and the relationship between women's nationalist participation and increased attention to women's rights. When Moore spoke for William Jennings Bryan and the Democrats years later, the *Baltimore Sun* referred to her Land League days, describing her as "the first Catholic woman in her own country to take the lecture platform for the discussion of political matters."[119] Unfortunately, little evidence remains of her activities in Ireland or America, but she certainly became an active reformer in the United States.

As advocates of Henry George's ideas, Moore and McGlynn both found themselves embroiled in a dispute with the Archdiocese of New York. Often inaccurately described as socialistic, George's land-reform theories aroused opposition within the Catholic Church. This hostility led to an open conflict when Father Edward McGlynn spoke at a political rally for George, leading to disciplinary action by Archbishop Corrigan. The case took a dramatic turn when McGlynn received a letter ordering him to Rome and he refused to go. A popular priest, McGlynn's removal from his parish excited protest from many supporters.[120] And like in the Cleveland Ladies' Land League dispute a few years earlier, competing visions of clerical authority over political matters led to open rebellion against Catholic officials. As one parishioner explained to a reporter, "This movement is like the one they have just had in Ireland. The upper clergy have got to learn that we will not submit to their dictation in any other than spiritual matters."[121]

The crisis between McGlynn and the Catholic hierarchy had important implications for the Americanists, but McGlynn's rebellion also highlighted the support he had among women in the Irish

American community. According to press reports, women took an active role in the debates and protests. The *New York Times* reported a mass meeting at Cooper Union attended by a large number of "socialists" and a "large number of church-going Catholics, both men and women." Another protest meeting, held in the basement of the Saint Stephen's Church against the orders of the new pastor, appointed a committee of twenty-five men and ten women to meet with the archbishop. Among the acts of dissent in Saint Stephen's Parish were the following: altar boys refused to serve McGlynn's replacement at his first Mass; collectors would not pass the contribution baskets; the women who decorated the altars denied their services; and the servants at the rectory quit.[122] After McGlynn's suspension, Bishop McQuaid wrote to Archbishop Corrigan, "You will not fail to notice that pious women will be among the worst mischief makers. Reason and common sense seem to leave them when they get excited."[123] Women certainly did protest. The Sisters of Charity were also disciplined for staging a children's performance in support of Father McGlynn. In retaliation, Archbishop Corrigan closed the children's home that they ran in the parish.[124]

Already a seasoned speaker, Marguerite Moore addressed protest meetings and fueled the brewing rebellion, invoking her own experiences in Ireland and urging resistance. Moore expressed anger at the actions of the archbishop, reminding parishioners that the Irish people had encountered "Corrigans" too (she used the archbishop's name to mean a tool of the British). However, she insisted that they defeated such men by withholding financial support. Speaking to the women of Saint Stephen's Parish, Moore urged them to carry on the fight by refusing to donate money for parish maintenance until their priest returned. She asked them to be as true to McGlynn as McGlynn had been to them. In response, parishioners placed slips in the collection basket offering a cash amount to be paid after the restoration of Father McGlynn. Meanwhile, they raised funds to support Father McGlynn. Moore compared McGlynn's treatment by the archbishop to evictions in Ireland: Corrigan sent him "out into the world without a dollar in his pocket" on a cold winter's day. She also accused the archbishop of being a traitor to the Irish people for dining with the governor of Bermuda, whom she alleged had enforced anti–Land League policies in Ireland before being "driven from his native land by force of public opinion."[125]

With the land war in Ireland behind them, Henry George and Father McGlynn championed a new movement at home, founding the Anti-Poverty Society in March 1887. As George reportedly told followers, "No great social revolution was ever accomplished that did not begin as a religious movement."[126] The new organization grew to have branches in several major cities as well as Canada, Australia, New Zealand, and England. With McGlynn as president, the Anti-Poverty Society described its purpose as spreading: "The truth that God has made ample provision for the needs of all men during their residence on earth." George and McGlynn taught that "involuntary poverty is the result of human laws that allow individuals to claim as private property that which the Creator has provided for the use of all."[127] The Anti-Poverty Society held regular Sunday-night meetings, but Henry George assured his audience, "It is not proposed to start a church. . . . If the churches such as we have could abolish poverty, there would long ago have been none in this great city to suffer want." Instead, he assured them, they would do God's work by arousing "the religious sentiment to do what charity and creeds have not done—abolish poverty."[128]

Although the society was a nondemoninational organization, Father McGlynn and the Anti-Poverty Society appealed to Catholic members, and McGlynn maintained that their activities were compatible with Catholic teaching. He insisted that his convictions as a Catholic led to his involvement in the new organization. For example, he told one audience, "I am emboldened by a sense of duty—I feel that I would be recreant to my manhood and my Christian priesthood if I should fail in speaking the word that I am commanded to utter."[129] In McGlynn's most noted speech, "Cross of a New Crusade," he reassured followers that, as a servant of the church, he advocated policies consistent with Catholic teachings. He believed that God, the Creator, provided land and that all people had the right to "the general bounties of nature." In his interpretation, the new crusade reasserted divine natural law; private use of land must accommodate service of the common good.[130]

The organization drew membership across class and denominational lines. Leading members included James Redpath, a former abolitionist who also spent time in Ireland during the land war, and politician and newspaperman Louis Post, a strong supporter of Henry George. But early accounts of Anti-Poverty Society meetings suggested a large attendance by Catholics, and many of them were likely working class. For example, one resolution in support of McGlynn declared, "We, citizens of New York . . . of every condition in life, but chiefly working people, and of different denominations, but a large proportion of us devoted to the spiritual doctrines and sacraments of the Catholic Church . . . heartily approve of the action taken by the Rev. Dr. Edward McGlynn."[131]

In response to the controversy between McGlynn and Corrigan, Henry George wrote to a friend, "The great masses of the Catholics of this city stand behind him in spite of all the excommunications that can be leveled against him. The movement is strongest in New York just now on account of my campaign but it is booming al [*sic*] over the United States."[132] Despite this support of McGlynn, the issue divided Catholics, too. For example, the Catholic Club, which reportedly attracted prominent men in New York and wielded "a large influence in Catholic society," expelled Anti-Poverty Society members from its rolls in 1888.[133]

Early press accounts of Anti-Poverty Society meetings also suggest a large attendance by women, which became a source of some ridicule.[134] For example, a caricature appearing in *Puck* showed Father McGlynn riding atop a book labeled "H. George's Theories," while a crowd of women carried along this litter. Some women carried signs reading "Hail to McGlynn, while others waved handkerchiefs or bowed as the procession passed.[135] The *Puck* cartoon followed an earlier editorial describing McGlynn's mental attitude as characterized more by enthusiasm than by "depth of thought" and containing "a strong element of femininity." Dismissing the emotionalism of women, the article alleged that, like the woman who cried out at social injustice, McGlynn's indignation represented an "extravagant outburst of a man who is carried away by his feelings, and who wants, for the moment, to rend the universe, because a workingman has a hole in his overalls."[136] Such descriptions, like the charge that Irish nationalists collected most of their funds from servant girls, criticized the movement because of women's support. McGlynn's overly sentimental and allegedly irrational proposals attracted worshipping women rather than rational men. In an even more dismissive portrait of women activists, an article in the *New Haven (CT) Register* reported that "a great many young girls go to them [Anti-Poverty Society meetings] who have no interest in the subjects under discussion whatever, but find them a place where acquaintances can be made with ease and flirtations are unrestrained."[137] Such commentary does seem to confirm the presence of women, even if contemporaries are interpreting women's activism as frivolous or immodest.

Although critics derided them and failed to take their commitment seriously, women fulfilled an important role in the Anti-Poverty Society, raising money for the United Labor Party and participating in politics. Henry George's newspaper, the *New York Standard*, explained the "extraordinary zeal" of women in terms of the benefits the movement offered to "every man, woman, and child." The "Anti-Poverty girl" (like her predecessor in the Ladies' Land League) was asked to use her influence with men, to bring her sweethearts into the movement and refuse them her company if they declined.[138] As one announcement in the *Standard* reported, "The ladies of the society in New York are unanimous in embracing this opportunity to allow the disfranchised sex to do something definite toward helping on the canvass."[139] Women also contributed by organizing an Anti-Poverty Fair. One letter to the editor claimed that a group, composed largely of working-class women, raised fifteen thousand dollars. The *Standard* heralded the fair as "significant of the practical entrance of women into the field of politics," calling on supporters of women's suffrage to embrace the United Labor Party.[140]

Through their activities in the Anti-Poverty Society, women supported radical social change through land nationalization and raised funds for a political party, the United Labor Party. As in the Cleveland controversy over the Ladies' Land League, the participation of Catholic women in a political cause led to conflict. Several Irish American women, in particular, risked censure for their activities in support of the Anti-Poverty Society. Although the *Standard* described her decision as "unwise," a Mrs. O'Donnell called on Archbishop Corrigan while gathering subscriptions for the Anti-Poverty Society. In response, he reportedly seized her subscription book and, in the words of the *Standard*, "sentenced her to hell." The archbishop denied excommunicating Mrs. O'Donnell, but apparently he did not return the book.[141]

In July 1887, after refusing several orders to go to Rome, McGlynn received word of his excommunication. By January 1889, Archbishop Corrigan declared attendance at Anti-Poverty Society meetings a mortal sin. However, women continued to risk their good standing in the church. For example, one woman named Ellen Farrell willingly confessed her attendance at the forbidden meeting in the hopes of gaining an interview with the archbishop.[142] Theresa Kelly became the center of controversy after her sudden death. Born in Ireland, Kelly was a devout Catholic and an active member of the Anti-Poverty Society. She also ran a corset manufacturing business out of her house and taught Sunday school. Although the Kelly family owned a burial plot in the diocesan cemetery, her right to a Christian burial became a source of dispute because she had attended an Anti-Poverty Society meeting a few days before she died. Father Burtsell, the pastor of Kelly's parish and a close associate of McGlynn's, performed the funeral services and escorted her body to the cemetery. This activity aroused the opposition of the archbishop, leading to Burtsell's removal from his parish.[143] In 1889 McGlynn also reported the story of a dying woman whose friends came to him for help. He claimed that the woman had been denied the sacraments because of her sympathy with the Anti-Poverty Society. Her priest reportedly would not administer the sacraments without first securing a dispensation for her antipoverty activities. McGlynn accused the priest of demanding that she pledge not to attend any more meetings and take her children out of the public schools. Although no longer a priest, McGlynn promised to visit the woman and "minister to her faith."[144]

The McGlynn affair, and the many conflicts it inspired, erupted at a crucial time in the development of the American Catholic Church. As part of larger ideological debates within the church, and in the absence of an official doctrine on social reform, McGlynn developed his own plan to address the needs of the Catholic working class. His clash with Archbishop Corrigan, and the ensuing discipline from Rome, raised important concerns about a priest's freedom to express political views and the relationship between the Catholic Church and American institutions, a debate that ultimately resulted in papal condemnation of Americanism and the conservative consolidation of the American hierarchy. By the time McGlynn clashed with Archbishop Corrigan, a conservative bloc in the American church had begun to formulate a challenge to liberalism among the clergy. Even after his excommunication, McGlynn remained at the center of the struggle between liberals and conservatives, as the question of his restoration continued until the early 1890s. Father McGlynn was ultimately reinstated after a ruling that his views were not in conflict with Catholic teaching. Archbishop Corrigan effectively silenced him by sending him to a quiet parish in upstate New York.[145] However, the agitation for change represented by Father McGlynn left its mark.

Rerum novarum

The plight of Catholic workers, and their participation in radical agitation for reform in America and abroad, led Pope Leo XIII to begin working on an encyclical on the social question. Issued in May 1891, *Rerum novarum* addressed the conditions of labor and offered a program for social justice. The pope condemned the excesses of both capitalism and socialism but supported moderate alternatives, including labor unions and government regulation for the protection of workers. As one contemporary interpreter related the meaning of *Rerum novarum* in the American context, "[The pope] clearly lays down the inviolability of private property, especially in land." Yet he also showed "fatherly tenderness and sympathy" toward working people and encouraged organization based on religious principles and motives.[146] Building on an extensive network of Catholic institutions developed largely by women religious (school, hospitals, orphanages, and settlement houses), lay Catholics increasingly entered reform organizations, particularly as middle-class Catholics came to see reform as a means of gaining respectability for their faith.[147]

The decade of the 1880s was a particularly active one in the Irish American community. Although Irish Americans already had a history of supporting nationalist efforts in Ireland (including physical force), the campaign of the Land League to reform the land system in Ireland through parliamentary means opened up opportunities for women to serve a vital role in the movement. In Ireland women served as organizers, speakers, fund-raisers, and strategists. They led the movement after the imprisonment of the men. In America women became active in the Land League as well, and for many it was their first experience with politics and social reform. Despite initial criticism of the women's participation, women in the United States found fertile ground for their participation. The Ford-George wing of the movement in particular introduced women to radical ideas and popularized a movement for social reform in the United States, one that lasted beyond the brief life of the Land League.

1. Maud Malone at a suffrage rally, May 1914. Courtesy of the Library of Congress. https://www.loc.gov/item/ggb2005016079/.

2. Margaret Hinchey, ca. 1915–20. Courtesy of the Library of Congress. https://www.loc.gov/item/ggb2005023037/.

3. Women protesters. [*Picketers: In Memory of Irish Martyrs Slain by American Loans to England, Etc.*], ca. 1915–23. Courtesy of the Library of Congress. https://www.loc.gov/item/hec2013000556/.

4. Women protesters who were ejected from the House of Representatives, June 3, 1920. Courtesy of the Library of Congress. https://www.loc.gov/item/npc2007001719/.

5. Leonora O'Reilly and her mother. Courtesy of the Schlesinger Library, Radcliffe Institute, Harvard University.

6. Agnes Nestor, 1914. Courtesy of the Library of Congress. https://www.loc.gov/item/ggb2005015547/.

4

Propaganda, Protest, Purchasing, and Picketing

Irish American Women's Nationalist Strategies in the Twentieth Century

Our Picketers

The Doom of Ireland was writ
By Britain's blood-stained hand,
The very day and way of it
Were staged by her command;
But God who built the Firmament
Made valiant women too
And they did what their brothers meant
But lacked the grit to do.[1]

On the Fourth of July 1920, the people of Boston witnessed a new campaign for independence led by two hundred "Minute Women" dressed in white and wearing headdresses of orange, white, and green—the colors of the Irish Republican flag.[2] These women were part of a burst of political protest staged on behalf of Ireland in 1920. Irish American women lent a militant edge to Irish nationalist activities after World War I. As a result, women led drives to educate the American public about Ireland's claim to independence, capture international media attention, and threaten British commercial interests through boycotts. Despite resistance by male nationalist leaders, smaller nationalist groups placed women and economics at the center of their activism. This burst of protest in the twentieth century was the culmination of years of organizing and experience by Irish American women and some Irish allies, who brought their experiences as nationalists, suffragists, and labor organizers into the final mass movement for the Irish Republic. Although nationalist groups continued to attract a broad spectrum of the Irish American community, this final phase (like the Land League of the 1880s) led women to renewed visibility as American policy and American politics became crucial to solving the question of Ireland's future. Women had been active in Irish nationalism before, but the early-twentieth-century wave coincided with the development of women's political protest—women engaged in more direct, and at times more militant, forms of protest than they had in the past.

Women played their most important and openly political role in the nationalist movement during this era for several reasons. The final years of the suffrage movement, and labor women's support for suffrage, meant that a small but vocal group of Irish American women had become veteran speakers and campaigners in the long fight for women's rights. When the amendment was ratified in 1920, new women voters entered the national spotlight, seeking to capitalize on the momentum of their suffrage victory, and both political parties sought their loyalty. Women's visibility in the postwar era built on years of organization among Irish American women, but also marked the culmination of a shift in women's activism. While just a few years earlier many women were justifying their activities largely in terms of charity, service, and education, by the end of World War I Irish American women in the nationalist movement flexed their new political muscle by attempting to influence American foreign and domestic policies.

In the years surrounding World War I, Irish nationalism became a mass movement in the United States, but its revival started earlier with the final push for Home Rule, which began in the nineteenth century, and also with a wave of cultural nationalism, which became popular with Irish Americans in the early twentieth century as well. Both movements were transnational, but both also involved women in the United States building on years of experience in nationalist, ethnic, and fraternal organizing.

Cultural Nationalism in Ireland

Influences from Ireland combined to make the turn of the twentieth century ripe for an organized defense of Ireland and Irish American identity, particularly the Gaelic Revival and the reemergence of an organized Irish nationalist movement under the leadership of the reunited Irish Parliamentary Party. A movement to preserve national identity through language, literature, and athletics flourished in Ireland at the end of the nineteenth century, particularly after the defeat of the second Home Rule Bill in 1893. The Irish reacted to the threat of Anglicization by celebrating Irish identity and encouraging a revival of Gaelic culture. In 1893 Douglas Hyde became president of the Gaelic League, officially a nonpolitical organization dedicated to teaching the Irish language.[3] The organization ran language classes, sponsored festivals, and published a newspaper. Historians estimate that the Gaelic League expanded rapidly at the end of the nineteenth century, boasting an estimated 671 branches by 1908. Although not explicitly political, the Gaelic League fostered nationalist sympathies in its members and also provided women with opportunities to participate in public affairs, becoming "something of a magnet" for politically active women.[4] Although no central membership list exists, estimates suggest that in the 1890s, 15 percent of the overall membership was female, and by the early twentieth century almost 12 percent of the 813 branches had women officers. Women also formed a majority in some Irish branches and found opportunities for advancement and leadership in the movement.[5]

The early twentieth century was also a period of movement building for women in Ireland, who had been excluded from political nationalism since the decline of the Ladies' Land League. In addition to joining the Gaelic League, by the early twentieth century women were building separate women's organizations. The revival of women's nationalist organizing began with the formation of Inghinidhe na hEireann, which was organized by Maud Gonne in 1900.

Gonne, the daughter of a British officer stationed in Ireland, had supported greater participation for women in the movement since being turned away by the Celtic Literary Society and Irish National League for membership because of her sex.[6] The women of Inghinidhe na hEireann organized activities for children, taught Irish history, and in other ways participated in the cultural revival. Their primary goal was cultivating nationalist sentiments in the next generation. However, the organization also took on much more political and controversial topics. One of the major campaigns was an antirecruitment campaign to keep Irish men from enlisting in the British army.[7]

Cultural Nationalism in America

Although the American Irish ultimately had their own reasons for supporting a Gaelic cultural revival, influences from Ireland were many at the turn of the century, including speaking tours by Maud Gonne, Douglas, Hyde, and John Redmond. Gonne brought her messages of anti-imperialism and antirecruitment to the United States during the Boer War. On two tours between 1900 and 1901, Gonne raised relief funds for the Boers, publicized efforts to limit Irish enlistment in the British army, and condemned Anglo-American relations. On Gonne's second tour, the *Washington Post* announced her mission as "the forming of women's clubs to give moral and financial support to the movement recently started in Ireland for the perpetuation of Irish language, literature and art."[8] She urged women to organize for the preservation of Irish heritage. Women also formed auxiliaries to the Boer Relief Fund, responding to the call by raising money for Boer widows and children. For example, Miss Nora Maloney, president of the Clarewomen's Association, announced that her organization would hold a ball and reception, with proceeds donated to the widows and children of the Boers. Miss Ellen Ford appeared among the "patronesses" of a Shakespeare recital to aid the fund, and the Baltimore Branch of the Women's Auxiliary of the Boer Relief Society held a bazaar to raise money.[9]

As with other movements in Ireland, the Irish in America became a crucial source of financial support. Appeals for American dollars culminated in Douglas Hyde's tour of the United States in 1905 and 1906.[10] While Irish Americans responded to funding drives for the preservation of the Gaelic language in Ireland, the Irish in the United States also had their own unique concerns: Gaelic societies in America focused their efforts on preserving their distinctive Irish identity. The Gaelic League of America, established in 1898, federated existing Irish-language organizations in an effort to promote language classes and support the Gaelic League of Ireland. The organization also made significant contributions to the teaching of Irish history, the cultivation of traditional art and dance, and the crusade against Irish caricatures in America.[11]

The Gaelic League of America also welcomed women and worked to bring its message to a wider audience through other Irish societies, including the Ancient Order of Hibernians. In 1905 Miss May T. Quinn addressed the New York Gaelic League in a speech titled "Daughters of Erin, and Their Relation to the National Movement." She called on Irish women to take interest in Ireland's struggle and spoke of the "somewhat widespread conviction" that women have no place in the nationalist movement. Quinn urged women, "Let no opportunity pass, no day go over without doing something to bring the day of [Ireland's] deliverance nearer." She also encouraged women to use their influence on the men: "Use your powers of example on the careless brothers, husbands or lovers, and show them that if they will not take up their country's burden you are ready and willing to shoulder it."[12]

Women made ideal workers in this campaign, and it also provided an outlet for their vision, service, and nationalist beliefs. One speaker told the Brooklyn Gaelic Society, "I believe one of the reasons why the Gaelic movement has taken such a strong hold upon our people is that the women have been allowed to participate in it on terms of equality with the men." He outlined several roles for women. As mothers, women could "inculcate race pride, which is the very foundation upon which love of country and everything that pertains to Nationality . . . rests." Women also needed to be vigilant about their children's education, seeing "to it that the mental food supplied their children

. . . is not the kind likely to produce in them false ideas regarding their race."[13] Although the rhetoric here focused on women's traditional roles in the home, the movement did provide opportunities for women to become active in the community.

In the United States, there was no national organization like Inghinidhe na hEireann, which had arisen out of the desire of Irish women to play a role in the nationalist movement. However the Ladies' Auxiliary of the Ancient Order of Hibernians was rapidly developing by the turn of the century. Although it was an auxiliary, the LAAOH won the right to handle its own money and elect its own officers in 1906.[14] The AOH in the United States was independent of the AOH in Ireland, and the women's auxiliary in the United States has a much longer history, since women in Ireland could not join the AOH until 1910, whereas the American LAAOH was officially recognized in the 1890s; local branches go back even further.[15] In the United States, the national LAAOH claimed fifty thousand members by 1907.[16] Therefore, these women were organized, interested, and ready to play a role in the nationalist-inspired campaigns of the twentieth century.

Among historians of Irish America, one of the most noted cultural campaigns is the battle against the stage Irish, which was part of a larger campaign to protect and defend Irish American identity. A variety of Irish organizations, including the Gaelic League and the AOH, joined forces to rid American popular culture of these offensive stereotypes. Although accounts of the protests usually focus on the men, Irish American women were able to define their own ways of protesting, arguing for respectable protest, while embracing political motives and means.

The Stage Irish

In the late nineteenth century, Irish men generally appeared in American cartoons as "an inferior, animalistic, racial type" or a "laughable ethnic fool." The roots of Irish caricature appeared in Britain, where humorists depicted the Irish with apelike features that suggested evolutionary backwardness. In addition to the obvious visual features like a slanted forehead, protruding jaw line and pug nose, the behavior of this fictional Irish man suggested several other ethnic traits, including laziness, drunkenness, violence, and stupidity. Such depictions of the Celtic "race" found a receptive audience in America by the 1870s and 1880s.[17] Irish immigrant women appeared most often as domestic servants and shantytown wives. While the young, fresh-faced recent immigrant generally appeared absentminded and irresponsible, a more sinister stereotype predominated. In illustrations Irish women shared the apelike features of their male counterparts, while stereotyped as bossy, uncouth, and untrustworthy maids who stole from their employers and threatened physical violence toward the middle-class housewives who depended on hired help.[18]

Onstage, these stereotypes appeared as early as the 1820s. The stage Irishman and a later version—the stage immigrant—flourished in the mid-nineteenth century. Such characters were usually named Pat or Paddy, had thick brogues, and were prone to blunders and boisterousness.[19] Although some protest appeared in the Irish press in the 1880s, Irish organizations did not take unified action until the beginning of the twentieth century. The AOH joined the Gaelic League and other Irish societies to eliminate offensive images of Irish men and women from American popular culture.[20] Controversy first erupted in 1902 over a play called *McFadden's Row of Flats* (written in 1897), which featured an Irish character with a monkey face and green whiskers. The play met with protests in cities across the country, including Denver, Chicago, Philadelphia, and New York.[21] Some protests took the form of resolutions and boycotts, but when these methods failed, theater audiences hissed and hurled rotten eggs and tomatoes. Eighteen men were arrested in Philadelphia and four in New York before the managers agreed to censor the offensive scenes. On the surface those individuals involved appear to be mostly men. The actors certainly were, and so were the ones who were arrested.

The battle against the stage Irish continued with similar protests against a popular vaudeville act called the "Irish Servant Girls," in which brothers John and James Russell engaged in "knockabout comedy" while dressed as maids. The brothers began performing the skit in 1876, enjoying steady success until changing attitudes on the part of audiences and the opposition of Irish societies forced them to alter their routine. The sketch featured whiskey-drinking women, vulgar conversation, and horseplay. In one of the offending scenes, a character "divest[ed] herself of so much clothing that she cast away all decency" in the process. Reportedly, two hundred men, representing ninety-one Irish societies in New York, forced the Russell brothers off the stage with rotten eggs and vegetables after their committee's appeal to the theater owner failed to bring satisfaction. Twenty-two men were arrested, but the *Irish World* defended the respectability of the men—they were not rowdies but men of intelligence, character, and property.[22] Although the AOH expressed concerns about the respectability of egg throwing, many saw the action as justified, and protesters received favorable coverage in the Irish press.

While newspaper coverage portrayed respectable Irish men forced to extreme measures in defense of Irish womanhood, women rarely appeared in the articles. No women got arrested for hurling rotten eggs or tomatoes in the theater, but they did protest in ways they considered proper. Under the leadership of first-generation immigrant Mary McWhorter, the Chicago LAAOH declared war on the stage Irish in June 1904.[23] In her denunciation of the Russell brothers, McWhorter agreed that they needed to rid the stage of the gross misrepresentation of Irish working girls, but questioned the use of the "decayed egg as a means to this end." She suggested that other and more effective methods might be found, calling for the cooperation of the men and women of all Irish societies in Chicago to boycott theaters where the offensive characters appeared. Another LAAOH leader, Ellen Ryan Jolly, succeeded in getting an offensive character removed from a play in Pawtucket, Rhode Island. In the battle over the stage Irish, Jolly protested to the manager about a "shrieking, drunken women, with wildly disheveled red hair," a character she believed unnecessary to the plot. The play, titled *The Factory Girl*, featured a character named Kitty Fogarty who was apparently "fond of her cup." Jolly had also protested a similar caricature at this theater earlier.[24]

For the leaders of the LAAOH, these examples involved less controversial methods of protest, allowing women to become more involved. The LAAOH had a gendered way of protesting. Their rhetoric outlined the kinds of protests women could be expected to engage in, where women's strengths were perceived to lie, and what would be respectable conduct for women. For the women of the LAAOH, this campaign allowed them to chart out their philosophy of protest, while also blurring the lines between fraternal and nationalist work. The women also took aim at postcards with Irish caricatures sold for Saint Patrick's Day. On the issue of postcards, the LAAOH's first national president, Anna Malia, a schoolteacher from Scranton, Pennsylvania, who was born in England of Irish parents, said, "The Ladies' Auxiliary can do much good, dear Sisters, by using its influence in a gentle, refined, but determined, manner in helping to put down such misrepresentations." She credited the cooperative efforts of the AOH and the auxiliary with driving out the repulsive stage Irishman and even more repulsive stage Irishwoman, calling on members to demonstrate their indignation by refusing to purchase such articles and showing proprietors their mistakes in "a dignified, yet determined manner."[25]

Respectable protest also included exerting political pressure, but for auxiliary women this idea meant nudging Irish men to act rather than calling directly for political rights. For example, in Chicago, the Irish American community held a mass meeting and appointed a committee to meet with the mayor and school board after a public high school entertainment included a student-drawn caricature of "Mrs. Mulcahy," a stern-looking, stout woman, with pudgy arms and cheeks and a small, flat nose. Mary McWhorter responded that the Ladies' Auxiliary of Chicago was "a monument of disapproval" of the city's public schools; they expressed their dissatisfaction by sending their children to parochial schools. However, she further pointed out that although Chicago had an Irish Catholic mayor, the number of Catholics on the board of education had dropped. She urged the women of the auxiliary to "see that your husbands and sons, fathers and brothers, put on their thinking caps between now and the next election."[26] McWhorter, who was not a suffragist, relied on indirect means of political influence, but her strategies would evolve as the nationalist movement began to revive in the twentieth century. As leaders of the LAAOH in the early twentieth century, both Jolly and McWhorter became active in nationalist organizations through the World War I period.

Revival of Home Rule and the Home Rule Crisis

The rise of cultural nationalism coincided with and complemented the renewed push for Home Rule in Ireland, and as in other nationalist movements, Irish Americans participated enthusiastically. The setbacks of the 1890s had split the movement when allegations of Parnell's affair with a married woman, Katherine O'Shea, led to calls for his resignation. Parnell refused, but even after Parnell's death in 1891, the Home Rule ranks remained divided.[27] A new wave of political nationalism began in Ireland with the founding of the United Irish League in 1898, which had one thousand branches in Ireland and more than one hundred thousand members by the fall of 1901. However, Irish women continued to be excluded from the Home Rule movement; only one branch of the United Irish League admitted women.[28] As one recent history of women nationalists asserts, "Not only did the Irish Parliamentary Party discourage interested women, it positively set out to alienate them."[29] Along with the revival of the Home Rule movement came the reunification of the Irish Parliamentary Party under the leadership of John Redmond. As Parnell had in the nineteenth century, Redmond pursued a parliamentary strategy that depended on the power of the Liberal Party in Britain.[30] Also like Parnell and Hyde, Redmond turned to the Irish in America for financial support. On a tour of the United States, Redmond founded the United Irish League of America in 1901 to raise funds for the Home Rule movement.[31] By 1902 the UILA boasted two hundred branches, attracting leading members from upper- and middle-class Irish America.[32]

Although women have rarely been mentioned in histories of this phase of the nationalist movement, they took part in the UILA from the beginning. The precedent of the Ladies' Land League, and the recent expansion of women's activities in the public sphere, eased the way for them. The moderate tone of the movement also allowed women to participate without criticism. League president John F. Finerty, who also published the *Citizen* in Chicago, told women that "they can do much for our cause." At the first national convention in 1902, women attended as delegates; a few women appeared as members of the general committee, including "Miss Davitt" and "Miss Ford." At the 1904 national convention, eleven women delegates attended, and one, Miss Mary O'Flaherty, was elected to the national executive committee. By 1906 Sabina Davitt, Mary O'Flaherty, and Ellen A. Ford were all listed among the executive committee. O'Flaherty, described in the *Boston Pilot* as one of the best-known Irish women in New York, had reportedly been an active nationalist "for many years" by then, and of course Davitt and Ford had also been active in the Ladies' Land League.[33] As these reports indicate, the United Irish League of America attracted experienced nationalist women, many with connections to the Land League or Irish National League of America. For example, Dr. Gertrude B. Kelly, who would become a leading member of the Irish Progressive League, was active in the UILA before that.

Local branches also attracted a number of women. Although their numbers may have been small, women organized auxiliaries or requested membership in male-run branches. For example, the *New York Times* reported that the second New York branch organized with a membership of 315, including 65 women.[34] When a number of women expressed interest in joining the Parnell Branch in Brockton, Massachusetts, the leadership "impressed upon" its members that the membership of ladies was desired, because "this has not been fully understood." The Maryland Central Branch reportedly made "a radical departure from its original plan by admitting ladies to membership" when a number of women sent in applications and paid dues, and the Michael Davitt Branch in Washington, DC, elected Miss Ella Gleason, "one of Washington's most popular young ladies," as secretary.[35] In Chicago the president of LAAOH Division 18 "deemed it almost a sacred duty on the part of every patriotic son and daughter of the Irish race to join the United Irish League."[36] Several Massachusetts towns also had leagues with women members by 1902, including Peabody, Gardiner, and Lynn.[37]

Other branches organized as separate women's auxiliaries. The women of Boston organized two auxiliaries in 1902, and Philadelphia organized its first ladies' branch in 1906, under the leadership of Miss Nellie Smythe, who was also president of a division of the LAAOH. In Boston Mrs. Finley, county president of the LAAOH, promised her support at the first meeting of the St. James Auxiliary of the United Irish League of America, organized in January 1901 with 30 members at the request of P. J. Flatley.[38] Flatley, president of the Boston Central Branch, "hoped that the splendid example set by the ladies" would be widely followed by the women of Boston. He called the participation of the women an inspiration and recalled the contributions of the Ladies' Land League. The following year, the auxiliary became an independent branch, known as the St. James Branch. By its second anniversary, the branch had 90 members, most of them women. Over the next few years, membership averaged between 65 and 80 members. One of the most recognizable members was Katherine Conway, then the associate editor of the *Boston Pilot*.[39]

Although most of these women are too difficult to trace, a brief sketch of one woman suggests the depth of her commitment to Irish affairs and the variety of organizations through which she offered her services, exposing one woman's contribution to a richly developed web of activism in the Irish American community. The president of the St. James Branch of the UILA, Mary J. Donovan served the Irish cause in a number of ways. In addition to repeatedly being elected to lead the St. James Branch and serving as a delegate to the national UILA conventions, Donovan taught Gaelic and served as president of the St. James Branch of the Gaelic League. One division of the Ladies' Auxiliary of the Ancient Order of Hibernians reported, "We have attached to our Auxiliary a class for the study of Irish language, with Sister Mary J. Donovan as the teacher, who is also our Corresponding Secretary."[40] She also served as an agent of the Irish Cottage Industries Committee, selling Irish-made lace directly to consumers, with the proceeds benefiting Irish industry.[41]

Donovan served actively in both the UILA and the Gaelic League, causes that she saw as intimately linked. In her address greeting Joseph

Devlin, member of Parliament, in 1902, Donovan emphasized her ethnicity. "A large number of us are Irish by birth," she said. "Our faith, language, habits and training are all derived from Ireland, and are still dear to our hearts." She made a plea for preservation of Irish language and history, asking Devlin to urge his audiences to study both. She also argued through the pages of the *Irish World* that Ireland could not be an independent nation "without [the] unity of its people and possession of that one true birthright, its language." She insisted that the United Irish League sought both.[42] Cultural nationalism and political nationalism were not mutually exclusive, but the crisis of World War I would lend urgency to nationalist debates and ultimately destroy the United Irish Leagues of Ireland and America as a new generation of nationalist organizations revived the republican dream.

The outbreak of World War I effectively ended the Home Rule movement as events in Ireland took a rapid and ultimately tragic turn. By 1910 the strategy of the Irish Parliamentary Party had begun to yield results. Electoral shifts as a result of parliamentary elections placed the IPP in a strong position; the Liberal Party needed Irish votes. Then, in 1911, when the Liberals defeated the House of Lords in a struggle that stripped the Lords of their veto power, Home Rule seemed ensured.[43] However, as the deadline for Home Rule approached, Ulster reacted with the threat of armed resistance, leading Irish nationalists to found their own military wing—the Irish Volunteers—in November 1913. By mid-1914, the Volunteers boasted a membership of 160,000.[44]

The situation escalated when Prime Minister Herbert Asquith offered a compromise to the Unionists—the temporary exclusion of Ulster from the Home Rule Bill. The outbreak of war complicated matters further, as John Redmond pledged Irish support for the British war effort in 1914, dividing the Irish Volunteers. Most Volunteers enlisted in the British army, but a small revolutionary nationalist minority prepared for armed resistance. The creation of a military body in Ireland and the threat of partition also mobilized Irish women, leading them to their most visible role in the nationalist movement since the Ladies' Land League of the 1880s. They founded Cumann na mBan (Irish Women's Council) in 1914 to raise money for the Volunteers and train in first aid.[45] The new organization had sixty branches in its first year, and in 1915 Cumann na mBan appointed an organizer who toured the country to encourage women to establish new branches. Inghinidhe na hEireann also became a branch of Cumann na mBan.[46]

The formation of the Irish Volunteers established an alternative to the Irish Parliamentary Party's quest for Home Rule, called for a new nationalist movement with widespread appeal across social and political lines, and developed a renewed role for women. While women began to prepare for the use of force in Ireland, Irish American women also took a more prominent position in protesting events in Ireland. Redmond's support for the British military and the threat of partition in Ireland alarmed Irish American nationalists and destroyed the UILA. For example, William Bourke Cockran, a lawyer, Democratic politician, and member of the national executive committee of the United Irish League of America, reported that Irish Americans had been "shocked beyond expression" at the plan for partition and held a large protest in New York, called "exclusively by women."[47]

This rally to protest the "mutilation of Ireland" was planned by Dr. Gertrude B. Kelly and Anna McAuliffe (vice president of the Interborough Association of Women Teachers).[48] The women, as leaders of the United Irish Women of New York, represented an impressive alliance of women professionals and reformers, including teachers, doctors, and journalists. Among the leading members were reformers and nationalists, including Marguerite Moore, Leonora O'Reilly, Ellen Ford, and Sarah McPike (president of the St. Catherine's Welfare Association and a Catholic suffragist).[49] Like the nationalist movement as a whole, they represented a broad assortment of women activists. Some, like Kelly and O'Reilly, represented a more radical tradition. When Gertrude Kelly wrote to thank Leonora O'Reilly for appearing at the meeting, she credited O'Reilly's name with attracting a great many and her speech with holding them once they got there. As for the content of O'Reilly's speech, Kelly reported that, although most praised the "silver tongue," O'Reilly's speech seemed to frighten some of her conservative friends, who associated her rhetoric with the Industrial Workers of the World. A member of the audience also wrote to O'Reilly, explaining that she heard her at Carnegie Hall and thought she detected a "tang" of suffrage and the IWW.[50]

Kelly and other Irish nationalist women of New York became more visible as the United Irish League of America began to crumble. She denounced Redmond privately and publicly. In a letter to Cockran, she asked, "Is Ireland after a nine hundred years' struggle for a separate nationality to end by being a colony? Is there anything we can do here to help the matter?" In print, she asked, "as a woman, an Irishwoman, and a physician, spokeswoman of hundreds, thousands of my sisters at home and abroad," if the Irish Parliamentary Party had gone mad. Who would be left to enjoy the benefits of Home Rule if Ireland sacrificed its young to the war effort?[51] Kelly noted the changing allegiances of Irish nationalists as well as gender differences: "We women have hesitated to give our adherence to the physical force party, not that we did not sympathize to the utmost with their aims, but that in our capacity as consecrators of the race, we hoped to call a halt to the immolation of Irish youth." However, she echoed the changing sentiments of many nationalists when she declared that if Irish men must fight, she would rather see them shed blood in defense of Ireland.[52] At a meeting of the United Irish League of America a few months earlier, Kelly, as a representative of the United Irishwomen of New York, reportedly presented a check for "$100 worth of bullets for the friends of Queen Mary who may try to defeat the cause of political liberty."[53]

Kelly was not alone in her criticism of Redmond. The *Irish World* printed several letters from women who opposed the enlistment of Irish men in the British army, including one from Rose McDermott, who would later lose her brother Sean McDermott after the Easter Rising. McDermott expressed her pleasure at seeing Irish women "awake to the wrong perpetuated by parliamentary leaders" and called on them to "protest such treason, and use their influence with their countrymen to persuade them to stay in Ireland and protect it." Like Kelly, McDermott called for arming the Volunteers.[54] Another letter writer, Margaret Kain of Philadelphia, a veteran of the Ladies' Land League and the United Irish League of America, declared, "We are willing to die for Ireland as we are willing to live for it" and prayed that the "boys at home" would not cross the English Channel.[55]

In the midst of the outcry over Redmond's position and the urgency of war, Irish American women, like their Irish counterparts, took a more visible stand, embracing familiar strategies such as fund-raising, philanthropy, and education. Dr. Gertrude B. Kelly, now described by the *Irish World* as "always in the forefront where Irish Nationality is concerned," established the first American branch of Cumann na mBan (First American Auxiliary), stressing the need for education and publicity. At that time, her public rhetoric in the nationalist movement did not yet show her radical roots. Dr. Kelly and Dr. Madge McGuinness issued a call to "Irish mothers and daughters to form an international league for the protection of Irish nationality." In organizing branches of Cumann Na mBan in the United States, Kelly and her associates built on not only the work of women in Ireland but also a network of Irish Americans organizations, some of which had been admitting women since the late nineteenth century. Their notice in the *Irish World* assured readers that "enlightened public opinion is to play an important part" in the "adjustment following this great war." They appealed to a wide range of Irish American women's groups, including the LAAOH, county societies, and literary and dramatic groups to cooperate and "inaugurate a comprehensive propaganda" for the liberation of Ireland.[56]

When Cumann na mBan first organized in New York, Mary Colum and Sidney Gifford Czira were there to represent Cumann na mBan of Ireland. Colum, an Irish literary critic who settled in the United States, was an original founder of Cumann na mBan of Ireland. Czira was an Irish journalist who arrived in the United States in 1914 with a mission to help spread the word for the Volunteers and Cumann na mBan. When Czira met Kelly for the first time at a lecture sponsored by the Gaelic League, Kelly arranged for her to speak about the Volunteers. Mary McWhorter also helped by arranging for Czira to attend a session of the LAAOH's convention.[57] After the first meeting, the *Irish World* stressed the broad appeal of the cause, reporting the attendance of "all forms of Irish national thought" at the first meeting, including Redmondites and anti-Redmondites, conservatives and revolutionaries, men and women.[58] Veteran speaker and activist Marguerite Moore rallied the women with her declaration that the men of Ireland would not fight England's battles. Moore reminded her audience of the service rendered by the Ladies' Land League; she told them "as the women came to the rescue then they would come to the rescue now." Irish women had always taken their place beside the men and sometimes replaced them in the struggle for liberty, she explained. Moore also appealed to women's sense of moral responsibility, warning the mothers of Ireland that they must prevent their sons from joining the British army, an army that she claimed was characterized by corruption and sexual impropriety. In other words, Irish women must guard against the corruption of their men and protect the purity of the Irish nation.[59]

As in previous bursts of nationalism, many supporters defined the role of women in fairly conservative terms. An account in John Devoy's newspaper, the *Gaelic American*, stressed the traditional role of women in the new organization: "This Cumann Na mBan [*sic*] is no Suffragette affair, as we understand 'Suffs' on the European side. It is a banding together of the mothers and daughters of Ireland to support their men folk in the mighty struggle for independence." Mary Colum also echoed these sentiments when she asked for the moral and material support of Irish women in America, claiming that "the women who joined the organization in the greatest numbers were mothers of families who rarely ventured into public affairs—women who . . . wanted a free country to bring up their children in, and opportunities for their sons and daughters in their own country."[60] This statement is not to suggest that nationalist women were not suffragists. Many, including Colum, were. However, the issue had been divisive. Colum had already defended the organization against criticism from Hanna Sheehy Skeffington and the Irishwomen's Franchise League, which considered the auxiliary position of Cumann na mBan a step backward for women. In response, Colum explained that branches of Cumann na mBan were “not the auxiliaries or the handmaidens or the camp-followers of the Volunteers—we are their allies.” She insisted, “As an organization we must confine ourselves within the four walls of our constitution.”[61]

Irish American women had a long tradition of nationalism by then, but in the United States Cumann na mBan was the first women’s nationalist organization since the formation of Ladies’ Land League branches in the 1880s. Sarah McKelvey, president of the second American branch of Cumann na mBan (Cumann na mBan, Inc., was formed in June 1915) and a supporter of John Devoy, had also been active in nationalist activities for many years before joining Cumann na mBan.[62] As a member of the Gaelic League, McKelvey tried to arouse interest in the Irish language and introduce Irish dancing in New York. She was also remembered as a leader in the war on the stage Irish and the push against Saint Patrick’s Day postcards. The *Gaelic American* described McKelvey and Cumann na mBan, Inc., as the “allies and ‘comrades in the fight’ with the Irish Volunteers” and praised McKelvey’s name for being “held in such high esteem in Irish organizations in America, that it will be a rallying cry of Irish women to join the organization over which she presides.” The column highlighted the need for organization among Irish American women for “patriotic purposes” and dismissed the leadership of Redmond and the Irish Parliamentary Party: “Many Irish women in this country have made blunders in the past through having lost touch with Ireland,” the writer insisted. “They have supported false leaders and reactionary parties who were deliberately strangling that very movement for Irish freedom which the Irish American women were seeking to foster.”[63]

The appeal for Cumann na mBan, Inc., for the support of Irish American women involved three strategies: appealing to the strength and dedication of Irish women, citing the past patriotic contributions of Irish women to the nationalist cause, and pointing to the sacrifices of those Irish who came before them. Rose McDermott, an officer in the new branch, called on Irish women in America, who were “blessed with that high and proud spirit upon which the hint of danger acts as fuel to fire," to support the men of Ireland in resisting conscription into the British army. In particular, Cumann na mBan, Inc., also appealed to the Ladies' Auxiliary of the AOH to cooperate in the struggle.[64] They invoked the past—the spirit of Ireland's women patriots—and reminded Irish American women, who enjoyed "freedom and comforts," to "stop and consider just one or two instances of the sacrifices that have been made by our mothers in the past."[65] According to the article, this new role for women built on a history of women's activism and sacrifices for Irish freedom.

Easter Week and Its Aftermath

As Irish American women escalated their attempts to support Irish nationalism by founding women's organizations and educating audiences on the situation in Ireland, Redmond's rapid rebuke by nationalists in the United States also signaled dramatic change in the course and strategy of the nationalist movement. Physical-force nationalism, under the leadership of John Devoy and Clan na Gael, had been relatively weak during the heyday of Home Rule, but American neutrality during the early years of World War I, and the split in nationalist forces in Ireland, gave the Clan a chance to revive the movement for armed rebellion in Ireland. Nationalist leaders in the United States called an Irish Race Convention in 1916.[66] John Devoy already knew about plans for a rebellion in Ireland (and had met with many of its leaders) when more than two thousand delegates attended the first Irish Race Convention in New York.[67] Women were represented at the meeting by the LAAOH. Ellen Ryan Jolly and Mary McWhorter both addressed the crowd. Responding to an editorial claiming that the Irish Race Convention would be attended by few real women, only viragos who outrivaled the men, McWhorter assured her audience, "I am not an accident. I come from the other side, and left Ireland at a time when it had a stormy period." Ellen Ryan Jolly told the crowd that her friends wanted her to "be moderate," but she asked, "Ah, how can I be moderate when I start to talk of the most brutal of all countries in the world—England?"[68] As a result of the first Irish Race Convention, a new nationalist organization emerged, the Friends of Irish Freedom; the FOIF accepted men and women, boasting 275,000 members (including federated societies) by 1919, although its numbers were much smaller in the beginning. The FOIF was run by a small executive committee of men, most of whom also belonged to the Clan. Among the few women on the original board of directors were some of the most prominent women in the Ladies' Auxiliary of the Ancient Order of Hibernians, including Ellen Ryan Jolly, Mary McWhorter, and Charlotte Holloway (a national lecturer for the AOH).[69]

Through the FOIF, John Devoy and his close associate Tammany judge Daniel Cohalan controlled the direction of the movement, deciding how to allocate funds and directing strategy. While the FOIF opposed American involvement in the World War I, Devoy and the Clan secretly supported revolution in Ireland, which began when a small faction of the Irish Volunteers in alliance with the Irish Citizen Army, under the leadership of James Connolly, started an armed revolt in Dublin during Easter weekend in 1916.[70] The leaders of the Easter Rising authored a proclamation for the new Irish Republic, which was read from the steps of the General Post Office by Patrick Pearse. The proclamation guaranteed equal rights and equal opportunities to all citizens, a pledge insisted upon by James Connolly.[71] As one Cumann na mBan participant (Eileen Gifford, who spent two months in jail after the Rising) later told a New Jersey audience, "The Declaration of the Irish Republic was broader than that of the Declaration of Independence . . . because it declared for the equality of men and women for labor and for nationality. Labor suffrage workers and the Nationalists fought side by side during the uprising."[72]

After the surrender of the rebels, fifteen men were charged with treason and quickly tried and executed (including a wounded James Connolly). Although armed resistance initially found little support among the Irish at home and abroad, the execution of the leaders evoked widespread sympathy, leading to a shift in public opinion.[73]

In the United States, the FOIF organized a major demonstration as public opinion united against British policy in Ireland, and news of the executions swayed many Irish Americans toward physical-force nationalism.[74] Irish Americans began to rally around the fallen leaders and the ideals of the Irish Republic. Frank Walsh, a progressive Democrat, who served under President Wilson as chair the Industrial Relations Committee in 1913 (and would later cochair the War Labor Board in 1918), wrote to Leonora O'Reilly, "Those Irishmen did not die in vain. The tragedy stirred countless thousands of us mutton heads, who have been maundering about Home Rule, into a sudden realization of the real Irish question. Connolly had it to the utmost; the others better than any of the Irish patriots who have ever gone before."[75]

Some in the American labor movement were also sympathetic to Connolly. After the executions, the Illinois State Federation of Labor, New York's central body, and the Detroit Central Labor Organization all condemned the executions. In New York, Irish-born labor leader Thomas Rock denounced the executions "of men who surrendered as prisoners of war" and called on President Wilson and the State Department to demand reparations for the murder of American citizens.[76]

In Ireland women's role in the nationalist movement changed after 1916. The women of Cumann na mBan in Ireland and the Irish Citizen Army had participated in the Easter Rising as cooks, nurses, couriers, and (occasionally) snipers. Countess Markievicz, an officer in the Irish Citizen Army, received a death sentence for her role in the fighting, although it was commuted because of her sex. With the revolutionary leadership either dead or in prison, women in Ireland moved to keep the republican movement alive, first by providing financial aid to the dependents of the martyrs and second by educating the Irish public and gaining international allies for Ireland's claim to independence. Kathleen Clarke, widow of Tom Clarke, organized the Irish Volunteer Dependent's Fund just after the execution of her husband.[77] Irish women also played an important role in the propaganda battle in the United States, as some of those individuals who were directly affected by the executions began to appear before American audiences.

The movement to support the widows and children of executed Volunteers quickly moved to the United States as well. After the Rising, Cumann na mBan, First American Auxiliary, declared, "The women of Ireland are standing with and behind the men in their fight for freedom. The spirit of both remains unbroken." The women of Cumann na mBan asked women to respond, because "the saving of women and children is essentially woman's work."[78] Despite these appeals to charity, the rhetoric at the relief meeting, chaired by Gertrude Kelly, suggests that some Irish American women were also challenging the narrow definition of women's role in the movement and calling explicitly for political rights. A suffragist named Mary Donnelly (discussed in chapter 6), acknowledged the role women could play in partisan politics, encouraging women to organize for relief work in Ireland, but also pointing to the need to organize "for political power in America which will be effective in helping our kinsmen when the peace conference meets at the Hague." Marguerite Moore also spoke and was introduced as "the first suffragette." She praised men who were willing to fight "that the flag of the Irish Republic may be kept afloat and Ireland may be free."[79] Leonora O'Reilly represented the interests of organized labor at the meeting. She instructed her audience to "be worthy of this martyr by understanding the part labor has played in Irish history and must continue to play until labor comes into its own everywhere."[80] As such rhetoric suggests, activists were mixing Irish nationalism with other reform goals such as the solidarity of labor and the political rights of women. Furthermore, although the nationalist movement expanded dramatically in this era, the women who appeared at the podium had a long history of activism and were experienced speakers by then. Another political veteran, Mary Elizabeth Lease, appears to have been a member of the FOIF and Cumann na mBan. At a protest meeting a few months earlier, she urged the audience not to rest until the Republic of Ireland was established.[81] Although Lease led a fairly quiet life in New York by then, she resurfaced to speak for the Irish Republican movement.

As in the Land League era, Irish nationalism in the World War I era united otherwise diverse groups (at least temporarily). Likewise, various factions struggled to control the message and the strategy of the movement. Although fund-raising remained an important role, politics and public opinion were also central concerns for Irish nationalists. While the divisions among the leadership would ultimately split the FOIF, women and workers became independent voices in the political struggle for Ireland. Irish American nationalists, under the direction of the Friends of Irish Freedom, sought to influence public opinion and government policy, initially to keep the United States out of the war and later to secure a place for Ireland at the peace talks. The FOIF encouraged cooperation with other ethnic groups in opposition to American involvement in World War I, and Judge Cohalan used the FOIF to oppose President Wilson's reelection in 1916. The FOIF had more success in drawing crowds and media attention.[82] Through a series of meetings and publicity, they were able to bring Irish citizens—Irish women—before American audiences. In the court of public opinion, women played a significant role.

One of the most powerful sources of pro-Irish propaganda came from Irish citizens, particularly the women and families of the Easter Rising. These heroic women had taken part in the fighting or lost loved ones to the cause. These women carried on the work and memory of the men who died by appealing to American audiences in person and in print. In New York, the women of Cumann na mBan, Inc., declared their "sense of horror at the brutality of the English Government in cruelly murdering the leaders of the Volunteers after they had honorably surrendered," expressing their sorrow to two of the group's own members, Rose and Kate McDermott, who lost their brother Sean, one of the leaders of the rebellion.[83]

Several Irish Republican women also toured the United States after 1916. Two of the most dramatic stories were told by Nora Connolly and Hanna Sheehy Skeffington.[84] Connolly slipped out of Ireland just after the Rising and made her way to the United States, where she recounted the events of Easter week and the execution of her father. The *Irish World* ran an article by Nora Connolly in August 1916, and she appeared at meetings of the Friends of Irish Freedom. The account of one meeting described Connolly as "a pale slip of a girl in a black dress" who told a packed audience at Faneuil Hall "a simple, sad story of how her father, 'Jim' Connolly, Commander-in-Chief of the Army of the Irish Republic, had been taken, sorely wounded, from his bed . . . and propped up against a wall and shot dead."[85]

Hanna Sheehy Skeffington appeared at her first mass meeting in the United States a few months before American entry into World War I. Skeffington and her husband, Francis, were leading figures in Irish reform circles and published a newspaper. Both were committed suffragists, nationalists, and pacifists; both served time in jail for their political activities; both went on hunger strikes. During Easter week, Francis Sheehy Skeffington was arrested while trying to organize against looting in Dublin. Although noncombatants, he and two other journalists were executed without notice or trial. Hanna Sheehy Skeffington decided to take her story to American audiences with the financial support of the FOIF. Although denied a passport, she and her young son entered the United States in disguise. Between January 1917 and June 1918, she spoke at more than 250 meetings throughout the United States on the topic of British militarism.[86]

America's entry into the war changed everything. The Friends of Irish Freedom and other Irish nationalists attempted to distance themselves from their earlier statements in support of Germany, emphasizing their loyalty and patriotism. Many Irish nationalists altered their strategy from opposing American involvement to reflecting President Wilson's rhetoric of supporting self-determination for small nations. Clan leaders Judge Daniel Cohalan and John Devoy refrained from directly challenging American policy, focusing instead on making Ireland's case a consideration in the war.[87] As Irish Republican Patrick McCartan recalled, "The feeling generally became such that Irish organizations, which periodically passed resolutions about Ireland, were afraid to meet."[88] Hanna Sheehy Skeffington recalled, "We Irish exiles in the United States . . . thought . . . that our meetings would have been suppressed, and that we ourselves would be sent to prison or deported."[89] There were arrests. In September 1917, police in New York arrested eight people at a Friends of Irish Freedom meeting, including Margaret Curley, a relative of Boston mayor James Michael Curley.[90] Citing harassment, Cumann na mBan, Inc., protested "the action of Chief Flynn of the American Secret Service for his brutal insults to a Sister Member in her home, while he with two other men raided her apartment and stole her Irish Republican flag."

The women resolved that the women of Cumann na mBan "are not the kind that can be terrorized."[91] The *Irish World*, *Gaelic American*, and *Freeman's Journal* (New York) were all banned from the mail.

Hanna Sheehy Skeffington was removed from a meeting by police in San Francisco in April 1918.[92] During her time in the United States, Skeffington canvassed politicians and lobbied Congress with the intention of blacklisting unsympathetic politicians. In a repressive wartime climate, she reported finding Irish Americans unresponsive but found support from "suffs, radicals and progressives."[93] While other nationalist groups moderated their activities during the war, Leonora O'Reilly recalled that the Irish Women's Council was "the brave group of women who have kept the flag of the Republic before the public and the torch burning for Ireland an independent nation when big business and big politicians were afraid to call their souls their own."[94] Membership in Cumann na mBan, American Auxiliary No. 1, overlapped with another group in which Dr. Gertrude Kelly played an important role: the Irish Progressive League.

Described by historian Francis Carroll as an alliance of "revolutionary [Irish] nationalists and left-of-center Irish Americans," the IPL formed in 1917. With US entry into the war, the strategy of nationalists had changed. The IPL intended to promote Ireland's right to representation at the peace conference following the war.[95] A small group of about 150 republicans led by poet and singer Peter Golden, the Irish Progressive League also had a significant core of women leaders, some American and some Irish citizens. Among its prominent women members were Hanna Sheehy Skeffington, Nora Connolly (daughter of James), Helen Golden (wife of Peter), Dr. Gertrude B. Kelly, and Margaret Hickey. Leonora O'Reilly also spoke under the auspices of the IPL. However, Katherine Hughes described Peter Golden and Dr. Kelly as the "salt of their movement."[96]

At the suggestion of Hanna Sheehy Skeffington, the IPL established the Irish National Bureau in Washington, DC, as a central organization for propaganda to promote the Irish cause with the US government. Katherine Hughes, a Canadian Catholic writer and public servant, oversaw the operation of the bureau.[97] Hughes became committed to Irish nationalism while working in London for two years. By the time of the Easter Rising, she was back in Canada and working on a book, but research trips to the United States brought her into contact with nationalists there. She attended the second Irish Race Convention in May 1918, where she told audiences that her trips to Ireland had led her to Sinn Fein. The Irish Progressive League hired her to run the bureau, but when the FOIF took over the funding of the bureau she was passed over for the top spot. Hughes remained on as secretary of the bureau and lecturer for the FOIF until returning to Canada in 1920 to mobilize Irish Canadian support for the Irish Republic.[98]

In its earliest phase, the Irish Progressive League had a significant socialist influence and chose to support socialist candidate Morris Hillquit for mayor of New York on the grounds that he was the only true friend of Ireland because he opposed the war.[99] Gertrude B. Kelly commended the stand taken by the Irish Progressive League "to preserve for America the rights so dearly won, of free assembly, free speech and free press." Kelly denounced the warlords, secret diplomatists, and, even more dangerous, the profiteers "who are fattening on the lifeblood of the people."[100] According to one historian, the tiny Irish Progressive League worked more aggressively during the war and became more critical of President Wilson and the US government than most other Irish American organizations.[101]

However, it is important to note that more moderate Irish American women also raised their political voices during this phase of the nationalist movement. As national president of the Ladies' Auxiliary of the Ancient Order of Hibernians and also a representative of the FOIF, Mary McWhorter attempted to influence President Wilson with a moderate and conciliatory message from Irish American women. The women of the LAAOH entered the debate as mothers of Irish American soldiers who fought and died for their country and the principle of self-determination. At the second Irish Race Convention in 1918, Mary McWhorter told her audience she represented seventy-five thousand Irish American women in the LAAOH and that

75 percent of their members had sons fighting in France or in training camps waiting to go overseas. She expressed her support for the American war effort but also insisted that "it is not inconsistent with our American patriotism to talk up good and strong, and to act for the little Republic of Ireland."[102]

Unlike many women peace activists who used motherhood as a justification of their antiwar stance, McWhorter demanded a political voice based on mothers' sacrifices in the war. This argument became the foundation of a "Mothers' Mission" to President Wilson. In her plea to the president, McWhorter focused on the desire of Irish American mothers to see their sons' sacrifices as meaningful: "Many of these mothers feel that if they could . . . present Ireland's case in the name of their boys . . . you would take up the cause of the Irish people . . . and see that they also are included among the peoples for whom you so nobly advocate the right of self-determination." She reminded Wilson that these mothers had "cheerfully given their boys for the sacred cause of the oppressed races on the Earth," and they "were positive" they could depend on Wilson to stand for justice for Ireland at the peace conference.[103]

McWhorter headed a committee of mothers to present the appeal, with six hundred thousand signatures, to the president. Denied a meeting with Wilson, she enlisted the aid of Congressman Thomas Gallagher and Senator James Hamilton Lewis of Illinois. McWhorter praised the representatives of her state but later told of the "terrible time" her committee had in its efforts to reach President Wilson. She warned her audience to stay vigilant on the issue of Irish self-determination. This time, McWhorter advocated a direct political strategy, urging the women of the Ladies' Auxiliary to organize public meetings in their states and send appeals to President Wilson and members of Congress. McWhorter had publicly opposed suffrage. In 1910 the *Chicago Daily Tribune* quoted her as saying, "I think all true women will agree with me that a woman has the most influence with a man when [she] is her own womanly self." She believed good women could clean up politics by exerting their influence on men but decried the uncouth and ignorant men whom women would be forced to encounter should they go to the polls. Although she did not specifically discuss suffrage during this campaign, she did endorse political pressure for the protection of Ireland, telling women, "This is the age of women. Senators and Congressmen are showing great regard for our opinion."[104] Illinois women already had the right to vote in presidential elections, but of course many states still did not have women's suffrage at the time.

By late 1918, as the war drew to a close, the FOIF and other Irish societies returned to prominence in the nationalist movement, adopting the strategy of appealing directly to President Wilson to include Irish self-determination at the peace conference.[105] When this strategy failed, the most serious opposition to President Wilson's postwar agenda came during the battle over the League of Nations. Irish American nationalists perceived the League of Nations as an Anglo-American alliance, and thus an obstacle to the Irish nationalist movement. They insisted that the covenant of the league would require America to defend its allies in territorial disputes, thus placing the United States in the position of supporting imperialism.[106] Devoy and Cohalan, who controlled the Clan and the FOIF, believed American politics and diplomacy could be used to win independence for Ireland. They advocated self-determination for Ireland, mirroring President Wilson's war rhetoric, while leading a fight against the League of Nations. Others, including Patrick McCartan and Eamon de Valera, both representing the Irish Republican government, wanted to finance the Irish revolution with money raised in America. Both men opposed the use of nationalist funds to influence American politics. McCartan believed that the Irish people had already exercised their right to self-determination through their support of Sinn Fein candidates, who swept to victory in the general election of 1918 and created a separate Irish Parliamentary body, Dail Eireann. McCartan sought recognition of the established Irish Republican government. This feud began to simmer even before Eamon de Valera, president-elect of the Irish Republic, arrived in the United States in the summer of 1919.[107] De Valera's presence exacerbated an already tense situation, and his challenge to the leadership of Cohalan and Devoy culminated in a complete split in the FOIF in 1920, when de Valera founded his own organization, the American Association for the Recognition of the Irish Republic (AARIR).

While these powerful men fought for control of the nationalist movement and the funds that had been raised, new strategies also emerged, reflecting the experiences of labor during the war. American labor initially supported neutrality in World War I, blaming the bloodshed on capitalism and the race for markets among European powers. American entry into the war, and the Bolshevik Revolution, led to wartime repression of radicals, but unions generally benefited from the wartime economy. Through the National War Labor Board, the government sought to regulate relations between workers and employers in war industries, and the leadership of the American Federation of Labor worked closely with the Wilson administration.[108]

However, this partnership did not reflect a change in the AFL's traditional attitude toward politics—voluntarism—that focused on trade union formation and collective bargaining rather than government legislation to improve working conditions and wages. Although the AFL continued to oppose independent political action, women workers and reformers had already embraced the strategy, and other progressive unionists began to advocate for the formation of a labor party in the United States. In the wake of massive defeats to strikers after the war, some of the strategies long advocated by radicals in the labor movement, including consumer boycotts, consumer-producer cooperatives, and a national labor party, became more widespread.[109]

The final phase of the Irish nationalist movement, from 1916 to 1923, included substantive contributions by American workers, an aspect largely overlooked by historians, according to David Brundage, because most nationalist organizations were led by the middle class and because studies of the relationship between Irish nationalism and labor focus on dynamic personalities such as James Connolly and James Larkin (both Irish socialists who spent time in America). Yet Irish American labor leaders and the rank and file also provided important support to the movement during these years.[110] Dissenting voices within the trade union movement, including the Irish-born leader of the Chicago Federation of Labor, John Fitzpatrick, rejected Wilson's vision for international cooperation because they believed it would strengthen international finance at the expense of workers. Fitzpatrick and other Irish American labor leaders were committed to a new world order through international class struggle, advocating the cause through several movements, including support of Irish and Indian independence and a campaign to boycott British goods.[111] They offered an alternative vision of working-class internationalism, calling for the unity of workers around the world and rejecting imperialism.

Some of the most innovative political protests and propaganda efforts of 1920 were led by women, many of whom also had ties to labor, Irish Republicanism, and suffrage. After years of organizing, and armed with new political experience and status, a group of Irish American women moved to center stage in the struggle for recognition of the Irish Republic. These women founded organizations to disseminate propaganda, captured media attention through dramatic protests, and conducted a grassroots campaign to harness the power of American workers against British imperialism. These campaigns were led not by large and well-funded Irish American organizations, such as the Friends of Irish Freedom or the Ancient Order of Hibernians, but by members of the Irish Progressive League and other small, independent groups.

One such group surfaced in California. Although many studies of the Irish in America focus on the Northeast, San Francisco boasted a thriving Irish American community, an active labor movement, and strong Irish Republican sympathies. In the summer of 1920, the eyes of the Irish American community turned to San Francisco because of the Democratic National Convention.[112] The previous summer women in San Francisco founded the Women's Irish Education League (WIEL), which grew to more than two thousand members by 1922. At its first meeting, Charlotte Anita Whitney and Minnie McCarthy presided over a gathering reported at fifteen hundred people and drafted a protest against any peace treaty that did not include recognition of the Irish Republic. While little is known about McCarthy, Whitney had been active in the California suffrage movement, and California women had the vote. She joined the Socialist Party in 1914 and was arrested for criminal syndicalism in 1919.[113] Whitney was not Irish, but she had been asked to chair the group by Kathleen O'Brennan, a Dublin newspaperwoman and the sister-in-law of Eamonn Ceannt, who was executed for his role in the Easter Rising. Whitney recalled, "The fact that it was quite independent of any of the older Irish organizations that flourished in San Francisco, and that its sole aim was the movement for national freedom, quite distinct from any religious or political affiliations, brought us phenomenal success."[114]

A month after the organizational meeting, the WIEL began planning a statewide campaign to educate the public on conditions in Ireland and advocate for Irish independence, or, according to its stationery, "To Put Before the American People The Truth About Ireland."[115] The *Irish World* reported of the new organization: "The Women's Irish Educational League of San Francisco concerns itself with educational work along economic lines, and is typical of the best efforts of American womanhood organized to maintain the ideals of liberty immortality [*sic*] enunciated in America's Declaration of Independence." The WIEL held a debate on the League of Nations, encouraged the formation of similar organizations in Nevada, and contributed to the publishing of a labor newspaper called the *Rank and File.* In carrying out its educational mission, the league also established a circulating library of Irish literature, an exhibit for loan, and distributed copies of Laurence Ginnell's book advocating an Irish Republic to one thousand San Francisco attorneys.[116] Katherine Hughes of the Irish National Bureau also commended the work of the San Francisco women; she recommended organizing Women's Irish Education Leagues in various states: "Set the women working. American women can do anything they undertake," she wrote to Daniel Cohalan.[117] The league participated in protests and boycotts, but its influence was not limited to the West Coast. The WIEL also had a link to another women's nationalist group, the American Women Pickets for the Enforcement of America's War Aims. Kathleen O'Brennan worked with both organizations.[118]

The American Women Pickets for the Enforcement of America's War Aims

The American Women Pickets for the Enforcement of America's War Aims grew out of the urgent need for publicity.[119] In 1920 William J. Maloney, a former British medical officer (of Irish parentage) turned Irish nationalist, conceived of a plan to recruit women to lobby Congress. Maloney became visible in the nationalist movement in 1918 after writing a series of articles called "The Irish Issue" for the leading Catholic periodical, *America*.[120] By 1919 Maloney, Joseph McGarrity (a leading Clansman and wealthy businessman from Philadelphia), and Patrick McCartan led the opposition to the leadership of Cohalan and Devoy.[121] Maloney recruited about sixty Irish American women to poll members of Congress on their position concerning the Mason Bill, a measure to appropriate funds for the salaries of diplomatic officials to the Irish Republic, thereby recognizing the government's legitimacy. Hoping to attract international attention to conditions in Ireland and to prevent bloodshed on the anniversary of the Easter Rising, the women protested at the British Embassy in Washington, DC.[122] Maloney apparently envisioned the campaign as a temporary publicity stunt—even hiring actresses to take part and selecting women for their good looks. However, Maloney soon lost control of events.[123]

In a two-week campaign, women from all over the country—professionals, actresses, journalists, and reformers—staged a variety of protests in Washington, DC. Some were already members of the Irish Progressive League or the Friends of Irish Freedom. Gertrude B. Kelly did not travel to Washington, but she did pay for other women to travel there.[124] The women picketed the British Embassy, conducted a poll of congressional members, and protested at the State Department.

The first arrests occurred after women picketed at the British Embassy with signs reading, "England: American Women Condemn Your Reign of Terror in the Irish Republic" and "Congress: Prevent the Massacre Impending in Ireland by Abrogating All Treaties with

England." Ten members of the Pickets and two women bystanders were arrested. While John Devoy's *Gaelic American*, and the national leadership of the FOIF, ultimately condemned the women, the *Irish World* gave them favorable press, running a picture of two women who refused bail and went to jail with the caption "These ladies have sacrificed much, including personal liberty, for Ireland. Will not you sacrifice something and contribute your share to the defense fund for these heroines of liberty here and beyond the Atlantic."[125] The *Citizen* of Chicago described the original picketing campaign as "opportune, illuminative, efficient work" by women who had "plucked a valuable leaf out of the book of the American suffragettes."[126] A Washington, DC, branch of the Friends of Irish Freedom helped bail the women out of jail, and Frank P. Walsh offered legal defense to those women arrested.[127]

The tactics of the women protesters evoked memories of protests by the National Woman's Party who had picketed the White House a few years before. NWP members went on hunger strikes in prison after their arrests and were force-fed. Both the United States and Ireland had militant wings of the suffrage movement in the twentieth century. In a letter to Leonora O'Reilly, a friend relayed the comments of O'Reilly's former mentor Edward King, who said, "It [the picketing] was a really good trick for the Irish movement, but unless they get arrested they won't get enough publicity—it is too tame, so far." "Well," her friend commented, "they have got arrested since and I hope the prison treatment is not so inhuman [*sic*] as that which was meted out to the suffrage militants for that was horrible, but it did its work."[128]

Perhaps the most dramatic moment occurred when Mollie Carroll, an actress from Manhattan, flew over the British Embassy, "bombing" it with leaflets and landing front-page coverage. The *New York Times* reported that Pickets "rained down packages of leaflets, espousing the Irish cause," but their "bombing expedition . . . registered no hits. Low visibility and wind scattered the 'bombs' everywhere but on the embassy."[129] Although Patrick McCartan described Carroll as a "lovely little actress, charmingly garbed as an aviatrix," Carroll was not just a pretty face. She was an original member of the Irish Progressive League, and her mother may have been an active nationalist in Ireland.[130] With the same dramatic flair, Carroll and several other women chartered a tugboat to greet Sir Auckland Geddes, the arriving British ambassador. The tug circled his ship, bearing a sign with a quote from President Wilson: "What we seek is the reign of law based on the consent of the governed and sustained by the organized opinion of mankind."[131]

As Patrick McCartan recalled, the Pickets had been mobilized to apply pressure in one particular emergency. Both he and Maloney considered their efforts successful. Their campaign proved that a direct appeal could mobilize American sympathy for Ireland. The Pickets had captured America's attention and were shown "nightly in Moving Pictures all over America." However, when Maloney thanked the women for their service and "instructed the captain of the Pickets [Irish American journalist Gertrude Corless] to disband her force," she declined.[132] Corless and Kathleen O'Brennan, who had moved east in 1920, cooperated in the founding of a new independent organization, the American Women Pickets for the Enforcement of America's War Aims, in late April 1920.[133] Bands of women picketers led to a number of other campaigns in the summer and fall of 1920, including demonstrations in Philadelphia, Boston, New York, and Washington, DC.

These women chose to continue their work, conducting an independent campaign to aid Ireland and working outside the traditional power channels of the Irish nationalist movement. Gertrude Corless, head of the American Women Pickets, acknowledged the departure their strategies represented when the Pickets brought their campaign to Boston under a new (but equally patriotic) name—the Minute Women. According to the *Irish World*, Corless "spoke for the American women who were going to adopt other methods than the men in gaining their ends." She told her audience, "If the women are going to use the same old methods of experiences versus principles then the vote will be valueless."[134] If women voters wanted to bring a heightened sense of purpose and propriety to politics, why not start with justice for Ireland?

Women did not abandon traditional centers of power. Gertrude Corless focused her efforts on Washington, DC, attempting to flex the muscle of the new woman voter by lobbying for the Mason Bill. In a letter sent to every member of the Foreign Relations Committee, the American Women Pickets told their elected representatives, "We demand that justice be done to the 20 million Irish-Americans—and we are organizing in your several districts to fight your re-election in case of failure to go on record on this important decision." When the Mason Bill failed, the women went to Capitol Hill to confront congressmen directly.[135]

In June American Pickets burned a British flag in front of the American Treasury Department and marched to demand that the United States cut off loans to Britain. The Pickets announced their purpose as educating American public opinion to crush British militarism in Ireland.[136] Women reportedly cheered as the flag burned, and the *Irish World* quoted one protester as saying, "It's just another little Boston Tea Party." The same week, American Women Pickets appeared simultaneously in both the House of Representatives and the Senate. Approximately thirty female supporters of the Mason Bill interrupted the proceedings by shouting from the gallery. The *Irish World* reported that Mrs. B. J. Roddy, captain of the Washington, DC, pickets, joined the picketing after losing her son in World War I; she wanted to do "real work" for Ireland. She stood up in Congress and said, "I did not give my son to fight to save England or that the twenty million Irish in America should be insulted."[137] To get their message out, the pickets also began "billboard raiding," posting slogans to signboards late at night.[138]

Although the initial picketing received some favorable coverage in the Irish American press, the women's independent action aroused the opposition of nationalist leaders, especially the Friends of Irish Freedom and John Devoy's newspaper, the *Gaelic American*. The *Irish World* defended their activities on the editorial page. Under the headline "Shameless Criticism of Noble Women," one editorial condemned a "highly paid official of the F.O.I.F." who publicly denounced the "noble women" for "not fighting the vampire in a ladylike manner."

Apparently, the editorial asserted, the official believed the women were disrupting "the wise and statesmanlike plans" of nationalist leaders.[139] While this criticism reflected, in part, the fight for control within the nationalist movement, the FOIF official apparently also disapproved of the women's activities because they had transgressed gendered norms of respectable behavior.

By the summer of 1920, more criticism emerged. Daniel T. O'Connell, director of the Friends of Irish Freedom National Bureau of Information (in Washington, DC), issued a statement distancing the organization from the women: "The apparent determination of the women Pickets to engage at Washington and in actions which cause the public to believe perhaps that they act with the approval of those giving their best efforts to advancing the cause of freedom and independence for the people of Ireland makes necessary the statement . . . that these women act only as individuals and have no sanction whatever from any of the large bodies of American men and women of Irish blood who act by and through the direction of the Friends of Irish Freedom."[140] The day after this statement appeared in the *Citizen*, John Devoy attacked "Maloney's Pickets" in his newspaper. Although the group's leaders had severed their ties with Dr. Maloney, Devoy charged them with being under his pay and control. Devoy believed that Maloney, who had once served in the British military, was a spy. According to Devoy, Maloney attempted to "substitute for the skillful and intelligent work of capable Irish leaders methods which would bring the movement into contempt" and substitute "screams and hysteria for arguments." He called the women "a nest of wasps who revel in vile slander" and "misguided women" who carried out Maloney's plots without understanding the implications of his policies.[141] "Defense of the Pickets," which was signed by "Four of the Philadelphia Pickets," scolded Devoy for not distinguishing between the original Washington demonstrations and the ones led by Corless and the new group. The letter writers credited their own quiet protest by "patriotic and modest women" with getting the "desirable" publicity for Ireland that more sensational acts failed to achieve. Finally, the authors described the New York pickets as divided into "two factions, each clamoring for leadership." In publishing the defense, Devoy included an apology of sorts: "The *Gaelic American* did not attack the women Pickets individually or question their motives. It simply pointed out that the movement was started by an individual with sinister motives to serve [a] factious purpose." The newspaper's indictment of the pickets clearly indicated that Devoy saw the women's behavior as outlandish and improper, but he also implied that women did not comprehend the true complexity of the issues. The clever Dr. Maloney had presumably duped them.[142]

Although the LAAOH had no official connection with the picketing, Mary McWhorter came to the defense of the women. After a trip to Ireland, she wrote to the *Irish World*, "In speaking about the help the picketing in Washington was to the cause in Ireland, both Mrs. Gavan Duffy [Louise Gavan Duffy was one of the original members of the executive board of Cumann na mBan in Ireland] and Mrs. Sean T. O'Kelly waxed eloquent in their praise of the work of the dear ladies who were so brave. Both ladies expressed surprise that there should have been any criticism of these valiant women." No stranger to controversy as a woman nationalist, McWhorter sent her encouragement from Paris: "Dear ladies, keep on with your good work and don't mind the critics and fault-finders who mean well, no doubt, but who seem to think nothing is done right unless it is done as they advise or wish."[143] Echoing these sentiments, Kathleen O'Brennan, publicity agent for the Pickets, reported that Mrs. Laurence Ginnell had also praised the work of the Pickets, who "with their flashlight on the ugly sore of British Militarism had done much good in creating public opinion."[144] Both statements invoked the words of nationalist women in Ireland to support the actions of women in American.

The center of picket activity moved from Washington, DC, to New York when Gertrude Kelly, Margaret Warner, and Kathleen Sheehan, all members of the Pickets and the Irish Progressive League, participated in planning a rally at the docks as a farewell to Archbishop Mannix of Melbourne, Australia. The Irish-born archbishop had been critical of British rule in Ireland, leading two anticonscription campaigns in Australia during the war. Mannix intended to sail for

Ireland, although David Lloyd George publicly stated that the archbishop's entry into Ireland would be denied.[145] In what the *New York Times* called a departure marked by "disorders rarely if ever equaled at an American transatlantic passenger pier," Archbishop Mannix boarded his vessel, cheered by five thousand New Yorkers. Women pickets added dramatic flair to the event, dressed in white and wearing green caps. The women also distributed five thousand copies of a leaflet issued by the Women's Irish Education League entitled "Nine Things You Do When You Trade with England."[146]

The initial campaign of the Pickets in Washington, DC, with the support of William Maloney, had been carefully choreographed to make headlines and attract international attention. However, by the end of the summer, the Pickets began advocating a new strategy—the boycott, a strategy building on a boycott movement within organized labor. In the summer of 1920, the Labor Bureau, an auxiliary of the American Commission on Irish Independence, was created to harness the power of organized labor for the Irish nationalist movement and included among its goals enlisting labor's support for the recognition of the Irish Republic, publicizing the Irish cause, and campaigning for a boycott of British goods.[147] The Labor Bureau, under the leadership of John Fitzpatrick of the Chicago Federation of Labor, sought to secure the endorsement of the American Federation of Labor for the boycott at the AFL convention in June 1921. Although the plan failed, the Labor Bureau built a network of more than two hundred local organizations to advance the cause.[148] Among women's group, the Women's Irish Education League, the American Pickets, and the Irish Women's Purchasing League all supported boycott strategies even before the AFL's failure to endorse the resolution in the summer of 1921 demonstrated the need to bypass traditional labor channels and adopt a grassroots campaign.[149]

While elements within the labor movement sought to mobilize labor for the Irish cause, the conflict escalated in Ireland. British destroyers arrested Archbishop Mannix at sea. He was released but refused permission to land in Ireland. Then on August 12, Terence MacSwiney, lord mayor of Cork and a commandant in the Irish

Republican Army, went on a hunger strike after his arrest by British troops for allegedly possessing revolutionary documents. In reaction to the treatment of Mannix and MacSwiney, a few women, including Gertrude Kelly, Helen Golden (secretary of the IPL), and Eileen Curran (an actress with the Celtic Players), picketed the British Consulate in Manhattan.[150] Then on August 27, thirty women moved their protest back to the piers, encouraging longshoremen to boycott British shipping. This phase of the protest was led by Helen Golden of the IPL in an attempt to challenge the leadership of Gertrude Corless, who had made it clear that she wished to remain independent of other nationalist groups.[151] But Sidney Gifford Czira later recalled that the idea came from Carlo Tresca, an Italian American anarchist, who had faced deportation during the Red Scare for his work with the IWW.[152] If true, the pickets' radical connections were certainly kept quiet. The women moved from pier to pier, imploring workers to leave British ships and join them. The next day, the *Washington Post* reported that two thousand longshoremen walked off their jobs, although their union leaders declared the strike unauthorized.[153] The *New York Sun* called it "the first purely political strike of workingmen in the history of the United States."[154]

While women picketed in New York, Gertrude Corless was in Washington, DC, leading a delegation of women to see Secretary of State Bainbridge Colby. Corless did succeed in meeting with Secretary Colby the next day, and she sent a letter to John W. Davis, American ambassador to England, claiming to represent one million American women and vowing to spread the boycott of British ships to "every nook and cranny of the United States."[155] The combined efforts of Corless and the picketers demonstrates the influence of the boycott strategy, as nationalist women sought to use the economic power of the United States to cripple England's military might. While Corless lobbied in Washington, women picketing on the pier in New York appealed directly to working men, attempting to use the strength of labor to make an international statement. As Corless reportedly told Colby, "Americans who really believe in human freedom are never without weapons. They have shown that in the strike which ties up

British shipping in our ports; they will show it further in a nation-wide boycott of British products."[156]

The strike made front-page news in the *Washington Post* and *New York Times* but failed to significantly disrupt British shipping traffic. One ship left without six hundred trunks and baggage belonging to steerage passengers; another departed without its cargo; some lost crew members. The events of the first day culminated in a rally at which Frank Walsh and Eamon de Valera addressed the crowd.[157] The meeting celebrated the strike and extolled the power of labor. As one speaker, Tim Milligan of the Marine Firemen's Organization, recounted, the striking men "had a meeting and the opinion was freely expressed that sufficient resolutions have been passed on behalf of Ireland—resolutions have got to be backed up by some concrete power. . . . [T]he power of labor is the greatest power that exists in the world today."[158]

At another meeting, Leonora O'Reilly also celebrated the power of unity when she told striking longshoremen, "Brothers, if you remain on strike English ships will not be loaded. . . . Not only will Mannix land, but every English soldier will leave Ireland. They can no longer divide us on religious lines or on the lines of nationality. Labor is labor, the same the world over."[159] By early September, the picketing strategy had been extended to Brooklyn and Hoboken. In Boston Maura Quinn and four other women carried signs urging, "Labor Awake—Ireland Asks You for a Square Deal" and "Our Boys Died That Liberty Might Live—England Spits on Their Graves."[160]

The striking lasted over three weeks. In both Boston and New York, supporters established funds to aid the strikers. In New York, Leonora O'Reilly and Marguerite Moore promoted the boycott and raised funds for the striking longshoremen, and Gertrude Kelly acted as treasurer, administering the funds to the workers. In Boston the Minute Women were still trying to raise money for the strikers several months later. In January 1921, the Minute Women sought the help of Frank Walsh for a meeting "to secure aid for the men who joined the Boston longshoremen last fall in their protest against England's treatment of Lord Mayor MacSwiney." As a result of the protest, the men were out of work, and the women felt that "inasmuch as the Minute Women were to some extent instrumental in getting these men to stay out on protest . . . we should help them now if possible."[161]

Before the strike ended, the women Pickets received the thanks of Terence MacSwiney's wife, Muriel, who believed that the actions of the women, unlike the resolutions passed by many Irish organizations in England and America, were genuine efforts to save her husband's life. Terence MacSwiney died on October 25, 1920, on the seventy-fourth day of his hunger strike. At a massive memorial for MacSwiney in New York, the Pickets formed an honor guard. De Valera and New York governor Al Smith spoke to a crowd estimated at thirty-five thousand people.[162] Like the martyrs of 1916, MacSwiney became a symbol of commitment and sacrifice for the creation of an Irish Republic.

In this emotionally charged atmosphere, in between her work with the longshoremen's strike and a picketing campaign in Washington, DC, Leonora O'Reilly reported in her diary that she had started the "work of women as purchaser."[163] O'Reilly founded the Irish Women's Purchasing League, also referred to as the Irish Women's Co-operative League, in December 1920, as part of the campaign to boycott British goods and to tap the power of consumers, particularly women.[164] As O'Reilly wrote to the Women's Irish Educational League of San Francisco the same month, "We shall all do what we can to see that the blood of our martyrs shall not have been spent in vain. Isn't it glorious to know that from East to West from Atlantic to Pacific—at last our women are moving . . . realizing what power lies behind the pennies they spend." She also told Frank Walsh that she would "show Ireland what women are doing in America."[165]

O'Reilly appealed for the support of her friend Arthur Brisbane in promoting her new project. Brisbane, a journalist with William Randolph Hearst's newspaper empire, had his own column in Hearst's papers after 1917, syndicated in two hundred daily papers and many more weeklies.[166] She asked him to help "with your wisdom in the name of all that we hold dear to get something started," and she argued that "England has neither heart or soul but commerce. . . . England will listen when we show her we mean to have no commercial relations with her." O'Reilly called England the worst form of the disease—commercial empire—and sought to promote consumer and producer cooperatives through the promotion of local "home products."[167] By January 1921, O'Reilly reported to Frank Walsh, "We have a regular tea purchasing agency started—no English teas sold. . . . 50 women are working with me: not one of them getting a cent for the work they do 20% of all we earn is to go to Ireland to help the Irish rebuild their own industries in their own way."[168]

O'Reilly and the Irish Women's Purchasing League held a tea party in January, offering their own special blends. As she wrote to Frank Walsh, "England will get another Tea Party this time all the Gaels on earth will get a chance."[169] In February she reported selling six hundred pounds of tea and disclosed plans for another tea party to coincide with George Washington's birthday.[170] Her "1921 Tea Party" made the *New York Times*.[171]

The success and the fate of the Irish Women's Purchasing League are a bit unclear. In an unsympathetic portrayal of alternative nationalist efforts, historian Francis Carroll described such "independent projects by Irish-American groups" as "fiascos" that led to angry letters and the threat of lawsuits.[172] O'Reilly's organization sent seven thousand dollars to Ireland in its first year, but the movement failed after the J. B. Williams Company of Glastonbury, Connecticut, threatened legal action, demanding to be removed from the boycott list and claiming damages. The company denied any connections with British industry.[173] O'Reilly's correspondence with Frank Walsh indicates that neither actually knew the origin of the list of companies to boycott. O'Reilly maintained that she copied the list from "one Chicago got out," and Walsh replied that he had "not the least glimmer of an idea where the boycott list came from."[174]

By this time, the Pickets had also receded from view, and the Women's Irish Educational League ceased to make the boycott strategy a priority. In 1920 Charlotte Anita Whitney was put on trial for violating California's Criminal Syndicalist Act. According to Mary MacSwiney (the sister of Terence), there were two faces to the WIEL, "the nice mild Catholic group, and the Socialist group."[175] Under new leadership in 1921, the Women's Irish Education League sent a letter to members explaining that "owing to our increased activities the future policy of this organization will be devoted primarily to . . . educational and propaganda work." The League expressed its support of the boycott as "the greatest and most effective weapon against British cruelty and domination in Ireland" but no longer worked for it. Although the Women's Irish Education League moved away from the boycott strategy, another organization headed by Whitney, the American Irish Liberty League, continued to champion the boycott in the summer of 1922.[176]

The decline of these organizations, like their rise, reflected tensions within the American Irish nationalist movement as well as changes in the postwar political and social climate. The labor movement suffered serious setbacks in the postwar period. Between 1916 and 1922, American workers participated in strikes at levels far above any other previous period, and union membership nearly doubled. However, by the end of the depression of 1920–22, worker militancy rapidly declined. AFL membership fell by one-third, as workers faced a counteroffensive against their recent gains. In the words of historian David Montgomery, unions suffered "crushing defeats" between 1919 and 1922.[177]

Along with the rapid decline of the labor movement, the struggle between de Valera and the Cohalan-Devoy faction split the nationalist movement. Before returning to Ireland in late 1920, de Valera founded the American Association for the Recognition of the Irish Republic, splitting the Friends of Irish Freedom, as individual branches declared loyalty to one side or the other. The AARIR quickly eclipsed the FOIF, claiming seven hundred thousand members at its zenith.[178] However, when the Anglo-Irish Treaty created the Irish Free State in 1921, de Valera led republican forces in opposition to the treaty, and Ireland slid into civil war. As Irish men began killing other Irish men, the AARIR splintered and membership declined dramatically.[179] Yet a small group of republicans remained loyal to de Valera, including Gertrude Corless. After a period of inactivity, some of the Pickets returned to disrupt a meeting in support of the Irish Free State in 1923. That same year, Kelly and Corless signed a plea to President Harding to intervene on behalf of republican women political prisoners in the Irish Free State.[180]

Although women served the nationalist movement in a variety of ways, between 1916 and 1923 a small militant wing of the Irish nationalist movement in the United States sought to support James Connolly's vision of a worker republic in Ireland, while arguing for the international unity of the working class. As Gertrude Kelly told the *New York Times* in 1921, "The working class . . . has a greater question to solve than merely a political change. That class has to change the social system before a Republic could mean anything to it. That is the class that Connolly represented when he led the armies of the republic in 1916."[181]

Leonora O'Reilly, Gertrude Kelly, Marguerite Moore, and others represent the persistence of activism by the Irish American Left, which first embraced the Irish nationalist movement in the 1880s as part of a larger struggle for those Irish oppressed by capitalists, landlords, and imperialists. The radical faction of the nationalist movement receded during the heyday of the Home Rule movement, but Irish nationalists with connections to the labor movement became visible again in the World War I era, particularly after the fall of John Redmond and his parliamentary strategy. Although John Devoy and Judge Daniel Cohalan controlled the message of the FOIF, the voices of women and workers reemerged. Nationalists in the United States had always been a heterogeneous group. Dramatic developments in Ireland during World War I led to a shift in nationalist strategy, placing American policy at the center of a transnational struggle to win recognition of the Irish Republic. This meant that all women, not just the more militant faction, were encouraged to support political measures that would benefit Ireland. Meanwhile, more radical elements within the labor movement sought international worker solidarity, showing more interest in embracing political methods and using boycotts and general strikes to achieve their goals. By 1920 Irish American women had several reasons to embrace their new role as voters.

PART THREE

The Suffrage Movement

5

The Politics of Identity

Irish Americans and Woman Suffrage in the Nineteenth Century

In the mid-1890s, the *Catholic World* published two roundtable discussions, titled "The Woman Question." One of the contributors, a schoolteacher from New Hampshire named Mary A. Dowd, invoked the Irish struggle in her support of women's suffrage. Dowd maintained that "the best men" are not the ones who "urge that women cannot be trusted with more liberty for fear they will abuse it; and that they are so childish, weak-minded, and silly as to be incapable of using the ballot." She pointed out that Tories in England used the same arguments against Home Rule for Ireland. Dowd insisted she would abandon the movement if she believed it posed a threat to the home, arguing that since the church had not "set the seal of disapproval" on it, "we are free to advocate, as Catholics, what we believe to be one of the greatest reform movements of the age."[1] It may seem remarkable to find an author supporting suffrage and using a nationalist argument to do so. Admittedly, many of the other essays in the roundtable took a less favorable view of suffrage, but the existence of these roundtable discussions, and the support for suffrage that this writer conveyed, demonstrates that a shift in attention toward

This chapter is derived, in part, from an article published in *Women's History Review* 23 (Apr. 2014), http://www.tandfonline.com/doi/abs/10.1080/09612025.2013.849143.

women's rights issues went beyond the well-documented, and largely Protestant, suffrage movement.

Irish American women have their own suffrage history. Although Dowd's position may seem exceptional in the 1890s, a small group of Irish Americans (many of whom were Catholic) began supporting women's suffrage by the end of the nineteenth century. There are four main reasons Irish American women had increased contact with the suffrage issue in the late nineteenth century: in some cases the threat of nativism inspired Catholic women to vote for the first time, Irish nationalism in American established a place for women in politics and saw some early suffrage converts, Catholic women began to enter the temperance movement, and Irish American women's role as labor leaders led them to embrace the vote as a necessary strategy for helping working women (a trend that began in the nineteenth century but accelerated in the twentieth century as well). Although their numbers are small, Irish American suffragists were inspired by issues of identity and social class, embracing the movement out of their unique position in American society.

The Early History of the Movement

Our understanding of the suffrage movement is built largely on the histories of middle-class Protestant women who founded suffrage organizations and pursued political and educational tactics to win the vote. Without a significant presence of working-class women in the nineteenth-century movement, it is not surprising that historians don't find many Irish immigrant women involved. Their religion, ethnicity, and class status help explain their lack of interest or access to the movement. Yet it is exactly these identities that convinced some Irish American women to support suffrage. As chapter 2 demonstrates, Irish American women played a leading role in the labor movement, where their pioneering leadership brought them into the legislative arena and into alliances with middle-class Protestant reformers. Historically, a number of other factors also help explain the context in which Irish American women came to understand, discuss, and embrace the suffrage movement, including the development of suffrage organizations in Ireland and the United States, changes in gender roles within the American Catholic community, Irish nationalism, and anti-Irish and anti-Catholic movements in the United States.

Historians have written about the complicated relationship between suffrage and nationalism in Ireland. More than twenty years ago, Cliona Murphy's history of the Irish suffrage movement in the twentieth century filled a vacuum in women's and Irish history. Although British suffragists had received plenty of scholarly attention, the Irish movement had not. As Murphy explained, at that time most studies of Irish women focused on their role as auxiliaries to male nationalist organizations.[2] More recently, the edited volume *Irish Women and the Vote: Becoming Citizens* (2007) brings together the latest scholarship on suffrage activists and organizations in Irish history, placing women's political action at the heart of scholarly inquiry.[3]

Because the Act of Union (1801) dissolved the Irish Parliament and created one unified governing body for the United Kingdom, suffrage policies were debated at Westminster, but Irish politics also meant balancing the priorities of the Irish Parliamentary Party with the potential implications of women's suffrage. The first Irish suffrage organizations were founded in the 1870s, after the British Parliament rejected John Stuart Mill's proposed amendment to include women in the 1867 Representation of People Act. English women were granted the municipal vote in 1869. The early Irish movement was small and largely Protestant.[4] By the late nineteenth century, suffragists found themselves drawn into alliances with political parties over the Home Rule debates of the 1880s and 1890s, and many of Ireland's pioneer suffragists were Unionists.[5] Nationalist women also had a complicated view of suffrage, particularly when it was perceived as a distraction or threat to Irish liberty. The Irish Parliamentary Party viewed women voters with suspicion, fearing a potential obstacle to Home Rule. Their continued opposition angered both British and Irish suffragists, particularly during the twentieth century.[6]

In the United States, the topic of suffrage was first publicly discussed and endorsed in the women's rights movement of the 1840s and 1850s. The traditional narrative begins in the tiny town of Seneca

Falls, New York, where Elizabeth Cady Stanton, Lucretia Mott, and a small group of Quaker allies organized the first formal (but largely local) women's rights convention. By the 1850s, American supporters were holding annual national conventions. After the Civil War, conflict over the Fifteenth Amendment, which would enfranchise former slave men but not women, led to the creation of two suffrage organizations. Elizabeth Cady Stanton and Susan B. Anthony formed the National Woman Suffrage Association, while Lucy Stone led the American Woman Suffrage Association and began publishing the *Woman's Journal.* These two suffrage groups would unite in 1890 to form the National American Woman Suffrage Association (NAWSA). In the nineteenth century, most suffrage leaders were middle-class Protestants. One exception was Jane Campbell, born in Pennsylvania to Irish parents. Campbell, the daughter of a successful bookseller, was raised and educated in Philadelphia. She was active in Catholic charities, the American Catholic Historical Society, and the suffrage movement, serving as president of the Philadelphia County Woman Suffrage Society for twenty years and later founding the Catholic Woman's Suffrage League in 1915.[7] Although her Catholic faith distinguished her among nineteenth-century suffrage leaders, Campbell shared some similarities in terms of class and status; she was well educated and from a prosperous family.

Changes for American Catholics

Dowd's comments in the *Catholic World*, and the publication of the roundtable in general, reflect an important debate in Catholic America, one that did not go without notice in suffrage circles. Based on this roundtable, the *Woman's Journal* (a suffrage periodical published in Boston) pointed out that "some Catholic women are as good suffragists as could be desired."[8] In her study of Catholic lay reform, Deirdre Moloney identified the late nineteenth century as a period in which many Catholics saw the development of a significant Catholic urban middle class as "signal[ing] a shift away from traditional ethnic identities, a muting of the distinctiveness of Catholic traditions, and an embrace of modern values, particularly those related to gender roles." As Catholics sought social mobility, and struggled to maintain their ethnic and religious heritage, gender roles became one area of fierce debate.[9] While the "Woman Question" was gaining attention through Catholic publications, and a small group of liberal Catholic clergy promoted a public role for women, most clergy rejected suffrage and advocated a traditional view of womanhood. In 1900 the National American Woman Suffrage Association identified only six Catholic clergymen who supported suffrage.[10] Although the Catholic Church took no official position on the issue, Cardinal James Gibbons of Baltimore warned women to take care of their homes rather than carrying the "mud and dust" from the political arena.[11] The view of influential Catholic leaders gave the impression that the Catholic Church was opposed to woman suffrage.

The Irish American press was often critical. John Boyle O'Reilly, the influential editor of the *Boston Pilot*, who was also a hero in Irish nationalist circles for his Fenian activism in Ireland and escape to the United States, condemned women's rights as destructive and unnatural. He charged the movement with being an "unjust, unreasonable, unspiritual abnormality," with the potential to "reduce masculinity even by the obliteration of femininity."[12] The editorial staff of the *Pilot* from John Boyle O'Reilly to James Jeffrey Roche to Katherine Conway all opposed suffrage. Conway, an Irish American journalist and writer, began working for the *Pilot* under O'Reilly in 1883. She first published her opposition to suffrage in the 1890s, including participation in the roundtables published by the *Catholic World*.[13] Similar opposition found a home in New York's widely circulating Irish American press. Professor Robert Ellis Thompson, an Irish-born Presbyterian, wrote on the suffrage movement for the *Irish World*. In 1894, while New York State was debating the enfranchisement of women, he wrote, "Admission of women to the list of voters would intensify personal feelings in politics. Their natures are naturally more excitable than are men's. . . . Now we have quite enough of intense feeling on social questions in the present order of things. Let us do nothing to increase it."[14] Vocal opposition to suffrage among the clergy and in the press certainly circulated widely in the Irish

American community, but anti-Irish sentiment also contributed to arguments again it.

Anti-Irish Rhetoric and the Suffrage Issue

Although Irish American men were generally not supportive of, and could be outright hostile to, woman suffrage, the Irish American penchant for politics and the ascendancy of Irish American–controlled political machines such as Tammany Hall added to concerns over the impact that women voters might have. Popular prejudices against the Irish in America appeared frequently in popular culture, which included the resentment and anger over Irish political power. In the late nineteenth century, as we have seen, Irish men generally appeared in American cartoons as inferior, animalistic, lazy, violent, and inebriated.[15] While Irish men were depicted as dangerous and dim-witted, Irish American women appeared most often as domestic servants and shantytown wives. While the young, fresh-faced recent immigrant generally appeared absentminded and irresponsible, a more sinister stereotype predominated. In illustrations Irish women shared the ape-like features of their male counterparts, while stereotyped as bossy, uncouth, and untrustworthy maids who stole from their employers and threatened physical violence toward the middle-class housewives who depended on hired help. In her study of these stereotypical "Bridgets" and "Biddys," Maureen Murphy found more than one hundred such cartoons appearing in the 1880s alone.[16]

The Irish domination of urban politics, which provoked opposition in the late nineteenth century, also made Irish American women appear to be a looming threat. In particular, the issue of woman suffrage lent itself to a discussion of Irish political power and the potential influence of new women voters. Antisuffragists raised the specter of Irish American political domination, suggesting that "Patrick" had already taken over the machinery of urban governments, so why add "Bridget's" votes to the problem? As one antisuffragist explained, "We have suffered a good deal at the hands of Patrick and now the woman suffragists would add Bridget."[17] Suffrage activist and future president of NAWSA Carrie Chapman Catt also perpetuated anti-Irish sentiments when she reportedly dismissed Populist organizer Mary Elizabeth Lease as "having a reputation for being more important than she is." The *New York Times* quoted Catt as saying that Lease was "an Irishwoman, and to my mind she is an exact counterpart of the typical Irishman politician," certainly not a compliment in the 1890s. Catt further explained that she meant Lease's enthusiasm might carry her to the extreme, a statement that also suggested an acceptance of the Irish reputation for being fiery and hard to control.[18]

Fictional accounts of the suffrage movement also appeared in the press, revealing a fear of collective Irish political power. One such story warning of Irish American women's entry into politics received favorable reviews during a crusade against political corruption in New York. In 1894, the same year that anti-Tammany reformers in the city of New York combined to defeat Tammany Hall in the fall election, the New York State Constitutional Convention weighed a petition for woman suffrage.[19] In this political climate, an anonymous author (writer and journalist Thomas Janvier) published a short fictional work, outlining his vision of a future where women voted. "Women's Conquest of New York" detailed his vision of women's political tyranny, beginning with the founding of a league largely composed of "female domestics" (an occupation dominated by Irish women) and ending with the election of a female mayor named Bridget O'Dowd (with the help of Tammany Hall, of course).[20] A similar piece, appearing in *Ladies' Home Journal* the same year, described a married man's dream of universal suffrage. While the dreamer conceded that women voted intelligently, and initially "everybody was happy," a bombshell soon disrupted their tranquil home. His wife found herself summoned to jury duty, serving with her former domestic servant Bridget McNulty, who had recently been fired because "her civility was not so good a quality as her cooking." In the story, the jury was described as a virtual "Congress of Nations," which had been made possible by universal suffrage. The man in the story then vowed to oppose women's suffrage to spare his wife the ordeal.[21] Clearly, the author believed that women weren't ready to mix with different classes and races in the civic realm. In states with large Irish American populations, such as New York and Massachusetts, the question of women's suffrage was complicated by tensions between Catholics and Protestants, particularly in areas where Irish American men dominated political machines.

School Suffrage Controversies

By the time the Nineteenth Amendment was ratified in 1920, enfranchising women nationwide, more than half the states already had some form of suffrage for women in state elections. Many more had also granted limited suffrage for women, including school suffrage—the right to vote for members of the school board.[22] Massachusetts passed a law granting women the right to serve on school boards and vote in school matters in 1879, one of thirteen states (and three territories) to do so by 1880.[23] Decisions about women's political rights, then, were often made at the local and state levels and therefore were subject to local variables.[24] Thus, tensions between Protestants and Catholics had important implications for the suffrage movement.

At the height of the American Protective Association, more than one hundred nativist publications circulated anti-immigrant ideology during the 1890s, accusing them of threatening the American way of life. Often Irish immigrants appeared particularly ominous owing to their reported affinity for alcohol and political corruption, devotion to the Catholic Church, and a perceived propensity for violence.[25] As a result, Catholic women found themselves caught up in political battles, particularly over the question of who controlled the public schools.[26] In *Servants of the Poor: Teachers and Mobility in Ireland and America* (2004), Janet Nolan argued that Irish American women led their communities' advance toward "respectability and prosperity" with a mass movement into public school teaching at the turn of the twentieth century. Although their salaries were low, teachers held "significant social and economic importance within families as well as in their home communities."[27]

In areas where Catholics and Protestant competed over control of the public schools, local elections could get quite heated. Furthermore, the composition of the teaching force was changing, leading to even more anxiety. By the late nineteenth century, many of the teachers in public schools came from working-class immigrant backgrounds. For example, studies show that in Chicago and Pittsburgh, 50 to 60 percent of teachers came from working-class backgrounds. In cities with large Irish populations, Irish American women were the largest ethnic group by 1910. As Janet Nolan has demonstrated, teaching was an important source of social mobility for Irish American women, who made up a large percentage of the workforce in some urban school systems. The push for school reform, professionalization, and the control of experts led to conflict between Catholics and Protestants in urban school systems over who controlled the schools.[28] For example, in St. Louis school administrators and Irish American school board members clashed as early as the 1870s over the issue of hiring kindergarten teachers. In 1877 a formal system of certification was introduced for kindergarten teachers and assistants, allowing superintendent William Torrey Harris and kindergarten director Susan Blow to control the selection process and restrict hiring to "morally fit" women. John O'Connell, an Irish American sign painter who represented a heavily Irish district, led the fight against the plan, but he lost. O'Connell argued that school administrators discriminated against women from poor families; young women were being denied diplomas "because they were poor men's daughters and for nothing else."[29] Likewise, the Chicago School Board attempted to stem the tide of Catholic schoolteachers in 1903 by requiring that teachers be graduates of city-run normal schools or come to the city with two to four years of teaching experience. Although the school board reversed its decision a year later, attempts to limit the employment of Catholics in Chicago's schools continued, with entrance exams for Catholic school graduates and quotas for normal school graduates.[30]

In addition to the economic and professional interests of Irish American teachers, these controversies sometimes involved women as voters, when Catholics and Protestants clashed over school board elections. In these sporadic cases, while tensions flared, Catholic women were recruited to vote, but it did not lead to a long-term trend toward more Catholic women voting. The most significant showdowns occurred in Boston, where controversy erupted when the Massachusetts School Suffrage Association mobilized against one Catholic school board member, after the board voted to close a school that was too close to several liquor establishments. The Massachusetts School Suffrage Association alleged that liquor interests had swayed the decision, but targeting a Catholic school board member also inflamed Boston Catholics, so Democratic leaders sought to mobilize Catholic women for the election.[31] Echoing the reluctance of the archbishop to become engulfed in politics, the *Boston Pilot* reported, "If Democratic or Catholic women of Boston enter politics, their leaders will not be priests, but layman who perceive the danger that threatens their secular rights and see no other way to prevent it."[32] Fear of Catholic influence on the school board led to a second controversy after accusations of bias were directed toward a Protestant history teacher and the text he used. After an investigation, the text was replaced and the teacher reassigned, but not without mounting opposition to Catholic influence on school matters. In response, the Republican Party ran an all-Protestant ticket in 1888. Although the *Pilot* continued to oppose women's suffrage, another Irish periodical, *Donahoe's Magazine*, endorsed the Catholic women's vote, since "necessity demands it." The votes of Catholic women were seen as necessary to offset the votes of Protestant women, who, it was assumed, would vote on denominational lines. According to the writer, their votes were needed to "off-set the votes of these rabid women who hate the Catholics as the 'Devil does Holy Water.'" Voter registration drives on both sides of this controversy resulted in a tenfold increase in women's registration in Massachusetts, but more Protestant women went to the polls, resulting in a loss for Catholic interests on the school board.[33]

Similar controversies also occurred in the 1890s. In Worcester, Massachusetts, a superintendent was accused of favoring Catholics in hiring. He and his supporters were ousted with the aid of Protestant women voters.[34] In 1894 the *New York Sun* declared that the "first bitter fruit" of the Connecticut law allowing women to vote in school elections was growing, as "religious bigotry and intolerance" entered a number of local elections.[35] The following year, the *Irish World* boasted that "efforts of the APA to drive Catholic members from the Board of Education in Bridgeport, CT aroused the Catholic women of the city, and they made a noble use of the ballot in downing the bigots." In a retraction the following week, the paper declared that the APA men got in because Catholic women did not vote as instructed by Democratic Party leaders and Catholic clergy (vote for the independent candidates), highlighting the need for "political drilling in the warfare which must be waged against the A.P.A."[36] As the commentary in the *Irish World* implied, suffrage became a weapon in the war against nativism, if only temporarily. It also became an issue for some Irish nationalists.

The Political Nature of the Land League

As the previous section demonstrates, Irish American women first entered a mass political movement with the short-lived but widespread movement for land reform in Ireland. Through the Ladies' Land League, Irish American women gained their first experiences with public speaking, organizing, debating, and influencing public opinion. While these lessons did not translate into a large shift toward the suffrage camp, that period did lead to important contacts between the suffragists and nationalists. In addition to influential nationalist converts to suffrage (even in the nineteenth century), the role of women in the Irish nationalist cause did not go unnoticed by American suffragists, who reached out to Irish Americans in the nineteenth century through sympathy with the Home Rule movement.

Scholarship on Irish American women rarely discusses their explicitly political contributions, particularly to the suffrage movement, and with good reason: these women are hard to find. Yet the political nature of women's contributions to the nationalist movement beginning in the late nineteenth century also brought a small group of nationalists and suffragists together, as Home Rulers and suffragists sought alliances and converts in a uniquely American environment where Irish American men wielded political power and Irish American women continued to be active in the nationalist movement beyond the pinnacle years of the Ladies' Land League in the early 1880s.

Nationalism presented unique opportunities for women to become involved in political agitation on both sides of the Atlantic. In Ireland Michael Davitt urged the male leadership of the Land League to endorse the creation of a Ladies' Land League under the leadership of Anna Parnell. Anticipating a government crackdown on the men, Irish women fulfilled a very different function than the women of America, risking imprisonment for taking over the movement once the men were arrested.[37] Anna Parnell criticized women's lack of access to political power in 1880, and she also recognized the political nature of Ladies' Land League work. As Irish historian Margaret Ward has argued, there was feminist potential in the Irish organization, particularly in terms of women's determination to defend their role in the nationalist movement, but Land League women did not generally take a stand for suffrage.[38] However, controversy surrounding the activities of the Ladies' Land League in Ireland soon led to Irish women's exclusion from political nationalism.[39]

American Suffragists Reach Out to Irish Americans

While there are significant differences between the activities of the Ladies' Land League in Ireland and those in the United States, American women also engaged in political discussions and organizing. The Ladies' Land League was first organized in the United States, and Irish American women had a different role in the nationalist movement. When the Irish National Land League of America officially disbanded in 1883, the newly established Irish National League of America did not bar women. The INLA allowed many Irish societies (literary, fraternal, and charitable) to affiliate with the national organization, but since its goal of Home Rule gave it a definitively political mission, suffragists began to take notice. In an article entitled "Woman Suffrage to Help Ireland," the *Woman's Journal* applauded the North End Branch of the Irish National League for electing five women to the executive committee, describing it as "exceptional liberality of enlisting women in politics."[40]

Although the INLA was a much smaller organization than the Land League, forty women delegates attended the organizational meeting of the Irish National League of America, and Delia Parnell took a leading role in organizing women's branches. An active New York suffragist wrote to the *Woman's Journal* that "the writer was greatly pleased to make the acquaintance of Mrs. Parnell (in 1884)," and "She is truly a noble-minded woman; and meeting her has inspired us afresh to work for freedom."[41] As this comment suggests, suffragists saw the connections between their own political struggles and the subjugation of Ireland, but they also appreciated the political nature of Irish women's contributions to the nationalist movement. A week later, the *Woman's Journal* published a column entitled "Mrs. Parnell for Woman Suffrage," reporting on a meeting at which Delia Parnell demanded "the ballot for women in the strongest terms," much to the "surprise" of many in the audience.[42] The American-born mother of Charles Parnell held a special place in the hearts of many Irish Americans, and her conversion to suffrage is a significant development in the 1880s.

To convey their support for Ireland, American suffragists invoked the names of men and women who had made important contribution to the nationalist struggle in their rhetoric, thereby supporting suffrage for women at home and abroad. At one INLA meeting, New York reformer Hamilton Willcox (a lawyer, former abolitionist, and longtime suffragist) pledged suffragists' support for "Irish and other laboring women in America." Referring to the Ladies' Land League, Willcox called on Irish men to "remember the labors of Delia Stewart Parnell, Fanny Parnell, Anna Parnell, and other noble women; and not allow these and their sister to be disfranchised" in a free Ireland. At the same meeting, Miss Jeanie Macadam—identified as the granddaughter of a United Irishman, Samuel Neilson, who was also the treasurer of the New York Woman Suffrage Society—read a letter from O'Connell to suffragists Lucretia Mott and Elizabeth Cady Stanton and urged listeners to follow the example of Daniel O'Connell and stand up for women's equal political rights.[43] Descended from one Irish nationalist, she used the name of another beloved leader to compare the struggle of women in American to Ireland's movement for Catholic rights.

Therefore, despite popular prejudices against Irish American voters, supporters of woman suffrage did reach out to Irish Americans, at meetings and also in the press. Debates over Home Rule gave American suffragists an opportunity to build a connection with the Irish American community. In the pages of the *Woman's Journal*, suffragists expressed support for Home Rule for Ireland and compared the position of disenfranchised American women to the subjugation of Ireland.[44] As one letter to the editor urged, "We hope suffragists everywhere will show sympathy with the movement by peaceful and legal means for Irish liberty." The writer challenged Americans' lack of sympathy for recent Irish immigrants, indicting British misrule as the cause of their degradation, and insisted, "Woman suffrage and Home Rule are divisions of the grand army of Freedom, and should work together." Finally, the New York author praised Irish members of the New York Legislature and the leaders of the "Irish movement in America" for recognizing this relationship and continuing the legacy of Daniel O'Connell, the great Irish statesman who also "took on the woman question."[45]

Through the pages of the *Woman's Journal*, suffragists also praised events in Ireland and expressed support for the Irish Parliamentary Party in the 1880s. In 1884 Dr. Clemence Lozier, chair of the executive committee of the Woman Suffrage Party of New York, and her colleague Hamilton Willcox met with two Irish members of Parliament who were visiting New York. Willcox reportedly told them: "Last night I was on your platform as a guest and friend. . . . We come to ask you to convey to your comrades in the House of Commons the warmest thanks of the woman suffragists in America for their manly and generous support of woman's enfranchisement, and to express the hope that this noble example will be followed by every Irishman throughout the world." In return, Willcox expressed the warm support of suffragists for the Irish cause of self-government. Dr. Lozier agreed, saying, "We . . . are heartily friendly to freedom and equality for the whole human family."[46] An 1886 article titled "Women's Work for Ireland" repeated praise for women's fund-raising efforts for the Parnell Parliamentary Fund. President John Gleason reportedly said he was glad to see women "come to our aid. . . . [W]e will make them members as well as the men." When asked if they had the right to vote, he replied: "Most certainly . . . as they will also, I hope, when an Irish Parliament is in Dublin."[47]

In 1886 a suffrage speaker assured the Fifth Ward (New York) Branch of the INLA that woman suffragists "generally were friends of Irish liberty, and were seeking to secure fair play for Irish and other laboring women in America."[48] Such expressions of international sympathy and cooperation also suggest more immediate political priorities at home. Lucy Stone, the founder of the American Woman Suffrage Association and editor of the *Woman's Journal*, used the debate over Home Rule to call for rights for American women. While she insisted that men in Ireland deserve justice, she explained. "I hope that newspapers which urge the plea for Ireland may be moved to second the plea of women." These papers could "render essential service for the relief of women in the United States if they will . . . urge legislators to secure such measure of political rights as is within their power."[49] A few months later, Stone wrote angrily of Irish American opposition to women's suffrage, pointing out that supporters of Home Rule continued to vote against rights for women, and she demanded "fair play."[50]

While American suffragists appealed for political rights through the suffrage press at home, they also appeared in discussions of Home Rule in the British press. When the question of Home Rule occupied the attention of the Liberal Party in the 1890s, British suffragists disagreed on how to prioritize their demands. Many articles appeared in the press, debating the appropriateness of placing Home Rule before women's suffrage on the Liberal Party's agenda. For example, the *Woman's Herald* of London reported in 1892, "We say, without fear of contradiction, that the three reforms on which Liberal women have set their hearts are Home Rule, Temperance, and Women's Suffrage. It speaks volumes of their devotion to the first that they have subordinated the others to it." Women's Liberal Associations also banded together to petition Parliament in 1892 for a franchise bill, stating, "We cannot believe, when the Liberal and Irish Nationalist parties have urged women to enter political life, and to help in winning the battle of Home Rule for Ireland, that they will now discourage their efforts by refusing to admit that duly qualified women are entitled to the parliamentary franchise."[51]

Some prominent American reformers also weighed in on the issue, expressing sympathy for Ireland while insisting on the importance of the suffrage issue. An article on Frances Willard, president of the Women's Christian Temperance Union, appeared in the *Woman's Herald* in 1891. The author endorsed Willard's suffrage stance thus: "On the question of Home Rule and Federation she is sound. Surely she is right when she advises women who want their enfranchisement to work it out . . . by silence over any disputes and differences, and by constant cooperation one with the other."[52] While Willard seems to have minimized the dispute on her trip to England, Elizabeth Cady Stanton published a letter in the British press expressing support for Home Rule but urging women not to work for it ahead of suffrage. In March 1891, she wrote, "We do not place the Women's Suffrage question first because we think Home Rule of small moment, but because it is the larger question. . . . [I]f English and American women were enfranchised it would affect the status of women in every civilized nation."[53]

Stanton's autobiography, also published in the 1890s, expressed her admiration for Daniel O'Connell and her optimism for Irish self-governance. She recalled meeting O'Connell on her trip to London for the World Anti-Slavery Convention in 1840. At this convention, female delegates were barred from speaking, but O'Connell expressed his support for the women privately and publicly. He wrote to American abolitionist Lucretia Mott, "My mature consideration of the entire subject convinces me of the right of female delegates to take their seats in the Convention, and the injustice of excluding them."[54] Stanton observed that fifty years later, the people (of England) "are awakening at last to their duty, and, for the first time, organizing English public sentiment in favor of 'Home Rule.'" She concluded, "I trust that the day is not far off when the beautiful Emerald Isle will unfurl her banner before the nations of the earth."[55] By the end of the nineteenth century, American reformers and suffragists cultivated alliances with reformers abroad. In the case of Home Rule, the issue was complex. In the United States, suffragists expressed support for Home Rule and also appealed to Irish American audiences by invoking the names of important nationalist leaders. However, suffragists were also aware that the issue of women's suffrage had its own complicated context in Britain.

Irish American Nationalists Embrace Suffrage

While American suffragists expressed support for Irish Home Rule, some interesting alliances also formed between suffragists and nationalists, as the first generation of nationalists-suffragists emerged in the United States. In the state of New York, the weight of Irish Americans in politics may have influenced the cooperation of three seemingly unlikely allies: Marguerite Moore, Irish-born Catholic nationalist and suffragist; Lillie Devereux Blake, an American literary figure, Protestant, and leading New York suffragist; and Delia Parnell, Protestant mother of Charles Stewart Parnell and the daughter of American naval hero Charles Stewart. The presence of these three women together at Home Rule meetings and suffrage rallies presents a fascinating and virtually unknown chapter in the history of suffrage in the state of New York.

Of these three women, historians know the least about Marguerite Moore. With few published or private sources, her life story is difficult to piece together. However, Moore made significant contributions to the nationalist movement in Ireland before moving to the United States and quickly becoming immersed in nationalist and suffrage work in New York. As previously discussed, Moore began her political career in Ireland, where she distinguished herself as an organizer for the Ladies' Land League. She served six months in prison for her role in the Ladies' Land League and left Ireland a few years after its dissolution. In the United States, she remained committed to Irish nationalism, supporting Home Rule through the Parnell Branch of the INLA and continuing to champion the cause through the struggles of the World War I era.[56]

Once she settled in the United States, she quickly became active in politics and gained a reputation as a powerful speaker. Citing her own political experience during Henry George's 1880s mayoral campaign in New York City, Moore told readers of the *Woman's Journal*, "I have fought side by side with the men of the party to which I belong [the United Labor Party]. . . . In short, I have done all that a man could do in an election campaign, with the exception of smoking cigars and casting the ballot."[57] Moore also used her Ladies' Land League experience to open some doors in New York City politics. Appearing in 1894 at the Iroquois Club (a branch of Tammany Hall, the Irish American–controlled political machine that dominated New York politics), Moore left her suffrage petition book for signatures following a well-attended speech.[58] Later, Moore also took her powerful rhetorical ability to the campaign of William Jennings Bryan and the Democratic Party. In 1900 an article in the *Baltimore Sun* appeared, "She'll Speak for Bryan," explaining that Moore's Land League activities had led her to Henry George's land theories and ultimately into American politics.[59]

A committed suffragist, Moore carried her message to reform organizations, trade unions, and working women's societies.[60] Appealing for women's rights on behalf of working women, Moore told one audience, "It is not for ourselves we plead. Most of us have brains enough to take what we want. It is for those who are helpless, poor, and oppressed. We are not asking for woman's rights, but equal rights—equal pay for the men and women."[61] In 1886 Moore addressed the annual convention of the New York State Woman Suffrage Association. According to the *Woman's Journal*, she told her audience that she expected to find freedom for women when she reached American shores, but they did not even have the right of municipal suffrage, already enjoyed in England. She had hoped that her sons would become American citizens but did not want them to support a nation that rejected their mother.[62]

She also defended the rights of Catholic women to vote, arguing against fears that Catholic loyalties were dictated by Rome. In the 1894 New York suffrage campaign, some supporters expressed the belief that voters opposed women's suffrage for fear of the pope's influence in politics. Moore insisted that "Irish Catholic women ought to be proud that they can create such a disturbance." She reassured her audience that in Ireland, Protestants were regularly elected to office and reminded them that Charles Stewart Parnell was a Protestant.[63] Marguerite Moore and Delia Parnell were certainly associated in nationalist work, but Moore also worked closely with suffragist Lillie Devereux Blake.

Lillie Devereux Blake is primarily remembered today for her fiction, publishing a number of novels in book or serial form as well as a collection of short stories. She supported her two children with her writing after the death of her first husband. By the 1870s, Blake began lecturing for the suffrage movement and later wrote a regular column in the *Woman's Journal*.[64] Blake served as president of the New York State Woman Suffrage Association from 1879 to 1890 and the New York City Woman Suffrage League from 1886 to 1897. At a time when the suffrage movement emphasized petitions and nonpartisanship, Blake embraced political strategies in her suffrage work, including targeting a New York governor who failed to support a bill enfranchising women in school board elections and speaking for the Democratic Party. At the 1880 National Woman Suffrage Association Convention, Blake supported organizing women to campaign in the upcoming presidential election.[65] Although her suffrage strategies put her at odds with the nonpartisan emphasis of the movement, in 1880 Blake confided, "My great wish has been for a year past to gain political influence."[66]

In the state of New York, this strategy certainly meant fostering a good relationship with Irish American voters. To further illustrate these budding connections between Irish nationalists and suffragists, Lillie Devereux Blake appeared alongside nationalists such as Delia Parnell, Ellen Ford, and Marguerite Moore at Home Rule and labor rallies. Blake's paternal grandfather was from Ireland, but she lost her father at a young age and was raised by her mother. According to Blake's diary, she consciously used ethnic appeals to sway audiences. For example, in 1882 Blake reported that on a western campaign stop, she "spoke at what they call the 'Hall,' a disused saloon. . . . About a hundred men, twenty women . . . assembled, nearly all Irish. . . .

Told them I was a Devereux of County Wexford, and spoke of Fanny Parnell." Fanny Parnell's poetry, her role in the Land League, and her premature death in 1882 made her a heroic figure to many Irish Americans. Blake reported calling on every Irish man in Nebraska to support women's suffrage and claimed great results in converting her audience.[67]

Blake and Moore worked closely together in the suffrage movement, and Blake reported regularly on their activities through the pages of the *Woman's Journal.* Both also spoke in 1886 at a Fourth of July celebration in sympathy for Ireland. Thousands of union members (reportedly twenty thousand) gathered to urge support for Home Rule. Blake was in charge of a separate speaker's platform for women. During her speech, Blake declared the sympathy of American women with the women of Ireland, insisting that women in the United States longed to see Ireland free. The next speaker was Delia Parnell.[68]

Delia Parnell was born in Bordentown, New Jersey. She married an Irish man named John Parnell in 1835.[69] John Parnell died in 1858, leaving Delia to struggle financially while raising her children. She later returned to the United States, where she remained until her death in the 1890s. Parnell appears to have made several appearances for the suffrage movement in the 1880s. She was advertised as a speaker for the Woman Suffrage Party State Convention in 1884 in Buffalo, and she appeared the following year with Hamilton Willcox and Dr. Lozier in Albany, New York.[70] In her diary, Blake also mentioned two speaking engagements with Parnell. At one she reported introducing the women speakers with cabinet titles, including "Secretary of State Stanton . . . [and] Navy, Parnell."[71] Although it is difficult to know the extent of the women's relationship, when Delia Parnell died in 1898 Blake and Moore both spoke at the memorial service. According to one obituary, among the women invited to the service were those women who served in the Ladies' Land League and members of the Woman's Franchise Association.[72] This connection suggests that in addition to the cause of Irish nationalism for which her family is most known, Delia Parnell remained a committed suffragist until her death as well.

Delia Parnell, a Protestant, and Marguerite Moore, a Catholic, were both influential women in Irish nationalist circles, and both spoke publicly for suffrage. Another prominent woman nationalist, Mary J. O'Donovan Rossa, embraced suffrage as well. The wife of Jeremiah O'Donovan Rossa, a former Fenian who settled in the United States, Mary J. O'Donovan Rossa had close ties to physical-force nationalists in the United States. She was also a close friend of Marguerite Moore. Rossa became a suffrage convert in the 1890s and canvassed her neighborhood for the Brooklyn Suffrage League.[73] Although she maintained that women nationalists ought to work in an auxiliary capacity with the men, Rossa wrote to John Devoy in 1915, "I believe in votes for women, of course. Every women does these days, and I have always done so for every individual woman, no matter how silly or perverse, can think to the point where her affections or interests are concerned."[74]

Although including a few suffrage converts, even among the most influential women nationalists, does not suggest a significant shift in Irish American sentiment on the woman question, it does demonstrate a key point: Irish nationalism created a role for women in politics, and women's nationalist activities also exposed them to larger debates about women's rights. These issues certainly had significance beyond the Irish American community and did not go unnoticed by those individuals in the suffrage movement who sought to make alliances (and occasionally expressed frustration as well) with Irish American politicians and voters, particularly in states like Massachusetts and New York, where Irish American demographics and political influence made such potential allies very important. These connections emerged in the nineteenth century, particularly as Home Rule debates brought questions on the role of women to the fore, and they would resurface in the twentieth century as well.

Temperance, Labor, and Suffrage in the Nineteenth Century

While Irish nationalism inspired a significant political movement in the late nineteenth century, two other factors help explain the emergence of Irish American suffragists: the influence of temperance organizations and the growth of the labor movement. In both cases, these organizations developed in a context where American women as a whole were moving into reform work, but for Irish American women the influence of class and labor issues, as well as changes in the American Catholic community, also shaped these experiences. In the late nineteenth century, few male Catholic charities admitted women, and the ones that did organized separate women's auxiliaries. The leading Catholic philanthropic organization, the all-male St. Vincent de Paul Society, did not begin allowing women as auxiliary members until 1902. Some laywomen also saw the contributions of Protestant settlement-house workers as examples of the potential for female leadership in the realm of benevolence.[75] After 1880, as parishes began expanding to incorporate social, recreational, charitable, and educational goals, women also seized the initiative in creating benevolent and fraternal organizations. As Leslie Woodcock Tentler found in her study of Detroit, two trends in the 1890s demonstrate that "an important minority" among Catholic women had begun to see their roles in more expansive ways—large numbers of women joined benefit societies, and laywomen organized various groups dedicated to adult education.[76] In addition, more Catholic activists were embracing the view that philanthropy must include social reform—that relief was not enough to tackle modern social concerns.[77] As Deirdre Moloney suggested in her study of lay Catholic reform, middle-class activists, though of "relatively modest socioeconomic status" compared to their Protestant counterparts, sought respectability by tackling social problems. They believed that poverty and other social problems among Catholics reflected badly on their faith; however, they also feared the effects of Protestant reform programs on the Catholic poor.[78]

This trend presented opportunities for laywomen. An 1898 *Catholic World* article noted the existence of "fields for cultivation by the laity awaiting the united efforts of the Catholic women," fields where women could apply "spiritual and corporal works of mercy . . . uplifting thousands of the unfortunate."[79] In the first attempt to organize a national coalition of Catholic women, representatives of women's organizations met in Chicago, at the World's Columbian

Exposition in 1893, to form the Catholic Woman's National League. The *Irish World* reported that Eliza Allen Starr (a Catholic convert from a prominent Boston family) spoke in favor of the organization of a national society of Catholic women. Drawing comparisons and concerns over the influence of Protestant women, the writer of the article, Alice Timmons Toomy, argued that Catholic women were beginning to realize their duty to help the needy and join "the W.C.T.U. and other non-Catholic philanthropies because they find no organization in their own church."[80] As noted in chapter 1, Toomy supported the efforts of Catholic women in social reform, pointing out the needs for more organizations for Catholic women.

Temperance is an important example of a field where Protestant women had made great strides, but Catholic women had been discouraged from participating. The Catholic temperance movement in the United States first gained widespread appeal during the 1870s but as a largely male movement. American Catholics built on the work of Father Theobold Matthews, who began a temperance crusade in Ireland in the 1830s and toured the United States beginning in 1849. However, the American movement did not really develop until the 1870s. Catholic temperance advocates differed from their Protestant counterparts, particularly in favoring moral suasion and individual commitment over legislation. The Catholic Total Abstinence Union of America, founded in 1872, had ninety thousand members by the early twentieth century, but women did not join in large numbers, nor did they emerge as leaders until the 1890s. The leading woman in the Catholic temperance movement was Leonora Barry, the former Knight who retreated from the labor movement after marrying Obediah Lake in 1890. Catholic total abstainers emphasized manliness and masculine sociability, so women's role was often seen as influencing male family members. Yet Moloney found that women also added new activities that had not been part of Catholic temperance work before, including fund-raising for poor families, visiting sick or "fallen" women, and creating libraries.[81]

Although the Catholic movement had significant differences from its Protestant counterpart, the issue of suffrage does offer some parallels. The Woman's Christian Temperance Union (a Protestant organization) embraced suffrage as a tool in its fight for "home protection" under the leadership of Frances Willard in 1883. As the Catholic temperance movement gained in strength and women became more active, the issue of suffrage came up as well. In 1895 Father Thomas Scully, the director of the Catholic Total Abstinence Union of Boston, became the first Massachusetts priest to publicly support enfranchising women. When the Massachusetts Woman Suffrage Association (MWSA) wanted help in organizing Catholics, it asked Father Scully to suggest someone to lead the effort. Annie Murray, a Catholic journalist and friend of Alice Stone Blackwell, got the appointment and reported that she believed Catholic women were "generally not opposed." Scully spoke publicly for the suffrage movement and told a committee of the legislature that he believed "educated men and women of the Catholic laity" were "favorably disposed" to women's suffrage.[82] Catholic temperance women in Pennsylvania also investigated the suffrage issue. The Veronica League—a Catholic total-abstinence society—hosted Mrs. Lucretia Blankenburg, president of the Pennsylvania Woman Suffrage Society, in 1898 to speak on current issues.[83]

By the late nineteenth century, Protestant women made significant contributions to the temperance movement, and the WCTU's conversion to suffrage was an important part of their strategy to protect the home and family from alcohol abuse. As Toomy's remarks suggest, some Irish American women did have a history with the WCTU. For example, Mary Elizabeth Lease, who became a leading figure in the Populist movement, joined the WCTU in the 1880s. Like many activists who supported an expanded social influence for women, Lease argued that women's natural role as nurturers also made them particularly well suited for social reform: women could end political corruption, combat the liquor demon, and uplift humanity.[84]

Leonora Barry also began cooperating with the WCTU while working with the Knights of Labor, which had a strict temperance pledge and barred saloon keepers from membership. She even encouraged the Catholic Total Abstinence Union to work with the WCTU. In 1891 Frances Willard addressed the CTAU and invited a delegation to attend the WCTU convention as well. Despite these efforts at cooperation, the two women leaders were not able to overcome doubts about cooperation between the two organizations.[85] However, their efforts do suggest that Barry envisioned a widespread and unified movement, one that brought her beyond the labor movement and also beyond Catholic reform circles.

As we have seen, Leonora Barry played a pioneering role in the labor movement. As the first female organizer for the Knights of Labor, she was already committed to protecting the rights of working women through unionization. In 1887 Barry preached union organization as a means of self-help. As she reportedly told one audience, "When woman is forced from the home she must protect herself."[86] This emphasis on protecting working women also led to support for suffrage. Two years later, she predicted, "If women ever get the ballot it will be through the Knights of Labor." She pointed out the injustices done to women and insisted that the exploitation of female labor would continue until voters insisted on change, challenging male voters to elect reform-minded candidates but also advocating woman suffrage.[87]

She continued to lecture on suffrage after her departure from the Knights of Labor. In 1895 she reportedly told the Catholic Total Abstinence Union of Boston, "I'm not a suffragist and make no claim for woman's rights." Yet she added, "I cannot but realize if suffrage was granted to women what a power it would be against the saloon, and what a power it would be in the hands of honest Catholic women."[88] Like Mary Elizabeth Lease, Barry called for the vote in the familiar terms of social purity, home protection, and women's capacity to "lift up this grand republic of ours out of the mud of intemperance, of prostitution, of profanity and wickedness."[89] Although Barry was quoted as denying her connections to the suffrage movement, her rhetoric suggests the opposite. Furthermore, Leonora Barry Lake (she remarried in 1890) also toured Colorado during its 1893 suffrage campaign, with the support of the Knights of Labor.[90]

By the end of the nineteenth century, middle-class Protestant women were moving into social reform and suffrage work, and Catholics were beginning to develop their own reform initiatives. A few women, like Mary Elizabeth Lease and Leonora Barry, blurred those distinctions: they were suffragists and temperance activists, but they were also Knights. As Rebecca Edwards points out in *Angels in the Machinery: Gender in American Party Politics from the Civil War to the Progressive Era* (1997), there was significant support for woman suffrage among western Populists, and "almost every prominent Populist woman had worked, in fact, for the Knights."[91] As we have already seen in chapter 2, Irish American women made significant contributions to the labor movement in the nineteenth and early twentieth centuries. Their activism moved them to support legislation that would protect working women, and their efforts also brought them into alliances with middle-class Protestant reformers. Not surprisingly, then, the first Irish American labor suffragists emerged at the end of the nineteenth century as well.

Irish American labor activists added a new argument for woman suffrage: working women needed the protection of the ballot. The suffrage movement drew its membership largely from the middle and upper classes, particularly in the nineteenth century. With the exception of a brief attempt by Susan B. Anthony to organize working women in the 1860s, the suffrage movement did not reach out to wage earners until the early twentieth century.[92] Despite Anthony's attention to women workers earlier in the nineteenth century, Mary Kenney O'Sullivan described Anthony as "opposed to unions and strikes." In her autobiography, O'Sullivan recalled a night when she and Anthony shared a stage at the World's Fair. Anthony planned to speak on suffrage and O'Sullivan on "the Value of Labor Organization." They arrived to find the hall intolerably hot, but the janitor refused to open the windows. The women spoke to the manager, but when the manager also failed to cooperate, O'Sullivan suggested that they refuse to speak until the windows were opened. Their boycott worked, and O'Sullivan "couldn't resist the opportunity of reminding Miss Anthony that we had just won a strike."[93]

As O'Sullivan's teasing suggests, working women encountered obstacles in the overwhelmingly Protestant and middle-class suffrage movement. Despite their invisibility in the movement, leading working women like Leonora Barry and Mary Kenney O'Sullivan had already started to argue that voting rights were essential to improving the conditions of working women. In 1892 Samuel Gompers, president of the American Federation of Labor, recommended her appointment as the organization's first female organizer (a position she held for only five months), but O'Sullivan soon found herself at odds with Gompers over the needs of working women.[94] For example, an 1893 newspaper article predicted, "It is probable that President Gompers will get a raking over the coals today for having totally ignored the question of woman suffrage in his annual report to the convention." Although the American Federation of Labor had already passed a resolution for woman suffrage, the article accused Gompers of ignoring and belittling the cause. O'Sullivan, the article claimed, was "after Mr. Gompers with a sharp stick" on the issue.[95] In 1899 Samuel Gompers invited Susan B. Anthony to speak to the American Federation of Labor in Detroit, an address that was reportedly well received. Anthony asked the AFL to endorse a constitutional amendment (the Sixteenth Amendment) that would prohibit states from barring female voters.[96] Despite these gestures, the AFL generally devoted its energy to securing higher wages for skilled male workers and did not give much attention to the needs of working women.[97] Despite her differences with the American Federation of Labor, O'Sullivan would continue to support working women and suffrage. As she explained in a 1910 article, "There are only two ways that the individual worker, particularly the poor and uninformed worker, can make his claim for fair play heard—by organization and by legislation."[98] She worked tirelessly for both.

The roots of cross-class alliances among women began at the close of the nineteenth century. Irish American women began to move beyond organizations based on class (the labor movement) and organizations based on ethnicity (the nationalist movement) because they sought more political influence and needed new allies. Although few in number, they took an active part in social reform movements, sought a voice in shaping the agenda for industrial improvement, and lobbied for legislation that would benefit workers, including women's suffrage. Cooperation between middle-class women and working-class women became formalized in the early twentieth century with the founding of the Women's Trade Union League (to be discussed in the next chapter), but some of the same women were already crossing class, ethnic, and religious boundaries in the late nineteenth century. Likewise, the adoption of suffrage as a strategy to help working women, which became more prominent in the early twentieth century, particularly with the revitalization of the suffrage movement and a resurgence of labor activism, can be seen in the activities of some Irish American women years earlier.

6

Twentieth-Century Connections

Suffrage Tactics, Trade Unionists, and the Lessons of Tammany Hall

In 1912 *Literary Digest* published a surprisingly sympathetic portrait of the Irish American suffragist Maud Malone. "Militant Maud Malone," as she was dubbed, did not throw rocks as suffragettes were doing in Britain, yet she had been "howled at, booed at, insulted, ridiculed, [and] punched." Arrested several times by then for interrupting political meetings, Malone helped lead the first wave of militant suffrage activity seen in the United States, beginning with the first open-air meetings in 1907. A pioneer in new suffrage techniques, Malone continued her militant activities with another militant Irish American—Lucy Burns, serving jail time with other members of the National Woman's Party in 1917.[1] Yet Malone is virtually unknown in histories of the movement today.

So who was Maud Malone? According to *Literary Digest*, she had "the nose of a political economist" and large and fearless "true Irish eyes with the glint of humor in them." And according to the *Woman's Journal*, she came "of fighting stock."[2] Malone, a second-generation Irish American, led the Harlem Equal Rights League in the early twentieth century and joined a group calling itself the American Suffragettes. However, in 1908 she broke with organized militants, accusing them of a desire to "attract a well-dressed crowd, not the rabble."[3] She also helped organize the first union of library employees, the Library Employees' Union of Greater New York, which affiliated with the American Federation of Labor in 1917.[4] Although called the "Lone Suffragette" in the press because she single-handedly interrupted meetings and staged protests, as a suffragist and an independent wage earner she also represented a larger trend: the revitalization of the suffrage movement in the early twentieth century through new campaigning techniques and the increased participation of working women.

Irish American women became more visible in the suffrage movement in the twentieth century for a number of reasons. Beginning in the late nineteenth century, a small group of female labor leaders began to show more interest in political rights for women, a trend that continued to grow in the early twentieth century. Furthermore, as the National American Woman Suffrage Association accelerated its efforts to get suffrage on state ballots, particularly in the East, they faced the key challenge of getting union votes, ethnic votes, and Catholic votes. Speakers who could appeal to these audiences were in demand in several states. The resurgence of Irish nationalism in the United States during the final Home Rule battle and the international crisis of the World War I era also led to greater connections between events in Ireland and American politics, and finally, as more Catholic women sought a role in social reform, they also began to accept the argument that votes for women meant protection of home and family, elevation of the downtrodden, and the preservation of morality. Therefore, Irish American women made three important contributions to the suffrage movement in the twentieth century: they introduced or used militant techniques, provided important organizational and oratory support to the state campaigns, and participated in a separate Catholic suffrage effort.

Suffrage, Labor, and Progressivism

Working-class women and their reformer allies increasing saw suffrage as a necessary part of the struggle to secure rights in the workplace. Furthermore, the suffrage movement was changing, as a new generation of suffragists brought new campaigning techniques, some of them militant, to the effort. In another strategy change, suffragists also sought a closer relationship with working women.[5] Susan B. Anthony's death in 1906 marked the passing of the first phase of the suffrage movement. The era of Stanton, Anthony, and Lucy Stone had ended with only a few state-level successes. The movement, often described as being in the "doldrums," focused on education and not action. As Stanton's daughter Harriot Stanton Blatch recalled, "The suffrage movement was completely in a rut in New York State at the opening of the twentieth century. It bored its adherents and repelled its opponents. Most of the ammunition was being wasted on its supporters in private drawing rooms and in public halls where friends, drummed up and harried by the ardent, listlessly heard the same old arguments."[6]

Blatch offered a scathing critique of the movement her mother once led, but she had also spent years living in Britain. When she returned to the United States, she sought to bring a fresh perspective to the languishing cause. An early ally in the Women's Trade Union League, Blatch believed that working women were essential to the success of the suffrage movement, and she played an important role in revitalizing the suffrage movement by reaching out to new supporters and pioneering new campaigning methods.[7] In 1907 Blatch founded the Equality League of Self-Supporting Women, an organization centering on the needs of women in all occupations and professions. Inspired by her involvement with immigrant and trade union women through the WTUL, Blatch intended the new organization to serve the interests of women in the workplace. One of the new organization's first acts was to bring women wage earners before the New York State Senate Judiciary Committee.[8]

The suffragist movement's new emphasis on attracting working women also reached the National American Woman Suffrage Association. In 1908 NAWSA president Anna Howard Shaw invited Leonora O'Reilly to speak at the national convention in Buffalo, to "make that a good day for the industrial people," and to present "the needs of suffrage, and the advantages of it, to the working women of Buffalo." Although O'Reilly had to cancel her appearance owing to illness, she did send her speech. In it she told working women that "it is our

Sacred Duty to prepare ourselves by earnest study of the problems before us today that we may vote intelligently on these questions." But she also cautioned, "If these questions are left to our men folk only we haven't much to expect, in the way of progress, judging from the evidence against them. The questions which are primarily women's questions, questions which will take the intelligence of heart and brain the wonderful mother love of the human race to settle are: The Great Peace Question, The National Child Labor Problem, The Great Question of Industrial Organization." In closing, O'Reilly wrote to Shaw, these were her thoughts for "my own beloved people."[9]

As a leader in the New York WTUL, Leonora O'Reilly played an important role in the cooperation between labor and suffrage forces, particularly after the tragic fire at the Triangle Shirtwaist Factory killed 146 workers in the spring of 1911. After the fire, O'Reilly led the WTUL's efforts to improve fire safety in factories. She also accelerated her efforts to combine her labor activism with her feminism. O'Reilly founded the Wage Earner's Suffrage League of New York the same year.[10] The first Wage Earner's Suffrage League was founded in San Francisco in 1908. The organization's German American president told the San Francisco Equal Suffrage League, "We want the ballot for very different reasons from the ones you have for wanting it. Our idea is self-protection; you want it to use for someone else."[11] One of the San Francisco league's activists, Maud Younger, who served in the National Women's Trade Union League before returning to California, told the delegates that unions remained aloof from suffragists because they suspected that suffragists sought labor's support without supporting its goals.[12] Despite these tensions, O'Reilly wrote in her diary, "Must make plans to carry [illegible] fire & woman movement together. . . . The labor movement must be purified by a womans [*sic*] movement."[13] Her speeches and writings continued to emphasize the need for cooperation between labor and suffrage forces. "We are going to teach the whole people that the votes for women question and the Womens Labor Movement are absolutely inseperable [*sic*]," she wrote. Calling on working women to get involved in politics, she insisted, "It behooves us to learn how to play our cards well. This we mean to do."[14]

Women in other cities wrote O'Reilly for advice on organizing their own leagues. She explained, "Our Wage Earners League of NYC is only a very small wing of the WSP [Woman Suffrage Party of New York City] and at present our only work is to try and convert working women to the need of the ballot."[15] In regard to organization, she explained, "All we as a Wage Earners League insist on is that the League shall be officered and run by Wage Earning Women and that Wage Earning Women shall constitute themselves as Pioneers to take the message of Votes for Women into the places in which they earn their living."[16] O'Reilly explained the activities of the Wage Earner's Suffrage League as carrying the message to any meeting of wage earners, having working women give their own reasons that working women needed the vote, and trying to show why every organized working man should be involved in getting the ballot for women and forging a "great movement which is bringing women of all creeds all colors and all classes together to work for the solidarity of mankind." The New York Wage Earner's Suffrage League planned to hold one large meeting a year where, in O'Reilly's words, only wage-earning women would speak and give a "straight labor suffrage talk."[17]

In addition to propelling the growth of the wage earners' suffrage movement, outrage over the Triangle fire also led to political changes, as the Democratic Party in New York moved toward a more Progressive reform agenda and new leaders emerged, including future governor and presidential hopeful Al Smith (an Irish Catholic and a product of the Democratic machine). The Factory Investigating Commission, established after the fire, resulted in new legislation, enhanced the reputations of Smith and Robert Wagner (influencing their outlook on social welfare legislation), and established ties between the Democratic Party and leaders of progressive organizations and labor unions.[18] Although a change in attitude toward women's suffrage came slowly among Democrats, Tammany leader "Big Tim" Sullivan openly supported women's suffrage in 1911, arguing for the bill in terms of women's rights as workers. Tammany boss Charles Murphy also agreed to a suffrage plank in 1912.[19] This gradual adoption of women's suffrage characterized many urban machines between 1915 and 1919.[20] Al Smith's record also shows a shift in attitude. In 1916, in response to Leonora O'Reilly's inquiries about Smith, Margaret Finn wrote, "[I] am surprised to hear that he says there are no women who wish to vote in his district. Last year Smith recommended Democrats go on record for suffrage and said he would recommend it on account of widespread interest. Before that he personally opposed it in the assembly." But Finn also warned, "I do not think Al Smith is the man to *fight*, he has always stood for labor laws and civil service employees. Al Smith has a record of always helping the underdog. I do not know Mr. Smith but I think it will be better for our cause to leave him alone."[21]

Whether Democratic or Republican, political machines also changed during the Progressive Era. Urban machines proved adaptable to progressive reform. Large cities like Chicago, Jersey City, and Cincinnati adopted reforms, while machines still maintained power. In his study of political machines and women's suffrage, John Buenker argues that urban machines were pragmatic about "reform in general and woman suffrage in particular."[22] Instead of the reactionary attitude associated with machines, they proved dynamic and adaptable to reform when politics required it. He maintained that the machines' intransigence on the issue could be explained by their need to control their electorate and the belief that women were more idealistic about politics—more susceptible to the rhetoric of reform. However, in the last few years before the proposal of the Nineteenth Amendment, urban machines shifted their policy. While Tammany leaders lent considerable weight to the defeat of the 1915 suffrage referendum in New York City, by 1917 the Democrats took a neutral stance. Governor Al Smith later urged the ratification of the Nineteenth Amendment in the New York Legislature as an example to the rest of the nation. By 1919 most major Democratic and Republican urban machines accepted women's suffrage.[23] Machine politicians realized that enfranchising women would not significantly alter the political, economic, and ethnic composition of the electorate and might give them an advantage in urban areas. As one of Chicago's notorious bosses, "Bathhouse John" Coughlin, said, "It won't make very much difference at all."[24] These changes in the political landscape, combined with renewed activism for suffrage and labor reform, opened up opportunities for working-class women.

Suffrage Tactics and Working Women

The increasing participation of wage-earning women in the suffrage movement coincided with the first use of militant tactics in the United States. In 1907 Blatch's Equality League of Self-Supporting Women invited British suffragist Anne Cobden-Sanderson to speak, introducing American audiences to the militant techniques being used in Britain. A member of the Women's Social and Political Union, Cobden-Sanderson was a leader in a new wave of suffrage activism that focused on civil disobedience.[25] Founded in 1903 by Emmeline Pankhurst, the WSPU began to employ militant techniques to raise the visibility and effectiveness of the movement. This strategy also inspired militancy in Ireland, where Hanna Sheehy Skeffington and Margaret Cousins founded the Irish Women's Franchise League in 1908.[26]

Cobden-Sanderson's visit to New York also inspired American suffragists to begin experimenting with militant techniques. As a result of this visit, another British activist, Bettina Borrman Wells, founded the American Suffragettes to begin using more sensational techniques in the American movement.[27] As suffrage organizations in America began to introduce more militant tactics like open-air meetings and suffrage parades, working women emerged as powerful speakers for the cause. One of the goals of the American Suffragettes was to challenge standards of femininity. As Borrman Wells explained, "The time has come when we must eliminate that abominable word ladylike from out vocabularies." Instead she suggested women "get out and fight."[28] Irish American women proved themselves particularly well suited for the work of stump speaking on street corners, disrupting political rallies, and campaigning in urban neighborhoods. As Hasia Diner argues in *Erin's Daughters in America*, Irish American women, in particular, already found assertiveness in the economic sphere culturally acceptable.[29] Their needs as working women would also push them into the political arena, where they willingly defied class-based standards of female respectability.[30] Although not a suffragist, Mother Jones told a labor rally in 1914, "Never mind if you are not lady-like, you are woman-like. God Almighty made the woman and the Rockefeller gang of thieves made the ladies."[31]

Widespread stereotypes of "the fighting Irish" were common in press coverage of Irish American women, including suffragists. As we have already seen, suffragist Maud Malone was characterized by her ethnic background when covered in the press. For example, the *Women's Journal*, a suffrage newspaper, published an article entitled "Maud Malone Comes of Fighting Stock."[32] Many of these Irish American women accepted their reputations for argument and agitation. The press quoted them as being influenced by the struggles of the Irish abroad. Inspired by stories of Irish rebellion and nationalism, Margaret Haley embraced her reputation as one of the "fighting Irish."[33] Likewise, Leonora O'Reilly saw herself as a fighter. In a 1909 article, O'Reilly described herself as a Fenian who belonged to a family of revolutionaries. O'Reilly also joked publicly and privately about the Irish reputation for belligerence. An article in the *Cleveland Federationist* quoted O'Reilly's address to the Ohio State Federation of Labor's convention. She referred to herself as "the fighting O'Reilly from New York," rebuking her brother trade unionists for their chilly reception and their patronizing treatment of working women. Responding to a letter in the *New Canaan (CT) Advertiser*, O'Reilly wrote that "like the good Irishman" says, if she can't knock down her opponent, she will "stagger him at least."[34]

These women did not fit conventional images of femininity, but they also embraced the "fight." Their contributions to the suffrage movement were shaped by class and ethnic factors, including their ties to the labor movement, their activism on behalf of working women, and their assertiveness. Although Maud Malone is rarely mentioned in histories of the suffrage movement today, Ellen Carol DuBois has described her as a pioneer militant "who might have been as important an innovative force as Harriot Blatch."[35] Maud Malone came from a reform-oriented family. Her father, Dr. Edward Malone, and his brother, Father Sylvester L. Malone, both emigrated from Ireland as teenage boys, and both were close associates of Father Edward McGlynn. Edward Malone chose to study medicine in the United States, but he also became a committed Irish nationalist.[36] Malone also served on the executive board of the Anti-Poverty Society, a cause his son (also Sylvester Malone) recalled was more a religious than a political one. When he died in 1890, his burial in Calvary Cemetery, the same consecrated ground denied to other Anti-Poverty members, caused some controversy.[37] Dr. Edward Malone's funeral was held at Saints Peter and Paul's Parish in Brooklyn, where his brother, Father Sylvester Malone, served for fifty years.

Like her father and uncle, Maud Malone was a supporter of the land theories championed by Henry George and Father McGlynn, serving as president of the Women's Henry George League, but her biggest contribution was to the suffrage movement. She founded the Harlem Equal Rights League in 1905, dedicating the organization to women's economic, industrial, and legal rights. One of the group's yearly activities was to offer a polling place for women to vote in the November election. The *New York Times* reported five hundred voters in the 1906 mock election, quoting Malone as suggesting, "Women as well as men are vitally interested in all the issues of this campaign, and have the right to express their opinions upon them and to have those opinions counted."[38]

Malone also took the lead in organizing a suffrage parade under the auspices of the American Suffragettes. Although the women were denied a permit, the event was covered by the New York press and received some out-of-state coverage as well. According to the *New York Sun*, a "Big Crowd Gather[ed] to Stare at the Suffragettes." Although the parade began as a small gathering, the *New York Times* reported "Six Thousand Followers of Maud Malone and Mrs. Wells in Quick-step," despite the lack of a permit.[39] This figure reflects the number who reportedly joined in sympathy. Under the headline "Amazons Bluff New York Police," the *Washington Times* reported a "quiet walk up Broadway," and even the *Hawaiian Star* reported on the event.[40]

Maud Malone has the distinction of being the first American woman arrested for her suffrage activities. The American Suffragettes began holding outdoor meetings in the winter of 1908. Malone explained that she began organizing open-air suffrage meetings to avoid the cost of renting a hall. She recalled, "I took a leaf from the Salvation Army's lesson book. . . . I noticed they'd built up a great organization with nothing but street meetings at first." Socialists had also used the street meeting with success. As Malone pointed out, economic arguments were most effective with audiences on the Lower East Side—the one plea that worked with them "is the need of the working girls for the ballot."[41] She was first arrested in 1909 for holding a street meeting without a permit.[42]

Although Malone split with other militants, accusing them of exclusiveness and pandering to a society crowd, she gained notoriety as an individual and got arrested for interrupting political speeches beginning in 1909. She also targeted local politicians and even socialists, but her most dramatic targets were national political figures like Theodore Roosevelt and Woodrow Wilson during the 1912 presidential election cycle. In a widely reported incident, Malone stood up at a Roosevelt event in New York to demand that he answer her question on suffrage. Men in the audience reportedly hissed and threw "paper programs and other missiles" until she was ejected from the event.[43] On the eve of the election, Malone, who had converted to the Bull Moose Party by then, interrupted Woodrow Wilson's speech to ask for his position on women's suffrage. She was arrested and spent a night in jail. According to the *New York Tribune*, the magistrate called Malone a "scatterbrained, loose-tongued, ill-mannered virago."[44]

Malone invited other suffragists to attend her trial (which resulted in a guilty verdict and a suspended sentence), but her local notoriety caused friction with the National American Woman Suffrage Association. In response to this incident, the *New York Tribune* quoted Anna Howard Shaw, president of NAWSA, as saying, "Miss Malone is doing things in her own way, and she mustn't look for suffrage organizations or their members to stop their work to rally around her when she gets into trouble. . . . [S]he must be prepared to stand alone and take her medicine."[45] She certainly was a "lone" militant, in that she did not have the backing of other suffrage organizations. However, by the time Maud Malone was arrested, the tactics she adopted were also being discussed and implemented elsewhere. Another Irish American, Margaret Foley, also made important contributions to the suffrage movement in Massachusetts after becoming a popular speaker and studying militant tactics.

Like the other Irish American women in the suffrage and labor movements, Margaret Foley embraced her reputation as a fighter, cutting her organizational teeth in the labor movement and becoming a leader in the hat trimmers' union, before joining the Massachusetts WTUL. Foley was born in Massachusetts and raised in the working-class neighborhood of Roxbury. She joined the Massachusetts Woman Suffrage Association in 1909, the same year that the organization began to hold open-air meetings around Boston. In 1911 Foley and another Massachusetts suffragist, Florence Luscomb, went to England to observe militant suffrage tactics.[46] A few months later, Foley and Luscomb put their experiences to work, challenging politicians with questions about their suffrage stance.

As in the case of Maud Malone, the press identified Foley as a militant. The *Boston Evening Transcript* announced in a headline that Boston had its "First Suffragette—Miss Margaret Foley Who Heckles, and the *Boston Herald* called her "heckler-in-chief" for the MWSA.[47] One of Foley's first targets was Representative James McInerney, a suffrage opponent who was running for reelection. In an exchanged loaded with gendered insults, he reportedly asked her, "Why aren't ye at home, darning y'r husband's socks?" McInerney also offered to find her a husband, but after the candidate drove off, Foley insisted on saying a few words, reportedly drawing laughter by accusing McInerney of being a tool of the machine, incapable of making up his mind without consulting Irish Democratic boss Martin Lomasney. Foley claimed McInerney was not man enough to answer her questions.[48]

Likewise, when Foley reportedly threatened to cook another politician's goose, he retorted that he didn't believe she knew how to cook a goose, shifting the focus from a political contest to Foley's presumed shortcomings in the domestic sphere.[49] The candidate, Levi Greenwood, lost the election. Although many of the local politicians Foley heckled in 1911 were part of the local Democratic machine, she also disrupted Republican campaign stops. Four suffragists, including Foley, followed Lieutenant Governor Louis Frothingham by car, reportedly for twelve hours, leading the candidate to charge the women with working for the Democrats and the press to report his "harass[ment] by [a] militant suffragette."[50]

Not all the newspaper coverage was negative. Some in the press enjoyed Foley's antics. On the showdown between Foley and ward politicians, the *Boston American* mused, "It suggests some reputation as a 'heckler' when a heckling woman has only to appear in a street corner crowd to make the political candidate on the stump climb down . . . and hurry over to shake hands with her." The same newspaper credited Foley's political savvy for this success: "Margaret Foley wasn't born and brought up in Ward 17, the home of real politicians, for nothing."[51] Other columnists defended her femininity. One agreed that Foley was actually not "a rampageous virago, but a woman who cherishes her ideals and respects her grammar as sedulously as we do."[52] Another article reported, "Her voice is the only mannish thing about her and it is an excellent voice for a hall."[53] Foley, who was a trained singer, gained quite a reputation for her oratory. Her notoriety also led to opportunities for Foley's arguments to appear in print. The *Boston Daily Globe* ran two of her columns in 1913, which focused on the need of wage-earning women for political rights. She wrote, "Women need the vote to make it necessary for the Government to consult woman's point of view in the making and enforcing of laws, particularly the laws affecting women and children in the industrial world."[54]

Although Foley's approach to suffrage activities, militant by American standards at the time, left her vulnerable to attack for unwomanly behavior, it also made her well suited for her environment—the competitive world of local politics. Another Irish American woman who became an important suffrage worker and political organizer in New York City, Mary Donnelly, first gained press notoriety as an employee of society suffragist Alva Belmont. Belmont joined the suffrage movement in 1909 after the death of her second husband, Oliver Belmont, becoming an important ally and financier. She helped establish a NAWSA headquarters in New York and later embraced the more militant position of the National Woman's Party, which was led by Alice Paul and Lucy Burns.[55] Belmont created district branches, including the one in a busy retail section of East Thirty-Fourth Street, which opened in 1910 and served lunch for a small fee.[56] When New York women won the vote in 1917, the *Sun* ran a story entitled "Names of Suffrage Pioneers Not Forgotten in Victory." Among those individuals credited in the article was "Mary Donnelly with her Irish Blarney running that suffrage lunchroom . . . making converts hand over hand as she beat the high cost of living with her 5, 10, 15 cent portions of good meat, vegetables, coffee and pie."[57]

Before Belmont hired Mary Donnelly as superintendent of the Thirty-Fourth Street branch, she worked as an assistant matron at the Queens County jail. She was fired but later accused the jail of tolerating assault and mistreatment of female prisoners. By 1910, when the story of her accusations ran in the press, she was being described as "a militant suffragette."[58] The *New York Times* dubbed Donnelly "the politician's pride of the Fourteenth Assembly District," and the *New York World* called Donnelly "the best politician on the block," insisting, "She can call every janitor's child by name and has pinned a votes for women button on every express wagon horse east of Broadway."[59] But Donnelly had a falling-out with Belmont when her employer closed the lunchroom in the Fourteenth Assembly District to concentrate her efforts on one suffrage headquarters, located off Fifth Avenue. Although Belmont continued to employ Donnelly and run a lunchroom, Belmont also added a department of hygiene, staffed by women doctors, and sold cosmetics and toiletries.[60] Donnelly insisted that women wanted an affordable lunch, not cold cream and soap, which they could buy for less elsewhere. She wanted instead to revive the old lunchroom.[61]

In a show of support for militant methods, Donnelly also supported Maud Malone during her trial, attending the trial and reportedly arranging for a protest should Malone be imprisoned.[62] Donnelly remained active in New York politics after she left Belmont's employment at the beginning of 1912. She announced plans to drill a women's police force in preparation for the suffrage parade, paraded a mule-drawn cart on Wall Street for suffrage, and organized women speakers for the Bull Moose Party.[63] Carrying her dedication to workers' rights into the Bull Moose Party in 1912, Donnelly urged voters to support the eight-hour day and fight against child labor, in addition to campaigning for woman suffrage.[64]

As a working woman, Mary Donnelly supported suffrage and sought to improve working conditions and living conditions for laboring women. As a Catholic, she led a delegation of suffragists to seek the support of Cardinal John Farley of New York. She declared, "The Catholic Church is not against woman suffrage. It could not be, because it has always stood for the uplift of women against divorce, for the sanctity of the home, and the protection of little children. Woman suffrage stands for all these things." Yet she rejected the idea of a separate Catholic suffrage organization. Donnelly was quoted as saying that Catholic women had approached her to organize a separate group, but she refused on the grounds that suffrage was a democratic movement and not sectarian.[65] Although Donnelly denied the need for a separate Catholic organization, the renewal of state suffrage campaigns, and the priorities of NAWSA's Committee on Church Work, created the demand for speakers and strategies that would appeal to Catholic voters and ultimately did lead to some separate Catholic suffrage groups.

The most visible Irish Catholic among the more militant suffrage faction was Lucy Burns, who along with Alice Paul led the National Woman's Party (NWP) campaign after its break with NAWSA. Burns grew up in a big Irish Catholic family in Brooklyn. A highly educated woman, Burns pursued advanced studies in the United States and in Europe, where she became acquainted with the suffrage militancy emerging in Britain. From 1909 to 1912, she worked with pioneering British militants Emmeline and Christabel Pankhurst, participating in her first hunger strike and teaming up with Alice Paul, a Quaker from Pennsylvania who was also involved in the British suffrage movement.

Upon her return to the United States, Burns and Paul cooperated in pushing for a federal suffrage amendment, a strategy that would lead them to split with NAWSA in 1913.[66] Under the auspices of the National Woman's Party, Burns participated in controversial picketing of the White House, serving more time in jail than any other American suffragist. Another Catholic woman of Irish decent, Josephine Collins was arrested with members of the NWP in Boston in 1918.[67] Likewise, Catherine Flanagan, born in Connecticut to Irish immigrant parents, was arrested outside the White House in 1917. Flanagan, the secretary at the headquarters of the Connecticut Woman's Suffrage Association, embraced suffrage militancy despite criticism from some inside the Connecticut Woman's Suffrage Association, and in 1920 she was chosen to deliver official notice of Connecticut's ratification of the Nineteenth Amendment to Washington, DC. She also continued her political work after 1920 in the Irish nationalist movement, serving as secretary and traveling aid to Mary MacSwiney on her US speaking tour and then as secretary of the legislative committee of the American Association for the Recognition of the Irish Republic.[68] As the stories of Burns, Malone, Foley, Donnelly, and others suggest, Irish American women played a significant part in the creation and visibility of suffrage militancy in the United States. Although the controversial nature of this aspect of the movement ultimately led to divisions within the suffrage ranks, Irish American women also played a key role in the state campaigns.

The State Campaigns

During the nineteenth century, suffragists tried a variety of methods to enfranchise women, but the federal amendment strategy did not gain any traction, and the state campaigns were largely unsuccessful. Between 1870 and 1890, suffragists were able to convince only eight states to hold referenda on the issue, and most were defeated. Only two western states or territories granted women the right to vote: Wyoming and Utah. Between 1890 and 1910, only two more western states were added to suffrage column, but things began to pick up after that period. Still, no eastern states adopted unrestricted women's suffrage until New York did in 1917. In 1915 Carrie Chapman Catt took over the presidency of a NAWSA divided over the question of strategy. Her "winning plan" of the following year was to use states where women had the vote to put pressure on Congress and President Wilson to move on the federal amendment, thereby combining the two strategies.[69]

To win voters in large eastern States, NAWSA needed to reach out to new voters. Part of NAWSA's vision was the increased attention to Catholic voters. In the early twentieth century, NAWSA created the Committee on Church Work to reach out to Christian women, and Catt attended the Columbia Catholic Summer School, but the Committee on Church Work did not make Catholic women a priority until the 1910s, when chairperson Mary Craige began to focus the committee's attention on the Catholic community. She argued, "More and more I am led to believe that the most important work before suffragists today is church work, especially the organizing of the Catholic women, that they will make their demands so emphatic the church will see the wisdom of supporting the movement."[70] Of course, Catholic voters were a key constituency in many of the states where suffragists were trying to win, especially in the East.

As suffrage organizations prepared for campaigns in large states such as Massachusetts and New York, they mobilized support by developing a complex system of district, precinct, and ward leaders, modeling their efforts after political parties. Suffragists, while still nonpartisan, sought to use political tactics and campaigning strategies to reach voters.[71] Carrie Chapman Catt described New York as the "most intensively organized state in the union" after the creation of the Woman Suffrage Party in 1909, which suffragists modeled after the tight district oversight first perfected by Tammany Hall.[72]

To court male voters, the state associations of the National American Woman Suffrage Association constructed their appeals in part based on class, ethnicity, and religion. For example, in New York suffragists held "suffrage days" to appeal to certain professions such as firemen and barbers, sponsored street dances and block parties on the Lower East Side, and distributed "rainbow fliers" in seven different languages.[73] The *Woman Voter* reported in 1915 that one out of every three voters in New York was foreign born, and the Woman Suffrage Party was making every effort to reach them.[74] These efforts created a demand for suffragists with particular ethnic backgrounds and ties to organized labor. In this final phase of the suffrage movement, Irish American suffragists made significant contributions to state campaigns and also to the development of a separate Catholic suffrage movement.

In addition to the many suffrage volunteers, women also worked as paid speakers and organizers. Margaret Foley toured the country in support of the cause, as did Irish-born laborer Margaret Hinchey. In 1913 *Life and Labor*, the journal of the WTUL, described Hinchey as "a young Irish woman, clean of thought, pure of heart, [and] brave as truth itself," who came to the league after being blacklisted for labor activities.[75] The Wage Earners Suffrage League of New York issued a pamphlet titled *Senators vs. Working Women*, containing working women's arguments for suffrage. In it Hinchey celebrated the value of the home, but argued that working women did not have the luxury of being homemakers. She explained her participation in the laundry strike as an attempt to improve the family life of workers: "We wanted to give a chance to the mothers of families to get home in the evening to attend to their children and to care for them. We wanted to give a chance to the boy and girl that had left school too young to know anything to go out in the evenings to hear a lecture, or to go to some night school and get some education." And she appealed to patriotism and the legacy of Abraham Lincoln. If Lincoln was in the White House today, she argued, he would emancipate working women and their families by enfranchising them "in this great country under the banner of the stars and stripes, of which we are so proud."[76]

Suffragists needed to court the labor vote, so they relied on speakers who could appeal to working men. For example, Jeannette Rankin (the first woman elected to Congress) wrote to Margaret Foley from the Montana campaign: "One of the women that the Antis were planning to bring to Montana is an old friend of yours, Minnie Bronson, and I have heard that you are the best antidote for Bronson, so if she does come, we believe that we will have to have you. . . . I believe you could do a great amount of good in our labor towns." Rankin thought that if suffrage captured the labor vote, "there is no doubt we can win" and asked Foley if she belonged to a union.[77] The *Christian Science Monitor* reported that Foley was in demand in Montana, Nevada, New Jersey, and St. Louis. She spent two months campaigning in Nevada in 1914 for the successful suffrage referendum there.[78]

Rankin also requested the help of Margaret Hinchey to campaign in strong union areas. Rankin's colleague Mary O'Neill of the Montana Equal Suffrage Association acknowledged the value of labor ties when she wrote to Leonora O'Reilly, "Miss Rankin appreciates the splendid character and the ability of Miss Hinchey as a speaker in her direct appeal to the labor unions, and these we must largely depend here. . . . The union men here all seem to have heard of her work in New York. If the federated unions are appointed with the efforts of the members Miss Hinchey, being a member of the executive board of the WTUL, will be a[n] open sesame to the unions in this city and in the state."[79]

While Foley, Hinchey, and O'Reilly could all be counted on to speak the language of the labor movement, their ethnic background also provided an important asset in states with large Irish American populations as suffrage organizations sought to appeal to Irish American voters. Correspondence between speakers and the suffrage organizations that employed them clearly demonstrates this strategy. For example, the Women's Political Union of New Jersey wanted to arrange a Saint Patrick's Day suffrage meeting, requesting that Foley speak at "a big mass meeting at the labor lyceum for the evening of the March 16." Ida Porter Boyer of the Ohio Woman Suffrage Association also wrote to tell Foley that she had been requested for an Irish Day celebration in Cincinnati.[80] She also teased Foley, "I would like to see you on Irish Day with your green and white flag and I say that I am startled to think of Votes For Women on a grass-green background."[81] Harriet Taylor Upton, also of the Ohio Woman Suffrage Association, wrote of a fish fry, "I put you there because I have an idea it is a Roman Catholic affair." She continued, "I think you had better take your green flag to the fish fry instead of you golden yellow. Good luck to you. I hope that grass green flag has a shamrock stitched on one end of it."[82]

In 1915 Margaret Foley teamed up with Margaret Hinchey to campaign for suffrage in New York. As the *New York Times* reported, "Maggie and Maggie" offered "Irish Vim" to the campaign. But when Hinchey missed her appointment to shake hands with Foley, the *Times* remarked, "Where oh where is Maggie Hinchey of New York. . . . She may be talking suffrage in the trenches which her friends are digging, or over on the docks, or twenty stories up on the framework of some new building, in her search for votes for women.[83] Hinchey took her message to the Bowery, the trenches, and the pier, appealing to workers, not just in terms of class solidarity but also as an Irish immigrant woman. In 1914 she offered to "go down to Washington and I'll tell them that the Irish do want the vote." Hinchey also recalled a conversation with an Irish woman who said: "They have a nerve to say the Irish women don't want the vote. . . . There's a society for every County in Ireland and not an anti will get into one of them," the woman claimed.[84] The *New York Times* also reported on Hinchey's ability to appeal to Irish voters: "When Maggie got up, to speak, the Bowery succumbed to a man. 'Brothers' began Maggie, rolling her r's with good Irish Brogue. As she went on, her audience alternately wiped its tears and shook with laughter."[85] Hinchey also tried to reach subway workers, carrying a large green banner with "Votes for Women" printed on it in Gaelic lettering and handing out literature decorated with shamrocks.[86]

While suffragists sought the labor vote and developed new tactics to appeal to ethnic voters, they also courted the support of Catholic voters. In 1915 NAWSA's Committee on Church Work listed the organization of Catholic women as one of the movement's most important tasks.[87] In fact, a study of voting patterns in state referenda between 1910 and 1918 found no consistent patterns among Catholics across the country. While German American Catholics were the most consistently opposed, the Irish were "only to some degree opposed."[88] To win Catholic support, suffragists tried to dispel the belief that the Catholic Church had condemned the suffrage movement. Although not an accurate assumption, the opposition of individual church leaders, especially the pope and Cardinal James Gibbons of Baltimore, had been interpreted as an official church position. In 1910 Gibbons, a longtime suffrage foe, told the students of St. Catherine's Normal Institute not to follow in the steps of suffrage advocates "who have become mannish in their ways and who fight for a place in politics." However, the Catholic Church actually took no official position on women's suffrage.[89] In 1913 Gibbons clarified his position in response to criticism by suffragist Inez Milholland. Although he opposed the movement, the cardinal explained, "The mission of the Catholic Church is to define faith and morals. In other matters individuals decide for themselves."[90] For suffragists, this statement meant the need to educate Catholic voters and win converts.

For example, in 1912 the *Woman's Journal* quoted Margaret Haley, the teachers' union pioneer, as saying, "The Catholic Church does not oppose progress," and "If I believed it did I would not belong to it."[91] With the help of Catholic supporters, suffragists published their own literature to demonstrate Catholic support for suffrage. Flyers produced in several states offered arguments for suffrage by prominent Catholics, particularly members of the clergy. For example, Massachusetts circulated a pamphlet entitled *Eminent Catholics Declare for Suffrage*.[92] Similarly, the Woman Suffrage Party of New York City produced literature titled "Prominent Catholics for Equal Suffrage" and a poster that declared "Catholic Church not Opposed to Woman Suffrage."[93] Margaret Finn, a factory inspector and Catholic suffragist, wrote to her old friend Leonora O'Reilly about such flyers: "I had no idea before I saw it, that we had so many of my church people with us."[94] She reported making "good use of them," and the following year she described "working like a beaver for the WSP."[95] Likewise, the Pennsylvania Woman Suffrage Association put out similar literature, and in 1914 another Catholic suffragist, Margaret Hayden Rorke, compiled a booklet titled *Letters and Addresses on Woman Suffrage by Catholic Ecclesiastics*.[96]

In 1915 suffragists staged a dramatic pilgrimage to the home of Margaret Brent, a Catholic who was also the first woman in colonial

America to petition for a vote in 1648. A group of women traveled by wagon, which the press described as the "prairie schooner," to visit Brent's Maryland home, speaking at towns along the way. Mary O'Toole, the Irish-born secretary of the College Equal Suffrage Association in Washington, DC, joined the caravan for two weeks.[97] Mary O'Toole had moved to New York at the age of sixteen. She described her father as being "a farmer who was associated with Parnell in the Land League days." She became a lawyer, and later President Harding appointed her as the first female municipal judge in Washington, DC.[98] While a judge, and in cooperation with the NWP, she also sought to make women eligible for jury duty.[99]

To reach Catholic audiences, suffragists worked with Catholic organizations and clergy. For example, the Equal Franchise League of Pittsburgh wrote Leonora O'Reilly, "We are having a big Catholic picnic here and one of the Priests, head of the biggest Parish in the city offered to put a Catholic committee of women suffragists in charge of his tent." O'Reilly, who was not a practicing Catholic, responded, "Miss Margaret Hinchey of New York is our working woman suffragist, who has worked especially among the catholic [sic] women and has been successful, I believe, in making priests to see that our cause is just."[100] Hinchey worked with Catholic women in other state campaigns as well. During the New Jersey campaign, Hinchey spent almost three weeks making street speeches, visiting Catholic clergy, and attending meetings of Irish societies.[101] Also, while she toured Montana, one newspaper reported on Hinchey's talk that "a special invitation is extended to the Catholic women to be present at the rally tonight."[102]

In 1917 the state of New York passed a referendum enfranchising women. On the eve of the election, Margaret Hinchey wrote an article in the *Gaelic American*, arguing for support of woman suffrage on three grounds. Appealing to Irish nationalism, she reminded Irish New Yorkers that the recent rebellion in Ireland witnessed the construction of a new constitution, one that included woman suffrage. Next, she appealed to class solidarity and self-interest, demanding the vote not only because women must work but also because they were left defenseless when laboring men went to war and needed to protect the interests of all workers in the men's absence. Finally, Hinchey urged Irish men to vote for suffrage in the spirit of justice—to "be true to the teachings of Christ and the Catholic Church."[103]

Margaret Foley also sought to bring her suffrage message to Catholic women. An article in the *Boston Evening Transcript* explained Foley's mission as "awaken[ing] the women, who, somewhat restrained, it may be by a misinterpretation of religious duty, had thereby inadvertently added superfluous links to their chains."[104] She began conducting suffrage work among Catholics, both because the Massachusetts Woman Suffrage Association sent her out to do so and because Catholic groups requested her services. The Knights of Columbus of Malden, Massachusetts, invited Foley to serve as ring mistress for their society circus, assuring her, "You are perfectly welcome to speak on Woman's Suffrage at your own pleasure and make converts as you are able."[105] In Pennsylvania the Equal Franchise Federation of Pittsburgh planned a suffrage debate at a Catholic Orphans' Picnic. Organizers expected forty thousand visitors at the picnic. They informed her that Father Lynch offered suffragists two speeches a day.[106]

The increasing suffrage activity among Catholics also suggests increasing interest in the issue. A number of Catholic groups also endorsed suffrage. For example, the Catholic Student Association of America supported the measure before World War I. The Catholic Order of Foresters, the Catholic Women's League, and the Ladies' Catholic Benevolent Association also endorsed woman suffrage.[107] In 1912 one local chapter of the Daughters of Isabella, the ladies' auxiliary to the Knights of Columbus, asked Margaret Foley to educate them about suffrage. As the president explained, "We are very ignorant on the suffrage question, you know, living as we do in the country. And we are anxious to learn. For instance, we would like to know how the suffrage, if gained, would affect the status of the working girl, its advantages, etc. In short, we would be glad to know how far the Suffragists have progressed along labor lines and just what they aim to do."

The writer went on to explain that the Catholic women in Winchester, Massachusetts, did not associate with the existing suffrage association because "it is composed of the 'idle rich'—and not affiliated with our Society in any way." As their interest in labor issues suggests, members of the chapter came from more modest backgrounds. Their president reported that about one-seventh of their members were unorganized working women. The rest were mainly teachers, stenographers, nurses, and married women.[108] These Catholic women were interested in suffrage as a possible tool to improve the lives of women, including working women.

By the fall of 1914, the Massachusetts Woman Suffrage Association had begun a campaign to reach the labor unions, and the political climate was also beginning to change. As one representative wrote to Margaret Foley, "We are reaching the voters in great shape at political rallies, and are having telephone calls every day asking us to send speakers, especially with the Democrats. How times have changed! It does begin to look as though things were coming our way with a bang."[109] The Democratic Party's attitude toward suffrage had softened. In 1915 Mayor James Michael Curley, a powerful Irish American Democrat, endorsed women's suffrage as part of his larger reform agenda, claiming that women voters would support his social welfare policies.[110] Suffrage also had the support of Massachusetts governor David Walsh. However, the referendum lost by 132,000 votes, and since the MWSA no longer needed suffrage speakers, the board dismissed Foley just before the election.

Foley's working-class background had been seen as an asset during the campaign, but now it worked against her. Her confrontational style fitted well in the arena of local ward politics but limited her participation in the wider movement. As a result, Foley found herself without work and therefore also without an income when the MWSA stopped employing her. In 1918 she tried to prove her worth in a letter to Mrs. Anna C. Bird, chairperson of the executive board of the Massachusetts Woman Suffrage Association: "It is true as you say, that I know a great deal about the inside of the suffrage movement as well as a great deal about the inside of political matters. This I consider a very valuable asset. . . . Because of my absolutely fair record as a suffragist and trade unionist my statements are sure to carry weight with the public. I have proven this by my success in the political field." Foley had served the suffrage movement well, and she reminded Bird, "I am a well known Catholic in the largest Catholic city in the United States. . . . Many Catholics joined the suffrage movement because of my activities. Some now are asking why I am not active at the present time."[111] Foley had lost her place in the movement.

A letter from Alice Stone Blackwell, editor of the *Woman's Journal* and the daughter of Lucy Stone, explained why, citing the changing needs of the suffrage movement. Blackwell argued that Foley's services might be needed to defeat congressional or legislative candidates. Blackwell praised Foley as an unrivaled speaker but suggested that lobbying would not suit her: "in the quiet preliminary work of organizing . . . and nosing about under the surface to find out how candidates stand and to use 'indirect influence' for our friends and against our enemies, I do not suppose you would find your most effective field."[112] Foley's tactics and background made her a formidable opponent but also limited her opportunities in the suffrage movement, which was her income as well. She would, however, move on to cooperate with middle-class Catholics in the Margaret Brent Suffrage Guild, a Catholic suffrage organization founded in 1918.

Margaret Hinchey shared a similar fate after suffrage passed in New York in 1917. Without paid suffrage work, she found herself forced to go back to the laundry. Frustrated and bitter that her efforts on behalf of suffrage had been forgotten, she described herself as "a Clare girl who took all the sneers and hooting and got the church doors slammed in my face." Leonora O'Reilly had not forgotten Hinchey's contributions and did what she could to offer financial support through money raised in the Margaret Hinchey Fund.[113] To avoid the look of charity, O'Reilly suggested having Carrie Chapman Catt offer the check to Hinchey as payment for her services and a much-needed rest. O'Reilly wrote, "She is proud as the poor Irish can be when they have made good against mighty odds. . . . [T]herefore the wrong person meaning right might make such a blunder in the doing of this sisterly act that there would not be a scrap of whole bit of china left in the shop when she got through.[114]

O'Reilly's letters suggest that she believed Hinchey did play an important role in the success of the referendum. She explained, "Margaret is unique. . . . She has really played a significant part in getting the vote—She feels this so do others—There are as many misunderstand her usefulness as those who understand it."[115] Foley, Hinchey, O'Reilly, and others played an important role in the suffrage movement, particularly as state campaigns accelerated in the twentieth century. Their contributions to the labor movement, as well as ethnic and religious identity, allowed them to appeal to male voters across the country. As working women, all three found the benefit of cross-class cooperation and made significant contributions to the suffrage movement as a means of helping working women. However, the struggles outlined by O'Reilly, Hinchey, and Foley also suggest that this cooperation across class, ethnic, and religious lines could be very difficult as well.

The Development of a Catholic Suffrage Movement: Catholic Women and Uplift

Many working women, such as O'Reilly, Foley, and O'Sullivan, became suffragists because of experiences with workplace exploitation and their role as labor organizers. But some middle-class Catholics also sought the vote as a means of helping working women. As we have seen, Catholic discussion of the "Woman Question" increased in volume during the 1890s as part of larger debates on the role of women in the Catholic community. Part of this discussion concerned the role of laywomen in social reform. As previously discussed, beginning in the late nineteenth century with Pope Leo XIII's 1891 labor encyclical, *Rerum novarum*, a movement for social justice began to move slowly up the American Catholic hierarchy.[116] Through reform organizations, Catholic laywomen, like their Protestant counterparts, also expanded their social and political influence. Although many American Catholics retained conservative views of gender roles, some used maternalist rhetoric to support suffrage, protective labor laws, and other social welfare legislation.[117] For example, a prosuffrage article in the *Catholic World* from 1915 explained that Catholic women had risen to the challenge of protecting women and children from the perils of a modern industrial age. Therefore, the article stated, "The Catholic woman suffragist offers votes for women as a modern means of protection for the home" and a way to preserve "our Catholic ideal."[118]

A tendency, particularly among middle-class Catholics, to organize separate organizations along denominational lines led to the development of new suffrage groups, founded to work specifically among Catholics. A small group of British women founded the first Catholic suffrage organization in 1911. The Catholic Women's Suffrage Society began with nine women who joined together to "secure for women the Parliamentary Vote on the same terms as it is, or may be, granted to men." The following year, the Roman Catholic Woman's Suffrage League was founded in Brussels.[119] Women in Ireland also followed suit. In 1915 Mary Hayden, a professor of Irish history at University College, Dublin, helped establish the Irish Catholic Women's Suffrage Association, a nonpartisan and nonmilitant organization that sought to inspire Catholic women to work for suffrage and social reform. In their first annual report, the group cited Pope Leo XIII's encyclical as evidence that Catholics ought to pursue a social reform agenda.[120] In the United States, Catholic women also began organizing separate suffrage societies designed to reach out to Catholics, persuade them that the church did not oppose women's suffrage, and promote reform while forestalling radicalism. Jane Campbell, who had been involved in the suffrage movement since the late nineteenth century, organized the first separate Catholic organization—the Catholic Woman's Suffrage League—in Philadelphia in 1914, but Catholic suffrage groups were also founded in New York and Boston.

As head of the Catholic Committee of the Woman Suffrage Party of New York, Sara McPike also had extensive experience in the suffrage movement before creating a separate Catholic organization. McPike, whose parents were both born in Ireland, was the executive secretary of the advertising department at General Electric. She participated in the first suffrage parade in New York in 1907, drafted flyers and pamphlets to appeal to Catholics, and held a suffrage meeting at the Catholic Summer School in Cliff Haven, New York.[121] She also desired to create a separate Catholic organization like the one already operating in London, which was described in the American Catholic periodical *Ave Maria* by British suffragist Elizabeth Christitch in 1911.[122] In 1911 McPike joined prominent Catholic women to found the St. Catherine's Welfare Society. The organization recruited members from Catholic organizations and charities such as the Daughters of Isabella and the St. Vincent de Paul Society. The advisory board members were prominent women in New York, including Mrs. William Prendergast, wife of the New York City controller, and the first Mrs. Dudley Field Malone (daughter of US senator James O'Gorman of New York).[123]

Although not founded as a suffrage organization, the St. Catherine Welfare Association endorsed suffrage as a means of improving the position of working women, but McPike was opposed "to feminism and to militancy."[124] According to the *Woman's Journal*, the St. Catherine Welfare Association sought to give Catholic women knowledge of social and economic conditions. "In order to secure the weapons to obtain these much needed reforms," their agenda included "full citizenship for women." McPike and her allies held meetings and invited speakers on reform topics, including suffrage. For example, in 1914, the group sponsored suffrage talks by a Dublin suffragist named Gertrude Mary O'Reilly. O'Reilly gave a spirited defense of Catholic support for suffrage while dressed in the costume of ancient Irish women, which reportedly "lent picturesque-ness and racial interest to the meeting."[125] In 1915 the group announced that owing to the unsatisfactory progress of legislation for shorter hours and better pay for women, it would dedicate its meetings exclusively to suffrage.[126] As Sara McPike explained, "Believing that better conditions can only be secured through legislation, and that all disfranchised persons are at a disadvantage when seeking remedial legislation, the organization has concentrated its activities to date on the votes for women plank."[127]

Although McPike recognized the obstacles to Catholic support for suffrage, the women sought to demonstrate the compatibility of women's suffrage with Catholic teaching. As she confided to Irish American lawyer and politician William Bourke Cockran, "There is determined opposition by members of the hierarchy to woman suffrage. Men voters in the societies of the Holy Name and the Knights of Columbus are opposing the movement because of this."[128] In 1917 McPike led a delegation of twenty-four women, representing several Catholic organizations, to meet with Cardinal James Gibbons of Baltimore, a longtime suffrage opponent. Gibbons reportedly promised to give the subject "earnest consideration."[129] Also signaling a change in Catholic support for suffrage, the Ladies Catholic Benevolent Association sent a telegraph to President Wilson in 1917, declaring that "no harm has come either to religion or to the family through women voting . . . but on the contrary good has been accomplished."[130]

At times the efforts of Catholic suffragists met with opposition from some church leaders. In 1915 the women of St. Catherine's Welfare Association planned to carry votes for women banners with the picture of their patron saint in a New York City suffrage parade. However, members of the clergy reportedly notified them that doing so would be distasteful to representatives of the Catholic Church. The women thus agreed to change the banners to match other suffrage societies, thereby muting their distinctiveness as Catholic women.[131] Catholic suffragists in Philadelphia also encountered resistance when they attempted to address the German Catholic Federation and the American Federation of Catholic Societies and were denied time to present their case.[132] Furthermore, one Catholic women became a center of controversy after losing her job at a parochial school for marching in a suffrage parade. The *New York Times* reported that Aimee Hutchinson became a more ardent suffragist after being dismissed from her teaching position when the parish priest explained that her participation in the parade had set a bad example.[133]

Despite opposition, controversy, and setbacks, the 1917 New York suffrage bill passed. McPike continued to call for reform, describing the mission of the St. Catherine Welfare Association as continuing to "bring home to Catholic women the truth that free government, next to the Christian religion, is the greatest boon the human race has achieved and that suffrage is a sacred obligation." McPike warned Catholic voters that "unless they place themselves on the side of real social reform the Socialist Party, with its sinister doctrine in regard to morality," would gain strength. St. Catherine's offered a course of lectures to new voters to combat the influence of socialist women and outline the responsibilities of home-loving and God-fearing women.[134] Armed with the right to vote and new influence in politics, the reform mission of St. Catherine's developed an antiradicalism stance and ultimately entered party politics.

As one of the first women on the New York State Democratic Committee, McPike quickly moved to bring Catholic women, particularly working women, into the Democratic fold. In a 1918 editorial in the *New York Times*, she warned against feminist and Bolshevist elements she claimed were infiltrating women's organizations to influence the electorate, and she made a plea for women to join the Democratic Party because of its success at enacting progressive legislation and its support of working people. A few months later, she also called for working women to support Al Smith. McPike claimed that no one "who is familiar with the history of the labor movement in this state, and especially of the women's labor movement, will vote against the Democratic candidate for Governor."[135]

While the women of New York won the vote in 1917, the women of Massachusetts would have to wait for the federal amendment, the Nineteenth Amendment, which passed both houses of Congress in 1919 but was not ratified until 1920. Like the women of St. Catherine's, Catholic women in Massachusetts also organized to educate their coreligionists about their civic responsibilities. In a fund-raising letter from 1919, the Margaret Brent Suffrage Guild targeted "public-spirited Catholic[s]," explaining the purpose of the organization as "Americanization . . . teaching the foreign-born man . . . what [American] institutions mean." As a Catholic organization, the Margaret Brent Suffrage Guild sought to organize Catholic women "along civic lines, in order that they may be more completely informed in regard to the various departments of our government" and to prepare them for the vote. The guild believed its growth proved women's great desire for such knowledge and considered itself "the only organization in this State doing work of this kind among Catholic women."[136] The guild was led by Mrs. Frank (Evelyn) Scanlan (about whom very little is known, unfortunately), but the organization employed Margaret Foley to promote the development of the guild in Massachusetts.

As a paid organizer, Margaret Foley continued her suffrage activities with an emphasis on recruiting Catholic suffrage workers. In a letter to Scanlan, Foley reported on her progress in Cambridge. In fifteen days, she enrolled 500 women and gathered 147 names of women to be interviewed, representing homemakers, teachers, and businesswomen. Of those women, she identified 20 "splendid workers."[137] One Cambridge suffragist wrote to Foley, "I am sorry that you were obliged to come to [our] city without knowing any Catholic Suffragist for I am one of those born suffragists . . . and am very happy to offer to you my services for anything I may do for you personally, or for the 'cause.'" The writer also shared some names with Foley to begin organizing efforts in Worcester.[138] By 1923 the *Boston Daily Globe* reported that the guild had "branched out through the entire state" and claimed several thousand members.[139]

In addition to recruiting new volunteers, Foley also traveled to educate Catholic audiences. For example, she received a letter from the Notre Dame Alumnae Association of Peabody, Massachusetts, asking her to speak at their reunion in 1919. The author asked Foley to address between 150 and 200 women (and a few priests), informing her that the suffrage question was very little understood by some of the young women who, though eager to learn, had few opportunities. She also arranged for Foley to arrive early and address "our community of nuns who would be eager to learn something of this vital question." Afterward, the author assured Foley, "You made a real hit in our home city. The girls were awakened by your eloquence. . . . Our nuns bid me thank you a hundred fold. They were like children on Christmas morning so pleased were they with the treat your talk afforded them."[140]

Despite her successes, Foley became frustrated with differences over priorities and strategies. Like the St. Catherine's Welfare Association, the Margaret Brent Suffrage Guild was controlled by middle-class women who sought to uplift the Catholic working class. As the organizer, Foley did not make policy for the organization and found herself in conflict with the executive board. In 1919 she wrote to the board, criticizing its usurpation of her position. Foley had been instructed to "stop all church meetings and give entire attention to organizing the Catholic women along industrial lines." She rejected this policy and resented the board's failure to take her advice seriously. She had "tried in vain to point out the impossibility of gathering together in a separate group the Catholic women leaders of organized labor." The only way to organize Catholics separately, she maintained, was through the church. Closing on a somber note, Foley claimed that the work progressed slowly and that they were not reaching Catholic women, who were "still asking if the church is opposed [to suffrage]."[141]

The Margaret Brent Suffrage Guild represented an attempt to aid Catholic working women while also instilling American values. As suffrage became a reality, the guild changed its name to the Margaret Brent Civic League, vowing to continue its work for the interests of "Christian and constructive standards in the body politic." As guild president, Scanlan saw the organization as an alternative to the League of Women Voters, arguing that Catholic women could not accept some of the positions endorsed by the National League of Women Voters, including loans to Britain and compulsory physical training.[142] One guild meeting in particular suggests that Catholic votes were being courted to respond to the perceived threat of feminism. Speaking at a guild meeting in 1919, Father Jones Corrigan, a professor at Boston College, urged members to avoid the radicalism of some suffrage supporters. He warned of alliances with those individuals who "push their views on easy divorce, economic independence, free love and birth control." Instead, Father Corrigan told Catholic suffragists to use their votes to support moral reforms for the protection of the home, toughen divorce laws, and fight against "illegitimate maternity."[143] The activities of the Margaret Brent Suffrage Guild or

Civic League are consistent with larger trends in Catholic politics after 1920, as Catholic leaders embraced three main strategies: a public relations campaign to highlight the role of Catholics in American life, the fostering of interethnic unity, and a civics campaign to encourage voting and community activism—particularly by women.[144]

Nationalism Again: The Final Wave

For Irish American women in particular, whether working class or middle class, these experiences in politics and social reform culminated not only in the final push for suffrage but also in the final wave of Irish nationalism, which swept the United States in the World War I era. It is not surprising that the Margaret Brent Civic League opposed loans to Britain after the war. Its president, Scanlan, was also an Irish nationalist. As the two movements came to a peak, leaders in both camps sought converts and alliances, just as they had in the nineteenth century. For example, a letter from Edward Quinn, mayor of Cambridge, Massachusetts, to nationalist leader Judge Daniel Cohalan of New York demonstrates that nationalists considered the Catholic women suffragists to be useful allies. In 1920 the Margaret Brent Civic League sent a committee to seek the mayor's help in securing a speaker for their meeting. Quinn wrote to Cohalan, describing the organization as an organization of six to seven hundred women "who are interested in the things that please us." He believed a good address to them would help the nationalist movement.[145]

As we have seen, this relationship between suffragists and nationalists has a long history, as does the relationship between Irish and American suffragists. In her study of the collaboration between the Irish and American suffrage movements, Cliona Murphy writes that although it was "evident in the nineteenth century," these ties were especially "noticeable and of significance in the twentieth century." The Irish suffrage movement, which began in the 1870s, had a decidedly international awareness. As a founder of the Irishwomen's Suffrage Federation (a nonmilitant organization) and general secretary of the Irish Women Workers' Union (beginning in 1917), Irish activist Louie Bennett believed that "the women's movement is a world wide movement; that we suffragists are working for all women and that we recognise the bond of sisterhood uniting women of every nationality."[146] As debates over Home Rule extended into the twentieth century, the relationship between the issues of woman suffrage and Home Rule became more complex.

American women supported John Redmond's drive for Home Rule; however, the question of women's suffrage remained contested. The Irish suffrage movement also gained strength between 1910 and 1914, but the Irish Parliamentary Party made no allowances for the enfranchisement of women under Home Rule because Prime Minister Asquith was antisuffrage, and the IPP also feared upsetting the balance of power in Parliament. As one Irish member of Parliament explained, "Irish nationalist members are sent here primarily to win Home Rule. . . . [I]f we had good reason to believe that the carrying of a women's suffrage amendment would prejudice that cause we should be bound . . . to abstain from supporting . . . such an amendment."[147] The IPP's position angered some Irish and British suffragists. However, the issue also reached across the Atlantic because American fund-raising tours had been an important part of Irish politics since the days of Parnell.

American suffragists showed support for Irish women's suffrage. According to Cliona Murphy, women from the United Irish League of America confronted Redmond; they told him they would not raise funds for him unless he supported women's suffrage. Irish suffragists also publicized the support of American women. In May 1912, during a suffrage parade in New York, organizers also included a demand that suffrage be included in the Home Rule bill.[148] The *Irish Citizen* (published by Hanna Sheehy Skeffington), which published news on the American movement and letters from American suffragists, also covered the significance of this parade, reporting that "an immense demonstration of Americans, numbering 10,000 at least, took place in New York," including a demand that suffrage be included in the Home Rule Bill. The *Irish Citizen* further argued, "We trust the Irish Party will not be blind to the significance of the action of the American women."[149] Furthermore, in July 1914, Louie Bennett wrote to

Margaret Foley, asking for help in the effort to secure suffrage for women under the Home Rule government:

> Mr. Redmond will shortly visit America to try [to] raise funds for the Irish Volunteers, and this seems to me to afford a splendid opportunity for American suffragists to come forward + give a helping hand to the cause in Ireland, by presenting a petition to Mr. Redmond when he comes to America, or *better still*, organizing a deputation to wait on him, in order to urge upon him the necessity for the enfranchisement of Irish women . . . Politically, it would be of the greatest value to us, that the Irish Party should be met with the demand for the inclusion of Irish women under Home Rule on this side of the water as well as at home.[150]

These transatlantic connections are a convincing testimonial to the cooperation between Irish and American suffragists. As previously discussed in chapter 4, the presence of Irish citizens in the United States also became more influential in building relationships across the Atlantic; however, these alliance also carried over into the suffrage movement. When Hanna Sheehy Skeffington, a founder of the Irish Women's Franchise League, toured the United States, the focus of her speeches was on British militarism in Ireland, yet she also brought her commitment to suffrage to her speaking itinerary. In her first public lecture in the United States, she reportedly said of her husband, "He was an ardent suffragist . . . and was wearing a 'Votes for Women' badge when he died."[151] Her husband, Francis Sheehy Skeffington, had toured the United States a year earlier. In his first American speech, hosted by the women of Cumann na mBan, American Auxiliary No. 1, in 1915, Francis Sheehy Skeffington had criticized Redmond's intention to "exclude the women of Ireland from even the small measure of emancipation for Irishmen contained in the Home Rule Bill."[152]

During her stay in the United States, Skeffington worked with the Irish National Bureau in Washington, DC, which was established for the purpose of promoting the Irish cause with the US government and providing a central organization for propaganda. As a militant suffragist herself, it is not surprising that Skeffington would seek suffrage support, and the Irish National Bureau in Washington, DC, did reach out to the leadership of the National Woman's Party. For example, Katherine Hughes, secretary of the Irish National Bureau, wrote to Judge Daniel Cohalan, leader of the Friends of Irish Freedom, "I have met with some of the Women's [*sic*] Party leaders and told them frankly what I think of their apathy + indifference to our movement—and just as they are the kind to run close bargains themselves—I am going to have them line up their wing of the suffrage party (and it always has been the most active wing) to help us if we succeed in moving the Delaware group."[153]

In the battle over the "Susan B. Anthony Amendment," the National Woman's Party needed the votes of three Irish American representatives from Delaware. All three were antisuffrage. Harry Boland (an Irish envoy working in the United States to secure support for the Irish Republic) also wrote to Cohalan of "the advantage to our cause of securing the good opinion of the leaders of the Suffrage movement who can be of great assistance to Ireland in her fight for Recognition." Boland met with the men from Delaware, but they could not be swayed.[154]

Cooperation with the NWP appears to have continued, however. In 1922 John Finerty (president of the American Association for the Recognition of the Irish Republic) received a letter from the NWP headquarters, thanking him for arranging a meeting with Mrs. Muriel MacSwiney. MacSwiney, the widow of Terence MacSwiney, appeared as a witness before the American Commission on Conditions in Ireland, which held hearings in Washington, DC, from November 1920 until January 1921. MacSwiney also returned to the United States in September 1922 to raise money for the Irish Republican Soldiers' and Prisoners' Dependents' Fund, which had just been launched in New York City. The letter also expressed the organization's thanks for Finerty's "constant interest and cooperation," suggesting a more longstanding relationship with the NWP. In reply, Finerty maintained that both he and Muriel MacSwiney "have deeply appreciated the interest and cooperation we have received from the National Woman's Party, and that we will welcome at any time an opportunity to evince our appreciation in a practical manner."[155] A highly visible wing of the suffrage movement, the National Woman's Party appears to have caught the attention of Irish nationalists and cooperated to their mutual interest even after the suffrage amendment was ratified in 1920.

As the exchange between Finerty and the NWP suggests, American suffragists and Irish nationalists courted each other and formed alliances in both the nineteenth and the twentieth centuries. During the heyday of Home Rule, suffragists found the cause appealing, in part because of their common interest in freedom and political representation, but also because Irish American politicians and voters were an important presence in states like New York and Massachusetts. Suffragists praised the work of Irish American women in the nationalist cause, and some Irish American women embraced suffrage. Although many Irish American politicians and publications were still vocal in their condemnation of women's suffrage, a small group of leading nationalist women embraced the cause beginning in the 1880s and 1890s. The question of how women would be incorporated into a new Irish government drew the attention of suffragists on both sides of the Atlantic beginning in the late nineteenth century, but battles in the twentieth century became more intense as the Home Rule movement faded and Ireland drifted toward war. As Irish citizens toured the United States and lobbied in Washington, DC, to gain recognition for the Irish Republic, they found support and made strategic deals with suffragists.

These alliances are one of many contributions made by Irish Americans to the suffrage movement. During the state suffrage campaigns, women of varying class, ethnic, and religious backgrounds played increasingly important roles on the campaign trail, and the intersection between the labor movement and the suffrage movement is particularly important in this time period. Irish American women labor leaders embraced suffrage as part of their vision for reform, and they became powerful voices and effective campaigners as well. Part of bringing suffrage out its slump was the use of militant tactics, some of which were first introduced by Irish American women. And finally, the growth of separate Catholic suffrage groups and strategies also highlights the contribution of Irish American women to the movement. A long view of the suffrage movement shows that Irish American women's involvement in the movement increased in the twentieth century, but also that class, ethnic, and religious identities and priorities were all influential in shaping their participation.

Conclusion

In 1934 Mayor Fiorello La Guardia dedicated a playground to Dr. Gertrude B. Kelly, praising her humanitarian work and describing Kelly (and Jacob Riis) as a leader among the city's welfare workers. La Guardia seized the opportunity to condemn the existence of "suffering and hardship" in America, and he praised the promise of establishing playgrounds for children, but the impetus for naming the playground for Kelly in the middle of the Great Depression (two years after her death) came not from the mayor's office but from the *Irish World*.[1]

Like many Irish American women, Kelly was a committed Irish nationalist, but she was also an activist. Irish nationalism swept the United States in several waves between 1880 and 1921. Each movement encompassed different goals, leadership, and strategies, but women became active in all of them. Portraits of these activities also reveal struggles within an Irish American community attempting to define its identity, disseminate its values, and determine its relationship to American society. Although many Irish American women worked together in nationalist organizations, the activities of these women demonstrate that Irish American women activists differed among themselves in terms of class outlook and also in their attitudes toward participation in the larger context of American social and political reform.

The Ladies' Land League of the early 1880s marked the beginning of this trend. The Land League movement lasted only a few years. However, women's participation marked a watershed for women in public life, inspiring further activism on behalf of the Irish American community. These women shared a commitment to Ireland and to the preservation of Irish American identity. Their activities provoked debates, revealing competing visions of women's service, but women insisted that they could also be patriots. Diaspora nationalism provided opportunities for women to make significant contributions to the Irish American community, fostering ethnic pride, celebrating common identity, and examining the significant political and economic questions of the day.

Nationalism served as one catalyst to public life for Irish American women, who justified their activities in terms of service and patriotism, but the Gilded Age also marked a pinnacle of radical agitation among the Irish American working class. Through the Knights of Labor and the Anti-Poverty Society, workers challenged the excesses of American capitalism and adopted a reform agenda. Both organizations presented new opportunities to women, who again risked criticism for public activism, while taking part in movements for economic justice. Marguerite Moore, Leonora O'Reilly, Gertrude Kelly, and others became outspoken critics of industrial capitalism, while advocating for the rights of women, particularly working women. Their sympathies soon led them beyond the Irish American community and the labor movement to embrace reforms that had the potential to ameliorate the effects of industrialization and protect the most vulnerable.

Of course, one of the most debated reforms embraced by women in the Gilded Age and Progressive Era was women's suffrage. Histories of the suffrage movement rarely mention Irish American women, but there is ample evidence that some women activists in the Irish American community also embraced the suffrage movement. Furthermore, suffragists noticed the role that Irish American women played in the nationalist movement, leading to ethnic appeals and strategic alliances.

Also beginning in the late nineteenth century, women of the Irish American working class began to organize, unionize, and envision political strategies to counter the exploitation of industrial capitalism, leading, by the early twentieth century, to alliances across class lines to win women the vote, to institute protective labor legislation, and for some teachers to demand equal pay for equal work.

Some Irish American women also became active in their communities through ethnic and fraternal organizations. Women fought for the establishment of the Ladies' Auxiliary of the Ancient Order of Hibernians, which the national board of the AOH recognized in 1894. Over the next twenty years, the women's auxiliary established its own treasury, executive board, and a widespread network of organizations, but continued to define the role of women in fairly conservative terms.

The growth of the Ladies' Auxiliary coincided with a second wave of Irish nationalism. After the downfall of Parnell and the defeat of two Home Rule bills, cultural nationalism, the celebration of Gaelic tradition and tongue, helped revive the movement in Ireland. In the United States, the Gaelic Revival embraced Irish history, athletics, literature, and language. However, the movement also became manifested in attempts to improve the reputation of the Irish American community, and women played an important role in these campaigns. Despite the prevalence of rhetoric celebrating Catholic women's devotion to the home, they adopted a public agenda, developing an organized defense of the Irish American community. These women advanced a moderate and respectable portrait of the Irish American community, defining their roles in terms of service to faith and family, while proclaiming their loyalty to America.

Whether women came to their activism through the developing web of Irish and Catholic organizations or through the labor movement and ties to middle-class reformers, most of the women in this study embraced Irish nationalism in its various waves and strategies. The Irish in America generally supported the Home Rule movement until 1914, when events in Ireland took center stage. Optimism about the coming of Home Rule shattered with the outbreak of World War I. When John Redmond pledged the support of the Irish Volunteers to the British war effort, many Irish American nationalists balked. Increasing violence between 1916 and 1921 inspired more widespread support and sympathy for Ireland, but America's alliance with Britain complicated the position of Irish nationalists during the war.

The final phase of Irish nationalism in the United States was significant for Irish American women for several reasons. Unlike in previous waves of Irish nationalism where the focus remained primarily on Irish land policy or British parliamentary politics, during the World War I era nationalists in the United States turned their attention to influencing American policy, first to keep the United States out of the war and then to get Ireland representation at the peace conference and to secure recognition of the Irish Republic. As Irish Americans sought to flex their political muscle, women, who were becoming more integrated into politics as the suffrage movement intensified in the late teens, also joined the effort. Furthermore, as the leader of the LAAOH, Mary McWhorter became the spokesperson for Irish American motherhood. McWhorter and other nationalists intended to hold President Wilson to his war rhetoric, demanding self-determination for Ireland.

Like the alliances of the Land League era, the nationalist movement of the World War I era brought together a variety of organizations and opinions, although factionalism eventually split the movement in 1920. Furthermore, while the agitation of the Irish American working class had been an important part of the Land League, moderates dominated the nationalist movement during the push for Home Rule. Beginning with the founding of the Irish Progressive League during World War I, the Irish American Left reclaimed a visible position in the nationalist struggle. Irish American women combined their commitment to the causes of labor and Irish nationalism by promoting a boycott strategy. The movement to buy American goods was intended to benefit American labor while also crippling British industry, pitting the power of the American consumer against British imperialism.

By 1920 Irish American women activists had, like their native-born Protestant counterparts, developed a place for themselves in public debates and movements, accepting a role for women in politics. However, differences within the Irish American community led to different agendas and strategies. Some Irish American women had adopted a conservative construction of womanhood, organizing in defense of the Irish American community and the Catholic Church, while preferring to remain separated into Catholic organizations, while others had embraced Progressive Era reforms and attempted to navigate new opportunities for cross-class alliances.

Irish American women played a central role in the development and defense of Irish American identity between 1880 and 1920, although they did not articulate a unified vision of what it meant to be Irish in America. However, by the early 1920s, women found their political influence waning. The defeats to organized labor in the post–World War I era, the decline of Progressive Era reform, and the end of the suffrage movement quieted the voices of working women, while the LAAOH appears to have turned its attention to social issues such as opposing divorce, birth control, and the flapper.

The 1920s also brought many changes for the Irish America community as a whole. Irish nationalism declined as battles erupted between American nationalist leaders and Eamon de Valera's policies as leader of the Irish Republic, leading to a split in the movement. The settlement of the Anglo-Irish War in 1921 seemed to signal an end to the struggle, but when debates over the treaty that created the Irish Free State led to civil war between the Free State and republican forces in 1922, many Irish Americans became disillusioned.[2] Immigration restriction in the United States, and a shift in Irish immigration patterns, also reduced the number of first-generation Irish immigrants and led to the decline in the Ancient Order of Hibernians.

Priorities within the Irish American community had changed. In his study of the Irish in Worcester, Massachusetts, Timothy Meagher describes the Irish American community by the 1920s as leading the effort to forge a new group identity, one that was "militantly, oppositionally, Catholic and patriotically American."[3] By the 1920s, the era of women's activism was subsiding, yet lay Catholic women found a new national voice through the creation of the National Council of Catholic Women. Between 1880 and 1920, Irish American women, many of whom were Catholic, found their voices through ethnic and nationalist organizations. They insisted on coming to the defense of Ireland but also organized to support an Irish American community still struggling for acceptance. However, the booming industrial economy in America, and the land question in Ireland, also led some women to embrace reform efforts centered on the needs of the working class, in which Irish Americans were still heavily clustered. Working women had unique needs but also made significant contributions not only to the Irish nationalist movement but to the labor and suffrage movements as well.

Notes

Bibliography

Index

Notes

Introduction

1. "Irish Women's Council," *Irish World*, 23 Dec. 1916, 2; "Mrs. Moore Delivers Eulogy at Grave of Mrs. O'Donovan Rossa," *Irish World*, 26 Aug. 1916, 3; "Great Irish Meeting in Massachusetts," *Irish World*, 21 July 1917, 7.

2. Janet Nolan, "Women's Place in the History of the Irish Diaspora: A Snapshot," 78.

3. There were a few exceptions. Joe Doyle examined women's contributions to the final phase of Irish nationalism in his chapter "Striking for Ireland on the New York Docks," in *The New York Irish*, edited by Ronald Bayor and Timothy Meagher. For discussions of local Ladies' Land League activities, see also David Brundage, *The Making of Western Labor Radicalism: Denver's Organized Workers, 1878–1905*; and Timothy Meagher, *Inventing Irish America: Generation, Class, and Ethnic Identity in a New England City, 1880–1928*.

4. Thomas Brown, *Irish-American Nationalism, 1870–1890*, 23.

5. For more recent discussions of women in Irish nationalist organizations, see Mary C. Kelly, *The Shamrock and the Lily: The New York Irish and the Creation of a Transatlantic Identity, 1845–1921*; Ely Janis, *A Greater Ireland: The Land League and Transatlantic Nationalism in Gilded Age America*; and Catherine M. Burns, "Kathleen O'Brennan and American Identity in the Transatlantic Irish Republican Movement," in *The Irish in the Atlantic World*, edited by David Gleeson.

6. Fanny Parnell, "Ladies' Land League: A Permanent Organization to Be in New York City," *Irish World*, 25 Sept. 1880.

7. T. Brown, *Irish-American Nationalism*, 23.

8. Matthew Frye Jacobson, *Special Sorrows: The Diasporic Imagination of Irish, Polish, and Jewish Immigrants in the United States*, 20; Eric Foner, "Class, Ethnicity, and Radicalism in the Gilded Age: The Land League & Irish America," 6; Kelly, *Shamrock and the Lily*, 4.

9. Kelly, *Shamrock and the Lily*, 4.

10. Hasia Diner, *Erin's Daughters in America: Irish Immigrant Women in the Nineteenth Century*, xiv, 140; Margaret Lynch-Brennan, *The Irish Bridget*, 37, 92. Lynch-Brennan's study of first-generation Irish domestics included a chapter on the social activities of domestic servants, but except for a brief reference to their financial contributions to Fenianism, she does not mention nationalism.

11. Diane M. Hotten-Somers, "Relinquishing and Reclaiming Independence: Irish Domestic Servants, American Middle-Class Mistresses, and Assimilation, 1850–1920," in *New Directions in Irish-American History*, edited by Kevin Kenny, 228–29; Lynch-Brennan, *The Irish Bridget*, 82, 153.

12. Kelly, *Shamrock and the Lily*, 71.

13. Deirdre M. Moloney, *American Catholic Lay Groups and Transatlantic Social Reform in the Progressive Era*, 5, 204. Catholic women entered the world of social reform in the Progressive Era, although their experiences in Catholic temperance groups and settlement houses differed from those of Protestant women.

14. Paula Kane, *Separatism and Subculture: Boston Catholicism, 1900–1920*, 57, 1; Maureen Fitzgerald, *Habits of Compassion: Irish Catholic Nuns and the Origins of New York's Welfare System, 1830–1920*. Other examples include Suellen Hoy, "The Journey Out: The Recruitment and Emigration of Irish Religious Women to the United States"; Dorothy Brown and Elizabeth McKeown, *The Poor Belong to Us: Catholic Charities and American Welfare*; and Carol Coburn and Martha Smith, *Spirited Lives: How Nuns Shaped Catholic Culture and American Life, 1836–1920*. Coburn and Smith focus on the Sister of St. Joseph, a French order that included several ethnic groups, including the Irish. They argue that the Sister of St. Joseph had a dramatic impact on the lives of immigrants and native-born Americans through the establishment and maintenance of schools, hospitals, and other social services. Furthermore, they argue for the agency of women religious who battled a sometimes hostile American climate, advocated for their institutions with the members of the Catholic hierarchy, and sometimes defied secular and religious authority.

15. Kathleen Sprows Cummings, *New Women of the Old Faith: Gender and American Catholicism in the Progressive Era*, 11.

16. Moloney, *American Catholic Lay Groups*, 168–69.

17. David Montgomery, "The Irish and the American Labor Movement," in *America and Ireland, 1776–1976: The American Identity and the Irish Connection*, edited by David Noel Doyle and Owen Dudley Edwards, 216.

18. Janet Nolan, *Servants of the Poor: Teachers and Mobility in Ireland and Irish America*, 107.

19. E. Foner, "Class, Ethnicity, and Radicalism," 6.

20. Kane, *Separatism and Subculture*, 3, 63.

21. Meagher, *Inventing Irish America*, 13.

22. Moloney, *American Catholic Lay Groups*, 5, 204.

1. Life in the Irish American Community

1. Suellen Hoy and Margaret MacCurtain, eds., *From Dublin to New Orleans: Nora and Alice's Journey to America, 1889*, 97.

2. Kenny, *New Directions*, 14, 187.

3. Malcolm Campbell, *Ireland's New Worlds: Immigrants, Politics, and Society in the United States and Australia, 1815–1922*, 133; Kenny, *New Directions*, 14.

4. Hoy, "Journey Out," 65.

5. Diner, *Erin's Daughters in America*, 5–6.

6. "The Great Famine," in *The Encyclopedia of the Irish in America*, edited by Michael Glazier, 297; Diner, *Erin's Daughters in America*, 2.

7. Kenny, *New Directions*, 14; Tyler Anbinder and Hope McCaffrey, "Which Irish Men and Women Immigrated to the United States during the Great Famine Migration of 1846–54," 620.

8. Diner, *Erin's Daughters in America*, 5, 15.

9. Lynch-Brennan, *The Irish Bridget*, 25, 39.

10. Nolan, *Servants of the Poor*, 2.

11. Diner, *Erin's Daughters in America*, 71; Bernadette Whelan, "Women on the Move: A Review of the Historiography of Irish Emigration to the USA, 1750–1900," 907.

12. Lara Vapnek, *Breadwinners: Working Women and Economic Independence, 1865–1920*, 14, 16, 54.

13. Lynch-Brennan, *The Irish Bridget*, 84–85.

14. Patricia Kelleher, "Young Irish Workers: Class Implication of Men's and Women's Experiences in Gilded Age Chicago," in *New Directions*, edited by Kenny, 195–96.

15. "No Cold Day in Irish Wit," *Sunday Inter Ocean*, 26 Oct. 1890, 6.

16. "Did as She Was Told," *Washington Post*, 12 July 1902, 6.

17. David Montgomery, "The Irish and the American Labor Movement," in *America and Ireland*, edited by Doyle and Edwards, 207; David N. Doyle, "Unestablished Irishmen: New Immigrants and Industrial America, 1870–1910," in *American Labor and Immigration History, 1877–1920s: Recent European Research*, edited by Dirk Hoerder, 193.

18. Diner, *Erin's Daughters in America*, 99.

19. Vapnek, *Breadwinners*, 34, 131.

20. Diner, *Erin's Daughters in America*, 74–75, 77.

21. Timothy Meagher, *The Columbia Guide to Irish American History*, 95, 103; Diner, *Erin's Daughters in America*, 95.

22. Meagher, *Columbia Guide*, 104; Nolan, *Servants of the Poor*, 2.

23. Nolan, *Servants of the Poor*, 107; Diner, *Erin's Daughters in America*, 140.

24. Nolan, *Servants of the Poor*, 3–4.

25. Moloney, *American Catholic Lay Groups*, 1, 5. Paula Kane also identifies this period as an era of identity formation that "often merged ethnicity with religious identification." Kane, *Separatism and Subculture*, 63.

26. Penny Edgell Becker, "'Rational Amusement and Sound Instruction': Constructing the True Catholic Woman in the *Ave Maria*, 1865–1889," 60; Samuel Thomas, "Catholic Journalists and the Ideal Woman in Late Victorian America," 89.

27. Colleen McDannell, *The Christian Home in Victorian America, 1840–1900*, 74.

28. Moloney, *American Catholic Lay Groups*, 168–69.

29. Cummings, *New Women of the Old Faith*, 5.

30. "The New Woman," *Citizen*, 19 Jan. 1895, 1 (reprinted from the *New York World*); John Paul MacCorrie, "The War of the Sexes," *Catholic World* 63 (1896): 605–6 (emphasis added).

31. Mary J. Oates, *The Catholic Philanthropic Tradition in America*, 45.

32. Fitzgerald, *Habits of Compassion*, 57, 3. See also D. Brown and McKeown, *Poor Belong to Us*.

33. Oates, *Catholic Philanthropic Tradition*, 81; Moloney, *American Catholic Lay Groups*, 139.

34. John O'Grady, *Catholic Charities in the United States*, 319, 327; Leslie Woodcock Tentler, *Seasons of Grace: A History of the Catholic Archdioceses of Detroit*, 213.

35. Oates, *Catholic Philanthropic Tradition*, 55.

36. Jay P. Dolan, *The American Catholic Experience: A History from Colonial Times to the Present*, 205; O'Grady, *Catholic Charities*, 327; Mary V. Toomy, "The Work and Aims of the Queen's Daughters," *Catholic World* 67 (1898): 611.

37. "Catholic Women in Session: A Brilliant Gathering of Scholarly Catholic Ladies at the Columbian Exposition," *Irish World*, 3 June 1893, 1; Alice Timmons Toomy, "There Is a Public Sphere for Catholic Women," in "The Woman Question among Catholics: A Roundtable Conference," special issue, *Catholic World* 57 (1893): 675. Catholic women did join the Catholic Total Abstinence Union by the 1890s, but men dominated the movement. Moloney, *American Catholic Lay Groups*, 44, 62.

38. "Catholic Woman's National League of Chicago Issues Call for Convention," *Irish World*, 15 Mar. 1901, 7; Debra Campbell, "Reformers and Activists," in *American Catholic Women: A Historical Exploration*, edited by Karen Kennelly, 173–74.

39. Dale B. Light Jr., "The Role of Irish-American Organizations in Assimilation and Community Formation," in *Irish in America: Emigration, Assimilation and Impact*, edited by P. J. Drury, 114, 129; Kevin Kenny, *The American Irish: A History*, 148.

40. John Ridge, "Irish County Societies in New York, 1880–1914," in *The New York Irish*, edited by Bayor and Meagher, 294.

41. Michael F. Funchion, ed., *Irish American Voluntary Organizations*, 50–51, 57; Ridge, "Irish County Societies," in *The New York Irish*, edited by Bayor

and Meagher, 278; John Ridge, "Ancient Order of Hibernians," in *Encyclopedia of the Irish*, edited by Glazier, 27. Membership among the men peaked in 1908 with 132,000.

42. Ridge, "Ancient Order of Hibernians," in *Encyclopedia of the Irish*, edited by Glazier, 27; John Ridge, *History of the Ancient Order of Hibernians and Ladies' Auxiliary of Brooklyn*; Kerby Miller, *Emigrants and Exiles: Ireland and the Irish Exodus to North America*, 534.

43. Jo Ann Manfra and Robert Kolesar, "Irishmen, Elites, and Reformers," 27.

44. Rodger Streitmatter, "The Nativist Press: Demonizing the American Immigrant," 673, 679.

45. Mary B. Dolan, "The Ladies Ancient Order of Hibernians" (unpublished manuscript compiled by Dolan while she served as national historian of the Ladies' Ancient Order of Hibernians, 1994); "Society News," *Scranton (PA) Republican*, 5 Jan. 1921, 11.

46. *Irish World*, 22 Aug. 1914, 8; 29 June 1918, 8; "Ellen Ryan Jolly Honored," *Irish World*, 19 Feb. 1921, 3; "Sketch of Ellen Ryan Jolly," *National Hibernian*, 15 Aug. 1912, 3; John Jolly, 1920 Census, series T625, roll 1675, p. 201, heritagequest online.com.

47. *Chicago Citizen*, 13 July 1912; "Sketches and Portraits of Those Now in Office," *National Hibernian*, July 1916, 10–11; William H. McWhorter, 1920 Census, series T625, roll 310, p. 85, heritagequestonline.com. According to Ancestry.com, McWhorter immigrated in 1900, but this date conflicts with newspaper accounts.

48. Georgina Pell Curtis, *The American Catholic Who's Who*, 293; "Tribute to Miss Holloway," *National Hibernian*, 15 Dec. 1913; Charlotte M. Holloway, 1930 Census, series T626, roll 282, p. 74, heritagequestonline.com. In 1930, at age fifty-nine, Holloway remained single.

49. Taryn Benbow Pfalzgraf, ed., *A Critical Reference Guide from Colonial Times to the Present*, 219; "Auxiliary Board Meeting," *National Hibernian*, 15 Mar. 1911, 3.

50. Janet Nolan, "Irish-American Teachers and the Struggle over American Urban Public Education, 1890–1920: A Preliminary Look," 13, 18.

51. *Proceedings of the 39th National Convention of the Ancient Order of Hibernians* (1894), 81–82; John O'Dea, *History of the Ancient Order of Hibernians in America and Ladies' Auxiliary*, 3:1112; "Hibernians Denounce the A.P.A.," *Washington Post*, 18 July 1896, 1.

52. O'Dea, *History of the Ancient Order of Hibernians*, 3:1123.

53. *National Hibernian*, 15 May 1905, 8; 15 Sept. 1905, 7. The *National Hibernian* began monthly publication in 1901.

54. "Ancient Hibernians," *Knoxville Journal*, 16 July 1896, 8; "Fair Hibernians: An Interesting Reunion and Banquet of the Ladies' Auxiliary," *Citizen*, 12 Dec. 1896, 1.

55. Mary McWhorter, "The Ladies' Auxiliary of the Ancient Order of Hibernians: The Largest Irish Women's Organization in the World," *New World*, 23 Dec. 1905, 17.

56. *Proceedings: Ancient Order of Hibernians 46th National Convention, 1908*, 59, books.google.com.

57. *National Hibernian*, 15 June 1904, 6; Mary McWhorter, "The Ladies' Auxiliary," *New World*, 23 Dec. 1905, 17; "Great Assembly of Ladies' Auxiliary," *Gaelic American*, 18 Aug. 1906, 1.

58. *National Hibernian*, 15 Oct. 1906, 7; 15 Nov. 1906, 1.

59. *National Hibernian*, May 1901, 6; 15 Nov. 1907, 6; 15 Sept. 1907, 2.

60. J. Dolan, *American Catholic Experience*, 329; "The Pope's Encyclical," *Irish World*, 3 Jan. 1891, 5; Morgan M. Sheedy, "The Encyclical and American Iron-Workers and Coal-Miners," *Catholic World* 53 (1891): 853, 860.

61. J. Dolan, *American Catholic Experience*, 329, 335.

2. Radicals and Reformers

1. Leonora O'Reilly to Annie W. W. Allen, May 22, 1898, Leonora O'Reilly Papers, reel 1. Edward Bellamy published *Looking Backward* in 1888.

2. Meagher, *Columbia Guide to Irish American History*, 101.

3. E. Foner, "Class, Ethnicity, and Radicalism," 7–8; Meagher, *Columbia Guide*, 103; Kelleher, "Young Irish Workers," in *New Directions*, edited by Kenny, 188–89, 198–99.

4. Montgomery, "Irish and the American Labor Movement," in *America and Ireland*, edited by Doyle and Edwards, 207; Doyle, "Unestablished Irishmen," in *American Labor and Immigration History*, edited by Hoerder, 193.

5. Diner, *Erin's Daughters in America*, 99.

6. Rebecca Edwards, *New Spirits: Americans in the Gilded Age, 1865–1905*, 6.

7. For a study of Catholic social reform, see Moloney, *American Catholic Lay Groups*.

8. Vapnek, *Breadwinners*, 2, 10, 66–67.

9. Susan Levine, "Labor's True Woman: Domesticity and Equal Rights in the Knights of Labor," 324.

10. Kim Voss, *The Making of American Exceptionalism: The Knights of Labor and Class Formation in the Nineteenth Century*, 2.

11. E. Foner, "Class, Ethnicity, and Radicalism," 45.

12. Philip Foner, *Women and the American Labor Movement: From Colonial Times to the Eve of World War I*, 191; Susan Levine, *Labor's True Woman: Carpet Weavers, Industrialization, and Labor Reform in the Gilded Age*, 10, 101; Mary Blewett, *Men, Women, and Work: Class, Gender, and Protest in the New England Shoe Industry, 1780–1910*, 222.

13. Levine, *Labor's True Woman*, 32, 32, 107.

14. Ibid., 104.

15. "Female Labor Leader," *Irish World*, 18 Dec. 1886, 3; P. Foner, *Women and the American Labor Movement*, 188, 197; Levine, *Labor's True Woman*, 125. Rodgers went on to found the Women's Catholic Order of Foresters in 1892.

16. Brooke Speer Orr, "Mary Elizabeth Lease: Nineteenth-Century Populist and Twentieth-Century Progressive," 15, 36–37.

17. Blewett, *Men, Women, and Work*, 247–48.

18. Eleanor Flexner, "Leonora Barry," in *Notable American Women*, 102.

19. Vapnek, *Breadwinners*, 43–44; Levine, *Labor's True Woman*, 111.

20. Meagher, *Columbia Guide*, 110.

21. James Hennesey, *American Catholics: A History of the Roman Catholic Community in the United States*, 188; John T. McGreevy, *Catholicism and American Freedom*, 132.

22. Quoted in P. Foner, *Women and the American Labor Movement*, 200. The Knights abolished the women's department in 1890 when Barry stepped down, but by then the organization was rapidly declining and some of the most militant women had left.

23. Levine, "Labor's True Woman," 334.

24. "Mrs. Barry's Lecture," *New Orleans Daily Picayune*, 21 Nov. 1887, 2.

25. "Mrs. Leonora M. Barry," *New Orleans Daily Picayune*, 21 Feb. 1889, 6.

26. Vapnek, *Breadwinners*, 48; Kathryn Kish Sklar, *Florence Kelley and the Nation's Work*, 141.

27. R. Edwards, *New Spirits*, 6.

28. Vapnek, *Breadwinners*, 68–69.

29. Ibid., 70.

30. Ibid., 71.

31. Ellen Condliffe Lagemann, *A Generation of Women: Education in the Lives of Progressive Reformers*, 95; Meredith Tax, *Rising of the Women*, 98.

32. Vapnek, *Breadwinners*, 73.

33. Ibid., 94.

34. Annual report of the Social Reform Club, 1898, Annie Ware Winsor Allen Papers, Schlesinger Library, box 38. The 1898 report stated that wage earners made up not more than one-third of the membership, although the goal was one-half. Margaret Finn was also listed as a member. O'Reilly to Annie Winsor [Allen], Nov. 1896, in O'Reilly Papers, reel 1.

35. David Montgomery, "Workers' Movements in the United States Confront Imperialism: The Progressive Era Experience," 14; P. Foner, *Women and the American Labor Movement*, 294.

36. Victoria Bissell Brown, ed., *Twenty Years at Hull-House*, 19.

37. Gladys Boone, *The Women's Trade Union Leagues in Great Britain and the United States of America*, 58; Suellen Hoy, "The Irish Girls Rising," 77, 83.

38. Tax, *Rising of the Women*, 93; P. Foner, *Women and the American Labor Movement*, 294, 298, 300.

39. Eleanor Flexner and Janet Wilson James, "Mary Kenney O'Sullivan," in *Notable American Women*, 655.

40. "Mary Kenney O'Sullivan," in *Encyclopedia of the Irish*, edited by Glazier, 756; Allison M. Martens, "Working Women or Women Workers? The Woman's Trade Union League and the Transformation of the American Constitutional Order," 148.

41. Kathleen Banks Nutter, "'The Necessity of Organization': Mary Kenney O'Sullivan, the American Federation of Labor, and the Boston Women's Trade Union League, 1892–1919," 127, 135. Kenney's association with Leonora O'Reilly began in the 1890s. Flexner and James, "Mary Kenney O'Sullivan," in *Notable American Women*, 655–66; Louise Perkins to O'Reilly, 9 June 1894 [?], O'Reilly Papers, reel 4, frames 149–53.

42. Martens, "Working Women or Women Workers?," 149.

43. Margaret Dreier Robins to O'Reilly, 19 July 1914, O'Reilly Papers, reel 7, frames 122–31.

44. Martens, "Working Women or Women Workers?," 157.

45. Vapnek, *Breadwinners*, 46.

46. "Mrs. Barry on Child Labor," *Irish World*, 2 June 1888, 7.

47. Sklar, *Florence Kelley*, 141.

48. Tax, *Rising of the Women*, 99.

49. Margaret Finn to O'Reilly, 9 July 1912, O'Reilly Papers, reel 1, frames 340–43.

50. Sklar, *Florence Kelley*, 142.

51. Martens, "Working Women or Women Workers?," 157.

52. Nancy Woloch, *"Muller v. Oregon": A Brief History with Documents*, 6.

53. Sklar, *Florence Kelley*, 37–38, 46, 86.

54. Ibid., 235.

55. Woloch, *"Muller v. Oregon,"* 3, 8.

56. https://usa.usembassy.de/etexts/democrac/30.htm.

57. Clarke A. Chambers, "Agnes Nestor," in *Notable American Women*, 615; Suellen Hoy, "Chicago Working Women's Struggle for a Shorter Day, 1908–1911," 16.

58. Zelda Ermine Stewart, "Girls in Glove Factory Have Hard Work," *Chicago Daily Tribune*, 21 Jan. 1906, E2.

59. "Clubdom Extends Hand to Toilers," *Chicago Daily Tribune*, 21 Oct. 1905, 3; "Aids Girl Toilers," *Chicago Daily Tribune*, 22 Oct. 1905, 3; "Agnes Nestor, Leader and Educator," *Christian Science Monitor*, 19 May 1925, 8.

60. Agnes Nestor, *Woman's Labor Leader: An Autobiography of Agnes Nestor*, 64; "Four Girl Lobbyists Who Ran a Legislature," *Chicago Daily Tribune*, 25 July 1909, G6.

61. Hoy, "Chicago Working Women's Struggle," 13, 19.

62. Ibid., 32.

63. Nolan, *Servants of the Poor*, 3.

64. Kate Rousmaniere, *Citizen Teacher: The Life and Leadership of Margaret Haley*, 27; Marjorie Murphy, *Blackboard Unions: The AFT and the NEA, 1900–1980*, 38.

65. Meagher, *Columbia Guide*, 104; Nolan, *Servants of the Poor*, 2.

66. Marjorie Murphy, *Blackboard Unions*, 4, 50.

67. Karen Leroux, "'Lady Teachers' and the Genteel Roots of Teacher Organization in Gilded Age Cities," 179.

68. Karen Leroux, "'Unpensioned Veterans': Women Teachers and the Politics of Public Service in the Late-Nineteenth-Century United States," 35, 40.

69. Linda Van Ingen, "'One Can't Live on Air': Sarah McComb and the Problem of Old-Age Income for Single Women Teachers, 1870s–1930s," 173–74.

70. Leroux, "'Unpensioned Veterans,'" 36; David Farbman, "Developing an Esprit de Corps," 44.

71. "Catherine Goggin Killed by an Auto," *Chicago Daily Tribune*, 5 Jan. 1916, 1.

72. Rousmaniere, *Citizen Teacher*, 45–47; "Catherine Goggin Killed by an Auto," 1.

73. "Irishwomen of Chicago Form a Club," *Chicago Daily Tribune*, 27 Feb. 1898, 26.

74. Robert Reid, ed., *Battleground: The Autobiography of Margaret A. Haley*, 33.

75. Leroux, "'Unpensioned Veterans,'" 49–51.

76. Rousmaniere, *Citizen Teacher*, 54; Marjorie Murphy, *Blackboard Unions*, 63.

77. Reid, *Battleground*, 14; Rousmaniere, *Citizen Teacher*, 12, 14.

78. Rousmaniere, *Citizen Teacher*, 17; Louise Wade, "Margaret Haley," in *Notable American Women*, 115.

79. Reid, *Battleground*, 43.

80. David John Hogan, *Class and Reform: School and Society in Chicago, 1880–1930*, 203; Rousmaniere, *Citizen Teacher*, 61.

81. Marjorie Murphy, *Blackboard Unions*, 64.

82. "Gives Race to Jordan," *Washington Post*, 8 July 1914, 4.

83. Marjorie Murphy, *Blackboard Unions*, 65–67.

84. "Tells Teachers to Join Union," *Detroit Free Press*, 11 Oct. 1908, 11. Goggin gave this speech at the Women's Catholic Order of Foresters convention.

85. Marjorie Murphy, *Blackboard Unions*, 81.

86. Hogan, *Class and Reform*, 210, 211; Rousmaniere, *Citizen Teacher*, 175–76.

87. Patricia A. Carter, *"Everybody's Paid but the Teacher": The Teaching Profession and the Women's Movement*, 10, 21.

88. "City's Women Teachers Demand the Pay of Men," *New York Times*, 8 Apr. 1906, 22. I have not been able to locate Kate Hogan in the US Census. However,

given the number of Kate Hogans that are listed as Irish, it is quite likely that she was Irish American.

89. Kate E. Hogan graduated from New York University School of Law in 1894. *Women Lawyer's Journal* 3, no. 4 (1914): 27; *Albany Law Journal* 48 (Oct. 1893): 338; "Women Teachers Want Equal Pay with Men," *New York Times*, 30 Sept. 1906, 9.

90. Grace C. Strachan, Brooklyn Ward 24, Kings, NY, 1910 US Census, Heritage Quest; "Catholics in Schools," *Life*, 18 Nov. 1915, 952.

91. Carter, *Everybody's Paid but the Teacher*, 91–92.

92. Marjorie Murphy, *Blackboard Unions*, 74; Robert Doherty, "Tempest on the Hudson: The Struggle for 'Equal Pay for Equal Work' in New York City Public Schools, 1907–1911," 414.

93. Doherty, "Tempest on the Hudson," 418, 430.

94. Marjorie Murphy, *Blackboard Unions*, 65; Nolan, *Servants of the Poor*, 69.

95. "Teachers Federation President Is Cited for 'Lese Majeste,'" *San Francisco Call*, 17 Apr. 1907, 3; "Board of Education Will Try Dr. Mahoney," *San Francisco Call*, 18 Apr. 1907, 16.

96. Nolan, *Servants of the Poor*, 69; "Woman Wants School Named for Teacher," *San Francisco Call*, 24 Feb. 1911, 11.

97. John R. McKivigan and Thomas Robertson, "The Irish American Worker in Transition, 1877–1914: New York City as a Test Case," in *The New York Irish*, edited by Bayor and Meagher, 301, 315.

98. Ellen Carol DuBois, *Harriot Stanton Blatch and the Winning of Woman Suffrage*, 140–41. Because the parade was scheduled for a Saturday afternoon, Jewish women would not be able to participate. As a compromise, Blatch agreed to begin the parade an hour later. Blatch to O'Reilly, 23 Dec. 1911, O'Reilly Papers, reel 5, frames 1028–30; O'Reilly to Blatch, 28 Dec. 1911, O'Reilly Papers, reel 5, frame 1047.

99. Gertrude Kelly's obituary in the *New York Times* lists 1873 as the date the family came from Ireland. However, the obituary of her brother, John F. Kelly, gives the date as 1868. His obituary also records the date that their father, Jeremiah Kelly, became principal of a public school in New Jersey as 1872. "Death of John F. Kelly, Ph.D.," *Irish World*, 21 Oct. 1922, 12.

100. "Dr. Gertrude B. Kelly, Pioneer Woman Surgeon, Passes to Her Reward," *Gaelic American*, 3 Mar. 1934, 5; "Dr. Gertrude Kelly, Irish Patriot, Dies," *Irish World*, 24 Feb. 1934, 1. Kelly's obituary lists her mother as a teacher and labor advocate, but no other details are available. While there is no evidence that Gertrude Kelly participated in the Land League, her family did. Kelly's father, Jeremiah Kelly, served as president of the Jersey City Land League, reportedly one of the most radical branches. Although a description of one meeting mentions the presence of Jeremiah

Kelly, as well as Mrs. Kelly and the Misses Kelly, it is unclear who these women were. John F. Kelly (her brother) and Mrs. John Kelly of Hoboken also appeared at Land League meetings. Furthermore, her mother was described as a close associate of Fanny Parnell and Ellen Ford in the obituary of John F. Kelly. Even if Gertrude B. Kelly was not an active member of the Land League, she would certainly have been well aware of its activities. "Demonstration in Jersey City," *Irish World*, 25 Dec. 1880, 5; "Jersey City—Ladies' Land League," *Irish World*, 30 July 1881, 5; "New Jersey Demand," *Irish World*, 19 Mar. 1881, 5; "Death of John F. Kelly, Ph.D.," 12.

101. Frank H. Brooks, ed., *The Individualist Anarchists: An Anthology of Liberty (1881–1908)*, 3. For a discussion of Kelly as a feminist anarchist, see Wendy McElroy, *Individualist Feminism of the Nineteenth Century.*

102. *New York Evening Post*, 8 Feb. 1889, O'Reilly Papers, reel 9, frame 2.

103. O'Reilly to Frank Walsh, 29 July 1920, Frank P. Walsh Papers, New York Public Library, box 28.

104. O'Reilly diary, 2 Jan., 14 Jan., 10 Feb. 1906, O'Reilly Papers, reel 1.

105. Gertrude B. Kelly, "'Culture' and Thought," *Liberty*, 12 Dec. 1885, 7.

106. Gertrude B. Kelly, "'Philanthropic Ladies Providing Vacations for Hard-Working Young Women,'" *Liberty*, 17 Apr. 1886, 7; Gertrude B. Kelly, "Bourgeois Charity," *Alarm*, 19 Nov. 1887; Gertrude B. Kelly, "A Woman's Warning to Reformers," *Liberty*, 23 Jan. 1886, 7.

107. G. Kelly, "Woman's Warning to Reformers," 7.

108. Gertrude B. Kelly, "Anarchy No Disease," *Alarm*, 31 Dec. 1887; Gertrude B. Kelly, "The New Abolition: The Ever-Present Struggle between Truth and Falsehood Renders Every Age Heroic," *Alarm*, 5 Nov. 1887.

109. D. George Boyce, *Nationalism in Ireland*, 300–301.

110. Carl Reeve and Ann Barton Reeve, *James Connolly and the United States: The Road to the 1916 Irish Rebellion*, 160.

111. Ibid., 81, 84–86.

112. Lara Vapnek, *Elizabeth Gurley Flynn: Modern American Revolutionary*, 13–15; Elizabeth Gurley Flynn, *The Rebel Girl: An Autobiography*, 58.

113. Flynn, *Rebel Girl*, 74–76.

114. Reeve and Reeve, *Connolly and the United States*, 183.

115. Vapnek, *Elizabeth Gurley Flynn*, 24; Flynn, *Rebel Girl*, 62.

116. Anne F. Mattina, "'Yours for Industrial Freedom': Women of the IWW, 1905–1930," 170.

117. "Persons in the Foreground: The Indomitable Spirit of Mother Jones," 6; Flynn, *Rebel Girl*, 88.

118. Meagher, *Columbia Guide*, 271.

119. "Persons in the Foreground," 7.

3. Charitable Colleens or Voracious Viragoes?

1. "Necessity for Present Action," *Boston Daily Globe*, 23 Apr. 1881, 5.

2. Diner, *Erin's Daughters in America*, 158.

3. Kelleher, "Young Irish Workers," in *New Directions*, edited by Kenny, 187.

4. Meagher, *Columbia Guide*, 198–99.

5. Lawrence McCaffrey, "Irish-American Nationalism," in *Encyclopedia of the Irish*, edited by Glazier, 644.

6. David Brundage, *Irish Nationalists in America: The Politics of Exile, 1798–1998*, 63–64.

7. Ibid., 89, 102–3.

8. Kelly, *Shamrock and the Lily*, 57.

9. Robert Schmuhl, *Ireland's Exiled Children: America and the Easter Rising*, 17.

10. Parnell accepted leadership of the Irish National Land League in the fall of 1879 and in 1880 became head of the Irish Parliamentary Party.

11. Ely M. Janis, "The Land League in the United States and Ireland: Nationalism, Gender, and Ethnicity in the Gilded Age," 69–70.

12. Edward Thomas O'Donnell, "Henry George and the 'New Political Forces': Ethnic Nationalism, Labor Radicalism, and Politics in Gilded Age New York City," 242.

13. Kenny, *American Irish*, 173; "Clan na Gael," in *Irish American Voluntary Organizations*, edited by Funchion, 77; "Irish National Land League of America," in *Irish American Voluntary Organizations*, edited by Funchion, 190. The Clan also controlled the Land League's successor, the Irish National League of America.

14. E. Foner, "Class, Ethnicity, and Radicalism," 11–12.

15. T. Brown, *Irish-American Nationalism*, 23.

16. Jacobson, *Special Sorrows*, 20.

17. E. Foner, "Class, Ethnicity, and Radicalism," 6.

18. T. Brown, *Irish-American Nationalism*, 23.

19. Brundage, *Making of Western Labor Radicalism*, 44.

20. Janis, *Greater Ireland*, 3.

21. Jane McL. Cote, *Fanny and Anna Parnell: Ireland's Patriot Sisters*, 135; Diner, *Erin's Daughters in America*, 58. Diner described family relationships between men and women as "characterized by intense animosity."

22. Janis, "Land League," 91; Janis, *Greater Ireland*, 142.

23. "The Women Organizing," *Irish World*, 30 Oct. 1880, 8; Margaret Sullivan, "Miss Fanny Parnell," *Irish Nation*, 12 Aug. 1882, 2; "South Brooklyn's League," *Irish World*, 5 Mar. 1881, 8; Brundage, *Irish Nationalists in America*, 222; Janis, *Greater Ireland*, 143.

24. Margaret Ward, *Unmanageable Revolutionaries: Women and Irish Nationalism*, 12–13. Delia Parnell, the mother of Charles, Fanny, and Anna, was the

American-born daughter of American military leader Commodore Stewart and strongly anti-British. J. J. Prendergest, "To Ladies' Land League," *Irish World*, 11 Sept. 1880, 8; Mrs. Ellen Hagarty, "To the Ladies," *Irish World*, 18 Sept. 1880, 2 (emphasis in the original). Hagarty was a regular contributor (twenty-five cents) to Patrick Ford's "Spread the Light" campaign, a fund used to supply copies of his paper to educate people in Ireland on the land question.

25. The men's organization grew slowly until the arrest of Michael Davitt (February 1881) and passage of the Coercion Act (March 1881) aroused the sympathy of Irish Americans and spurred the rapid growth of the Land League.

26. "South Brooklyn's Leagues," *Irish World*, 15 Mar. 1881, 8; "Spreading the Light in Brooklyn," *Irish World*, 5 Mar. 1881, 7; "The Women of Worcester," *Irish World*, 22 Jan. 1881, 5.

27. "Ladies' Land League: An Interview with Mrs. Parnell," *Boston Daily Globe*, 22 Jan. 1881, 1.

28. "The Women of Worcester," *Irish World*, 22 Jan. 1881, 5; "Grand Work in Saint Louis," *Irish World*, 26 Feb. 1881, 8.

29. "Ladies' Land League," *Boston Daily Globe*, 22 Jan. 1881, 1.

30. "Irish Ladies' Land League Association," *Baltimore Sun*, 2 Feb. 1881, 2.

31. Janis, *Greater Ireland*, 179.

32. "To the Ladies," *Irish World*, 26 Nov. 1881, 5.

33. "Au Revoir: Miss Fanny Parnell's Farewell Entertainment," *Boston Daily Globe*, 20 May 1881, 4.

34. Fanny Parnell, "Ladies' Land League: A Permanent Organization to Be in New York City," *Irish World*, 25 Sept. 1880; Margaret F. Sullivan, "Miss Fanny Parnell," *Irish Nation*, 12 Aug. 1882, 2.

35. Parnell, "Ladies' Land League."

36. "Ladies' Land League," *Irish World*, 1 Jan. 1881, 4.

37. Ladies' Land League, "Women's Work a Potent Factor in the World's Progress and Should Be None the Less So in Ireland's Case," *Irish World*, 27 Nov. 1880, 2, reprinted from the *New York Star*.

38. *Irish World*, 11 Dec. 1886, 3. For more on Dougherty, see Meagher, *Inventing Irish America*.

39. Meagher, *Inventing Irish America*, 185; Janis, "Land League," 245.

40. *Irish World*, 18 June 1881, 8; "South Brooklyn's Leagues," *Irish World*, 5 Mar. 1881, 8.

41. "Jersey City," *Irish World*, 30 July 1881, 5; "Miss Parnell in Boston," *Boston Pilot*, 14 May 1881, 1.

42. Meagher, *Inventing Irish America*, 184.

43. James J. Kenneally, "Sexism, the Church, Irish Women," 7.

44. Cote, *Fanny and Anna Parnell*, 177, quoted in ibid., 7.

45. Wm. Markoe, "Bishop Grace and the Ladies' Land Leagues," *Boston Pilot*, 9 Apr. 1881, 2. The letter ran in the *Boston Pilot*, *St. Paul Pioneer Press*, and the *Boston Daily Globe*. The *Pilot* ran it above a rebuttal to the charges of Archbishop McCabe in Dublin, written by A. M. Sullivan a month before.

46. Boyce, *Nationalism in Ireland*, 192–223. Several Irish women took tentative steps to form leagues after reading Fanny Parnell's letter, and once Anna Parnell issued the official call to join, "the response was immediate and enthusiastic." Cote, *Fanny and Anna Parnell*, 160.

47. Margaret Ward, "Gendering the Union: Imperial Feminism and the Ladies' Land League," 80.

48. "Women Wanted to Speak in Ireland," *Boston Pilot*, 3 Dec. 1881, 4.

49. "Letter from an Irish-American Lady in Ireland," *Boston Pilot*, 19 Aug. 1882, 6.

50. M. Ward, "Gendering the Union," 81; *Irish World*, 20 May 1882, 7; M. Ward, *Unmanageable Revolutionaries*, 28. The *Irish World* encouraged readers to show their resentment of the treatment of women "with ten-fold determination." *Irish World*, 6 May 1882, 6.

51. Cote, *Fanny and Anna Parnell*, 161, 170.

52. *Irish World*, 26 Mar. 1881, 4; "Archbishop McCabe's Attack on the Ladies' Land League," *Boston Pilot*, 19 Mar. 1881. 5.

53. *Irish World*, 2 Apr. 1881, 5. The controversy between the two bishops resulted in Croke offering a tepid apology to McCabe for criticizing him in public. Cote, *Fanny and Anna Parnell*, 174–75.

54. "Women and the Land Agitation," *Irish World*, 26 Mar. 1881, 4.

55. "Ladies' Land League," *Irish World*, 2 Apr. 1881, 5.

56. "Ironsides Ladies' Land League," *Irish World*, 30 Apr. 1881, 8.

57. "An Appeal for the Ladies," *Boston Daily Globe*, 29 July 1881, 2.

58. *Irish World*, 24 Dec. 1881, 5; "Ladies' Branches Formed," *Irish World*, 16 Apr. 1881, 2; "Central Falls—Ladies' Land League," *Irish World*, 28 May 1881, 2; "Ladies of Worcester," *Irish World*, 30 Apr. 1881, 5.

59. O'Mahoney's obituary claimed she was the first Catholic woman "in these parts" to achieve success in the lecture field. *Boston Republic*, 12 Jan. 1918, 2.

60. "Ladies' Land League: An Interesting Interview with Mrs. Parnell," *Boston Daily Globe*, 22 Jan. 1881, 1.

61. "Jersey City," *Irish World*, 30 July 1881, 5.

62. *Irish World*, 18 Dec. 1886, 3.

63. "Land League Sympathy: The Boston Trans-Atlantic Branch Passing Resolutions on the Lawrence Strike," *Irish World*, 8 Apr. 1882, 6.

64. Montgomery, "Irish and the American Labor Movement," in *America and Ireland*, edited by Doyle and Edwards, 216.

65. O'Donnell, "Henry George," 227–28.

66. "Demonstration in New Jersey," *Irish World*, 2 July 1881, 8.

67. O'Donnell, "Henry George," 221, 229.

68. Ibid., 76, 82, 86.

69. Cote, *Fanny and Anna Parnell*, 141.

70. Ibid., 196.

71. Fanny Parnell to Patrick Collins, 25 Sept. 1881, Patrick Collins Papers, Burns Library, box 1, folder 54; Margaret Sullivan, "Miss Fanny Parnell," *Redpath's Illustrated Weekly*, reprinted in *Irish World*, 12 Aug. 1882, 2.

72. Cote, *Fanny and Anna Parnell*, 220.

73. Parnell to Collins, 25 Sept. 1881, Collins Papers, Burns Library, box 1, folder 54.

74. Fanny Parnell, "Land Nationalization," *Donahoe's Magazine*, reprinted in *Irish Nation*, 26 Aug. 1882, 2. The *Irish Nation* was published by John Devoy. Fanny Parnell died after battling a recurring fever in the summer of 1882.

75. Boyce, *Nationalism in Ireland*, 210; M. Ward, *Unmanageable Revolutionaries*, 27. For a historical biographical sketch of Moore, see Frances Willard and Mary Livermore, eds., *American Women*, 517.

76. O'Donnell, "Henry George," 265.

77. Funchion, *Irish American Voluntary Organizations*, 192.

78. Ibid., 192; "Live Ladies of Philadelphia," *Irish World*, 24 Dec. 1881, 5; "Manhattan Land League," *Irish World*, 31 Dec. 1881, 6; "Father Sheehy Ladies' Branch," *Irish World*, 4 Mar. 1882, 5.

79. O'Donnell, "Henry George," 267; Janis, *Greater Ireland*, 171.

80. "Good Reports from the Baltimore Ladies," *Irish World*, 11 Feb. 1882, 5; "The Ladies' Land League," *Catholic Mirror*, 21 Jan. 1882, 4. A response to this editorial claimed poor attendance at the ball by the men of the Land League, possibly as a result of the paper's stance. "Ladies' Land League," *Catholic Mirror*, 28 Jan. 1882, 4.

81. "Land League," *Chicago Daily Tribune*, 22 May 1882, 2; "Bishop Gilmour," *Chicago Daily Tribune*, 3 June 1882, 16.

82. "Excommunicating Lady Leaguers," *Washington Post*, 3 June 1882, 1.

83. "Bishop Gilmour," *Chicago Daily Tribune*, 3 June 1882, 16; "Indignant Lady Leaguers," *Washington Post*, 5 June 1882, 3; "Steadfast Irishwomen," *New York Times*, 12 June 1882, 1.

84. "Lady Land Leaguers Defiant: A Bold Reply to Bishop Gilmour's Recent Denunciation," *New York Times*, 5 June 1882, 3; "Steadfast Irishwomen: Large Meeting of the Cleveland Female Land Leaguers Despite the Bishop's Threat," *New York Times*, 12 June 1882, 1; "Sympathy for the Lady Leaguers," *Washington Post*, 20 June 1882, 4.

85. "Bishop Gilmour," *Chicago Daily Tribune*, 6 June 1882, 4.

86. "Bishop Gilmour Excommunicates Lady Land Leaguers," *Boston Pilot*, 10 June 882, 1; "Dr. McGlynn in Cleveland," *Irish World*, 2 Sept. 1882, 8; Kenneally, "Sexism, the Church, Irish Women," 11.

87. "The Bishop's Ban," *Chicago Daily Tribune*, 4 June 1882, 11.

88. "Dr. McGlynn in Cleveland," *Irish World*, 2 Sept. 1882, 8; Kenneally, "Sexism, the Church, Irish Women," 11.

89. "Ladies' Land League of Cleveland," *Irish World*, 17 June 1882, 4; "Bishop Gilmour and the Ladies' League," *Irish World*, 1 July 1882, 6.

90. Brundage, *Irish Nationalists in America*, 133.

91. "Archbishop Lynch's Opinion of the Ladies' Land League," *Chicago Daily Tribune*, 10 Aug. 1882, 3.

92. Dierdre Moloney, "Land League Activism in Transnational Perspective," 72; "Bishop Gilmour," *Chicago Daily Tribune*, 19 June 1882, 2.

93. Boyce, *Nationalism in Ireland*, 210.

94. Janis, "Land League," 288, 291.

95. M. Ward, "Gendering the Union," 85.

96. Janis, "Land League," 227.

97. Boyce, *Nationalism in Ireland*, 210; Henry George to Helen Taylor, quoted in M. Ward, "Gendering the Union," 85. Parnell's deal with Gladstone also jeopardized his relationship with male allies. M. Ward, *Unmanageable Revolutionaries*, 37.

98. Anna Parnell, *Tale of a Great Sham*, 131.

99. Janis, "Land League," 305.

100. "Irish Convention," *Columbus (GA) Daily Enquirer*, 28 Apr. 1883, 1; "Irish in Convention," *New York Times*, 14 Aug. 1884, 2; "Woman Suffrage to Help Ireland," *Woman's Journal*, 12 Apr. 1884, 119.

101. "A Noble Catholic Woman of Massachusetts," *Boston Republic*, 12 Jan. 1918, 2.

102. Meagher, *Inventing Irish America*, 184–85. While little else is known about Dougherty's background, Meagher points out that some of her closest allies in the Ladies' Land League were teachers, and one was a doctor.

103. Orr, "Mary Elizabeth Lease," 15, 36–37. Lease also supported the land theories of Henry George and worked for his second mayoral campaign.

104. Robert Emmett Curran, "Prelude to 'Americanism': The New York Academia and Clerical Radicalism in the Late Nineteenth Century," 51, 56.

105. Jay P. Dolan, *In Search of an American Catholicism*, 100–101; Cummings, *New Women of the Old Faith*, 7; Moloney, *American Catholic Lay Groups*, 16–17.

106. James Hennesey, *American Catholics*, 182; Cummings, *New Women of the Old Faith*, 7; Moloney, *American Catholic Lay Groups*, 16–17.

107. Dolan, *In Search of an American Catholicism*, 104, 106; Moloney, *American Catholic Lay Groups*, 17.

108. "Denouncing the Machine," *New York Times,* 23 Jan. 1888, 5.

109. Wendy Deichmann Edwards and Carolyn De Swarte Gifford, eds., *Gender and the Social Gospel,* 2–3; Eileen Lindner, "Redemptive Politics of Henry George: Legacy to the Social Gospel."

110. Edward Thomas O'Donnell, "'Though Not an Irishman': Henry George and the American Irish," 408–10, 414; E. Foner, "Class, Ethnicity, and Radicalism," 37. For an intellectual history of Father McGlynn, see Manuel Scott Shanaberger, "Reverend Dr. Edward McGlynn: An Early Advocate of the Social Gospel in the American Catholic Church, an Intellectual History."

111. O'Donnell, "Henry George," 271, 274, 477–49.

112. Henry George to Mr. Walker, 3 Aug. 1886, Henry George Papers, New York Public Library, reel 4; Henry George, Sept. 10, 1886, ibid.

113. Fred Nicklason, "Henry George: Social Gospeller," 660. George finished second, behind Tammany's candidate but ahead of the Republican candidate, Theodore Roosevelt. He also ran for secretary of state in 1887, but with much less success. He died in 1897, during his second campaign for mayor of New York. By 1890 131 single-tax organizations had been founded nationwide. O'Donnell, "Henry George," 564.

114. *Irish World,* 25 Feb. 1882, 1.

115. Willard and Livermore, *American Women,* 517.

116. "Our Unique Women," *Columbia (SC) State,* 14 Apr. 1891.

117. "Women Knights of Labor: Their Talks to the Men at Odeon Hall Last Night," *Washington Post,* 30 Mar. 1888, 2; "American Pauper Labor: Mrs. Marguerite Moore's Comparison of Ireland and America," *Washington Post,* 2 Apr. 1888.

118. Willard and Livermore, *American Women,* 517.

119. "She'll Speak for Bryan," *Baltimore Sun,* 22 Aug. 1900, 10.

120. Shanaberger, "Reverend Dr. Edward McGlynn," 227.

121. "Catholics Up in Arms: Excited Protests against Dr. McGlynn's Removal," *New York Times,* 18 Jan. 1887, 1; "A Catholic Revolt," *Christian Union,* 20 Jan. 1887, 5.

122. "Catholics Up in Arms," 1; Stephen Bell, *Rebel, Priest, and Prophet: A Biography of Dr. Edward McGlynn,* 54; "A Catholic Revolt," 5.

123. Bell, *Rebel, Priest, and Prophet,* 55.

124. Fitzgerald, *Habits of Compassion,* 155.

125. "At St. Stephen's," *New York Standard,* 28 May 1887, 8; "In Dr. McGlynn's Parish," *New York Standard,* 11 June 1887, 4. Henry George published the *Standard* from 1887 through the early 1890s.

126. "Cheering Henry George," *New York Times,* 9 May 1887, 5.

127. William T. Croasdale, "Story of Dr. McGlynn," *Independent* (New York), 4 Aug. 1887, 5; "Dr. M'Glynn Re-elected," *New Haven (CT) Register,* 27 Mar. 1888, 3.

128. "Anti-Poverty Crusade," *Christian Union,* 5 May 1887, 6.

129. Ibid.

130. Dominic Scibilia, "Edward McGlynn: American Social Catholic," 8–11. Four theology professors from Catholic University reviewed McGlynn's teachings and found them to be consistent with church dogma, allowing for McGlynn's reinstatement in 1892. After the founding of the Anti-Poverty Society, McGlynn and George quickly parted over differences on trade policy, and George severed his ties with the society.

131. "Isolated Priest," *New York Standard*, 25 June 1887, 3.

132. Henry George to McGhee, 6 June 1887, George Papers, New York Public Library, reel 4.

133. "Catholic Club: A Powerful Influence against the Anti-Poverty Society," *Washington Post*, 28 Feb. 1888, 1.

134. One letter writer to the *Woman's Journal* suggested that the reports on the prevalence of women at Anti-Poverty Society meetings were exaggerated. However, the letter writer never attended a meeting herself. Fanny Russell, "The Anti-Poverty Society," *Woman's Journal*, 17 Dec. 1887, 406.

135. One *New York Times* account, from April, reported the presence of "many ladies," and another suggested women "were in the majority." "Friends of Dr. McGlynn," *New York Times*, 15 Apr. 1887, 5; "In and about the City: Dr. McGlynn's Crusade," *New York Times*, 19 May 1887, 8; Samuel J. Thomas, "Portraits of a 'Rebel' Priest: Edward McGlynn in Caricature, 1886–1893," 23, 27. One man who attended several of McGlynn's lectures in 1892 described his audience as small but largely middle class and heavily female. Cited in Robert Emmett Curran, "The McGlynn Affair and the Shaping of the New Conservatism in American Catholicism, 1886–1894," 193.

136. "Just You Wait" (cartoon), *Puck*, 22 June 1887, 276–77; "Cartoon and Comments," *Puck*, 9 Feb. 1887, 392.

137. "Anti-Poverty Society: Where and How a Lot of Superfluous Energy Is Worked Off," *New Haven (CT) Register*, 24 May 1887, 4.

138. "The Campaign: An Advance All along the Line," *New York Standard*, 1 Oct. 1887, 1; "Sunday Night Politics: An Anti-Poverty Ratification," *New Haven (CT) Register*, 22 Aug. 1887; "Preaching Georgeism to Newark," *New York Times*, 10 Oct. 1887, 8.

139. "The Anti-Poverty Society's Coming Fair," *New York Standard*, 10 Sept. 1887, 2.

140. Hester M. Poole, "Correspondence," *Open Court*, 19 Jan. 1888, 700; "Advance All along the Line," 1.

141. "The Case of Mrs. O'Donnell," *New York Standard*, 1 Oct. 1887, 4.

142. "The Archbishop's Letter: Defiant Talk at the Anti-Poverty Meeting," *New York Times*, 21 Jan. 1889, 2; Kenneally, "Sexism, the Church, Irish Women," 13.

143. "Miss Kelly's Funeral: The Question of Her Burial in Calvary Not Yet Settled," *New York Times*, 27 Oct. 1889, 5; "Miss Kelly's Death: Renewing the Struggle for Church Burial for M'Glynnites," *New York Times*, 25 Oct. 1889, 5. This controversy followed another, in which a man who died at an Anti-Poverty Society meeting was denied burial in the same cemetery. Burtsell appealed the archbishop's decision to transfer him, but he lost. Anthony D. Andreassi, "'The Cunning Leaders of a Dangerous Clique'? The Burtsell Affair and Archbishop Michael Augustine Corrigan," 626–68.

144. "Wouldn't Absolve Her," *New Haven (CT) Register*, 7 Oct. 1889.

145. Richard Gilmour of Cleveland was among the conservatives.

146. Dolan, *American Catholic Experience*, 329; "The Pope's Encyclical," *Irish World*, 3 Jan. 1891, 5; Morgan M. Sheedy, "The Encyclical and American Iron-Workers and Coal-Miners," *Catholic World* 53 (1891): 853, 860.

147. Moloney, *American Catholic Lay Groups*, 4.

4. Propaganda, Protest, Purchasing, and Picketing

1. This is the first verse of a poem by Theresa Brayton, appearing in the *Irish World*, 7 Apr. 1920, 12. Brayton emigrated to the United States in 1895. She was a committed nationalist and published three volumes of poetry. She later returned to Ireland.

2. "Minute Women of Boston Parade for Irish Relief," *Irish World*, 24 July 1920, 12.

3. Boyce, *Nationalism in Ireland*, 237–38.

4. Senia Paseta, *Irish Nationalist Women, 1900–1918*, 20.

5. D. A. J. MacPherson, *Women and the Irish Nation: Gender, Culture and Irish Identity, 1890–1914*, 90.

6. M. Ward, *Unmanageable Revolutionaries*, 44.

7. Paseta, *Irish Nationalist Women*, 41.

8. *Washington Post*, 11 Feb. 1901.

9. "Maud Gonne Reception," *Irish World*, 20 Jan. 1900; "To Help the Boers," *Irish World*, 20 Apr. 1901; *Irish World*, 3 Nov. 1900.

10. Brundage, *Irish Nationalists in America*, 131.

11. Una Ni Bhroimeil, "The American Mission: The Gaelic Revival and America, 1870–1915," 1, 12, 86. Language organizations had existed for twenty years before the founding of the Gaelic League of America. Funchion, *Irish American Voluntary Organizations*, 132.

12. "New York Gaelic Society," *Irish World*, 11 Feb. 1905, 8.

13. James Reidy, "Influence of the Irish Woman," *Gaelic American*, 24 Mar. 1905, 5.

14. *National Hibernian*, 15 Oct. 1906, 7; 15 Nov. 1906, 1.

15. Paseta, *Irish Nationalist Women*, 64.

16. *National Hibernian*, May 1901, 6; 15 Nov. 1907, 6; September 15, 1907, 2.

17. Kerry Soper, "From Swarthy Ape to Sympathetic Everyman and Subversive Trickster: The Development of Irish Caricature in American Comic Strips between 1890 and 1920," 258, 263–64.

18. Maureen Murphy, "Bridget and Biddy: Images of the Irish Servant Girl in *Puck* Cartoons, 1880–1890," in *New Perspectives on the Irish Diaspora*, edited by Charles Fanning, 154, 166.

19. Maureen Murphy, "From Scapegoat to Grasta," in *Irish Theater in America: Essays on Irish Theatrical Diaspora*, edited by John P. Harrington, 22–23.

20. "The Stage Irishman: If Spirited Irishmen Do Their Duty the Insulting Monstrosity Will Disappear Forever," *Irish World*, 7 May 1887, 5.

21. M. Alison Kibler, "Pigs, Green Whiskers, and Drunken Widows: Irish Nationalists and the 'Practical Censorship' of *McFadden's Row of Flats* in 1902 and 1903."

22. For more on the Russell Brothers, see Geraldine Maschio, "Ethnic Humor and the Demise of the Russell Brothers"; "Irishmen Stop Act," *Irish World*, 2 Feb. 1907, 1; "Chase It from the Stage," *Irish World*, 9 Feb. 1907, 4. For more on gender and class in Irish comedy, see Kibler, "Rank Ladies, Ladies of Rank."

23. *Chicago Citizen*, 13 July 1912; "Sketches and Portraits of Those Now in Office," *National Hibernian*, July 1916, 10–11; William H. McWhorter, 1920 Census, series T625, roll 310, p. 85, heritagequestonline.com. According to US Census data, McWhorter immigrated in 1900, but this date conflicts with newspaper accounts.

24. *Irish World*, 11 June 1904, 10; *National Hibernian*, 15 June 1904; "Stage Woman Ousted from Pawtucket Theater," *National Hibernian*, 15 June 1906, 6; "AOH Woman Has Pawtucket Play Changed," *Boston Morning Journal*, 11 May 1906, 5.

25. "Auxiliary Affairs: Strong Letter from National President," *National Hibernian*, 15 June 1907, 1; "Report of Miss Anna C. Malia, National President Ladies' Auxiliary," *National Hibernian*, 15 Sept. 1908, 3; Mary B. Dolan, "The Ladies Ancient Order of Hibernians" (unpublished manuscript compiled by Dolan while she served as national historian of the Ladies' Ancient Order of Hibernians, 1994); "Society News," *Scranton (PA) Republican*, 5 Jan. 1921, 11.

26. "APAism in Chicago's Public Schools: High School Mummer as Stage Irish Woman," *New World*, 20 Jan. 1906; "Whitewashing Hyde Park High School," *New World*, 3 Feb. 1906, 15; Mary McWhorter, "Caricaturing Irish Womanhood," *New World*, 17 Feb. 1906, 8.

27. Brundage, *Irish Nationalists in America*, 128–29.

28. Ibid., 136.

29. Paseta, *Irish Nationalist Women*, 64.

30. Boyce, *Nationalism in Ireland*, 268.

31. Miller, *Emigrants and Exiles*, 453, 543.

32. Brundage, *Irish Nationalists in America*, 132, 134.

33. "Objects of the League," *Irish World*, 1 Nov. 1901, 4; "Noted Irish Woman Honored," *Boston Pilot*, 18 July 1903, 3; "Officers and Executive Committee of the United Irish League of America," *Boston Pilot*, 3 Nov. 1906, 7. Mary O'Flaherty's brother Edward O'Flaherty had also been an active nationalist. She belonged to a branch of the UILA named for him.

34. "The United Irish League," *New York Times*, 15 Apr. 1901, 7;

35. "Brockton's Live Branch," *Irish World*, 6 Sept. 1902, 3; "United Irish League: The Maryland Central Branch Decides to Admit Ladies to Membership," *Irish World*, 1 Feb. 1902; "Will Admit Ladies," *Citizen*, 25 Jan. 1902, 1.

36. "U.I.L. in Chicago," *Citizen*, 30 Aug. 1902, 5. Two hundred Irish women from Philadelphia proclaimed their love for America while pledging personal and financial support to the IPP, in 1908, after a visit from Redmond. The women of Iowa's LAAOH commended "the Irish Parliamentary Party, under the leadership of John Redmond, and wish[ed] him Godspeed." "Patriotic Ladies' Auxiliary, A.O.H.," *Irish World*, 26 Sept. 1908, 7; "Patriotic A.O.H. Ladies of Philadelphia," *Irish World*, 10 Oct. 1908, 6; *National Hibernian*, 15 Oct. 1910.

37. "United Irish League," *Irish World*, 7 June 1902, 7: "United Irish League in Lynn, Mass.," *Boston Pilot*, 29 Mar. 1902, 7.

38. "Another Ladies' Branch of the United Irish League in Boston," *Boston Pilot*, 15 Feb. 1902; "Ladies Organizing for Home Rule," *Irish World*, 3 Nov. 1906, 23; "Boston Central Branch of the United Irish League of America," *Boston Pilot*, 9 Feb. 1901, 5; "Patriotic Boston Women," *Irish World*, 16 Mar. 1901; "United Irish League: New Branches Springing Up All over the Country," *Irish World*, 1 Mar. 1902; "The St. James Branch of the UIL of A," *Irish World*, 25 Feb. 1911, 7.

39. "St. James Ladies' Auxiliary of Boston Central Branch, UIL," *Boston Pilot*, 29 June 1901, 5; "United Irish League," *Boston Pilot*, 24 Jan. 1903, 5; "St. James (Boston) Branch, UIL of America," *Boston Pilot*, 28 Jan. 1905, 8.

40. "Ladies' Auxiliary," *National Hibernian*, 15 Feb. 1905, 8.

41. Donovan served as president of the St. James Branch (UILA) for ten terms and then announced her retirement. However, she appears to have returned, because she is later reported as being elected to her thirteenth term (in 1913). *Irish World*, 25 Jan. 1913, 7; *Boston Pilot*, 8 Dec. 1906, 8.

42. "Translation of Miss M. J. Donovan's Irish Address to Mr. Devlin, M.P.," *Irish World*, 17 May 1902, 8.

43. Boyce, *Nationalism in Ireland*, 278–82; Francis Carroll, *American Opinion and the Irish Question, 1910–1923: A Study of Opinion and Policy*, 14.

44. Redmond demanded control of the Volunteers, and the Volunteers' provisional committee agreed in an effort to avoid a split in the movement. Boyce, *Nationalism in Ireland*, 283; Carroll, *American Opinion*, 33.

45. M. Ward, *Unmanageable Revolutionaries*, 88–90, 92.

46. Sinead McCoole, *No Ordinary Women: Irish Female Activists in the Revolutionary Years, 1900–1923*, 31.

47. Carroll, *American Opinion*, 23, 24; David Brundage, "'In Times of Peace, Prepare for War': Key Themes in the Social Thought of New York's Irish Nationalists, 1890–1916," in *The New York Irish*, edited by Bayor and Meagher, 330.

48. "Rally of Irishwomen," *New York Times*, 16 Mar. 1914, 18.

49. "Protest by Irish Women," *Gaelic American*, 21 Mar. 1914, 1; "Irish Women of New York Protest," *Irish World*, 28 Mar. 1914, 5. The *Citizen*, of Chicago, declared that the officers of the United Irish Women were not Catholic. "Irish Women Protest," *Citizen*, 2 May 1914, 1; "Talk of War Unites New York Irishmen," *New York Times*, 4 July 1914, 5.

50. Gertrude Kelly to Leonora O'Reilly, 1 Apr. 1914, O'Reilly Papers, reel 7, frames 68–69; Louise Quesada [?] (name is illegible) to O'Reilly, 25 Mar. 1915, ibid., frames 64–67. Leonora O'Reilly expressed interest in Sinn Fein as early as 1911. O'Reilly to her mother, 3 Mar. 1911, ibid., reel 3, frames 595–96. O'Reilly joined Cumman na mBan in 1915, although she apparently did not attend meetings at that time. Dr. McGuinness to O'Reilly, 9 Jan. 1915, ibid., reel 7, frame 252.

51. Kelly to Cockran, 2 Oct. 1914, William Bourke Cockran Papers, New York Public Library, box 5. Kelly's article appeared in the *Gaelic American*, 3 Oct. 1914, 2; the *Irish World*, 3 Oct. 1914, 3; and the *New York Evening Journal*, n.d. Clipping in ibid.

52. Gertrude B. Kelly, "Has the Party Gone Mad," *Gaelic American*, 3 Oct. 1914, 2. Francis Carroll described Kelly as "prominent in New York UIL affairs." Carroll, *American Opinion*, 48.

53. "Talk of War Unites New York Irishmen," *New York Times*, 4 July 1914, 5.

54. Rose McDermott, "An Irishwoman's Very Pertinent Question," *Irish World*, 24 Oct. 1914, 3. Other examples include Mrs. Grace, "An Irish Woman's Denunciation," *Irish World*, 26 Sept. 1914, 3; Elizabeth Costello, "A Sorely Disappointed Irishwoman," *Irish World*, 7 Nov. 1914, 3; and Mrs. E. Tobin, "An Irishwoman's View," *Irish World*, 9 Jan. 1915, 3.

55. Margaret Kain, "Prays Irish Boys Will Not Cross the English Channel," *Irish World*, 24 Oct. 1914, 3; "Miss Margaret Kain Dead," *National Hibernian*, May 1926, 8.

56. This quote from the *Irish World* suggests that by 1914, Gertrude Kelly was already well known in Irish nationalist circles. "Women Organize to Stop Recruiting," *Irish World*, 19 Dec. 1914, 2; Gertrude B. Kelly and Madge McGuiness, "A Call to the Women of Irish Blood," *Irish World*, 21 Nov. 1914; Madge McGuinness, "For Irish Nationality," *Irish World*, 12 Dec. 1914, 2. Marguerite Moore was also advertised to speak at this meeting.

57. Sidney Gifford Czira, *The Years Flew By*, 70–71.

58. "Women Organize to Stop Recruiting," *Irish World*, 19 Dec. 1914, 2; "The Cumann na m-Ban of New York," *Gaelic American*, 23 Jan. 1915, 3.

59. "Irishwomen Organize," *Gaelic American*, 19 Dec. 1914, 2, 8; "Women Organize to Stop Recruiting," *Irish World*, 19 Dec. 1914, 2.

60. "Women Organize to Stop Recruiting," 2; "The Cumann na m-Ban of New York," 3; Mary Colum, "A Call to Irish Women in America," *Gaelic American*, 23 Jan. 1915, 2; Mary Colum, "A Call to Irish Women in America," *Irish World*, 16 Jan. 1915, 2.

61. M. Ward, *Unmanageable Revolutionaries*, 97; Rosemary Cullen Owens, *Smashing Times: History of the Irish Women's Suffrage Movement, 1889–1922*, 104, 111.

62. "Sarah McKelvey Banqueted," *National Hibernian*, July 1925, 2. Other branches of Cumann na mBan followed. Springfield became the first town in Massachusetts to organize a branch in October 1915. Women in Haverhill and Roxbury, Massachusetts, made plans to organize by the end of 1915, and a San Francisco branch had been formed by April 1916. "Cumann na mBan, Inc.," *Irish World*, 16 Oct. 1915, 2; "Cumann na mBan, Inc.," *Irish World*, 18 Dec. 1915, 7; "Cumann na mBan," *Irish World*, 15 Apr. 1916, 3. In addition to pledging aid for the Volunteers, the San Francisco branch held meetings to promote the study of Irish language and history. Joanne Mooney Eichacker, *Irish Republican Women in America: Lecture Tours, 1916–1925*, 35.

63. The article on Cumann na mBan appeared first in the *Gaelic American* and then in shortened form in the *Irish World*. "Cumann na mBan Appeals to Irish-American Women," *Gaelic American*, 10 July 1915, 2; "Cumann na mBan," *Irish World*, 17 July 1915, 8.

64. "An Appeal to Irishwomen," *Gaelic American*, 19 Feb. 1916, 2; Rose McDermott, "Cumann na mBan, Inc.," *Irish World*, 19 Feb. 1916, 7. This is the same article, but the one in the *Gaelic American* appeared without the author listed.

65. "To Arm the Volunteers," *Gaelic American*, 30 Oct. 1915, 7; "Cuman na mBan, Inc.," *Irish World*, 6 Nov. 1915, 7. This is the same article, appearing in slightly different form. I have retained the misspelling of Cumann na mBan in the title.

66. Carroll, *American Opinion*, 14, 26, 46, 52.

67. Schmuhl, *Ireland's Exiled Children*, 30.

68. "Closing Session of Convention," *Irish World*, 11 Mar. 1916. McWhorter spoke at all three Irish Race Conventions. "Hours of Oration for Irish Freedom," *New York Times*, 6 Mar. 1916, 4; "The Great Irish Race Convention," *Irish World*, 11 Mar. 1916, 7.

69. Michael Doorley, *Irish-American Diaspora Nationalism: The Friends of Irish Freedom, 1916–1935*, 48; Miller, *Emigrants and Exiles*, 543; "Friends of Irish Freedom," *Irish World*, 11 Mar. 1916, 7. A month later, Jolly was the only woman asked

to speak at a meeting of the Friends of Irish Freedom in Boston's Faneuil Hall. "Mrs. Ellen Ryan Jolly's Letter," *National Hibernian*, May 1916, 7. More women were elected to the executive committee at the next convention in 1918. The number of LAAOH women on the board also increased. *Irish World*, 25 May 1918, 12. Mary Gallagher, president of Philadelphia's Division 23 of the LAAOH from its founding until the 1920s, also held a national position in the FOIF. "Philadelphia Hibernians Honor Mrs. Gallagher," *Gaelic American*, 9 June 1923, 8.

70. Boyce, *Nationalism in Ireland*, 305.

71. M. Ward, *Unmanageable Revolutionaries*, 109.

72. "Miss Eileen Gifford on the Dublin Uprising," *Irish World*, 27 Jan. 1917, 8.

73. Brundage, *Irish Nationalism in America*, 146–47.

74. Alan J. Ward, *Ireland and Anglo-American Relations, 1899–1921*, 117, 120; Miller, *Emigrants and Exiles*, 542.

75. Frank P. Walsh to O'Reilly, 23 Aug. 1916, O'Reilly Papers, reel 7, frame 697. For more on Frank Walsh, see Glazier, *Encyclopedia of the Irish*, 939.

76. Reeve and Reeve, *Connolly and the United States*, 291. The resolution, introduced by Rock, claimed that James Connolly and Thomas Clarke were American citizens. This protest by labor was also reported in the *National Hibernian*, June 1916, 7–10.

77. M. Ward, *Unmanageable Revolutionaries*, 119. Many of the women who joined this organization were also determined to keep the republican movement alive. Another aid society, the Irish National Aid Association, was founded by people who were not connected with the Rising. The two organizations eventually merged.

78. "Appeal to Women," *Irish World*, 24 June 1916, 3.

79. "Will Ask Devery to Drill Policewomen," *New York Times*, 10 May 1912; "Irish Women's Meeting at Cooper Union," *Irish World*, 15 July 1916, 5.

80. "Irish Women's Meeting at Cooper Union," 5.

81. "New York Irish Women in the Fight to the Finish for a Free Ireland," *Gaelic American*, 27 May 1916, 7. For membership references to Lease, see "O'Rahilly Branch, FOIF," *Irish World*, 29 July 1916, 8; "Friends of Irish Freedom," *Irish World*, 17 June 1916, 7; and "Irish Women's Council," *Irish World*, 8 July 1916, 5.

82. Doorley, *Irish-American Diaspora Nationalism*, 53, 55, 58.

83. "Cumann Na mBan, Inc.," *Irish World*, 27 May 1916, 7.

84. Mary and Muriel MacSwiney later toured the United States, as did Constance Markievicz and Mrs. Margaret Pearse.

85. Nora Connolly, "Bold Exploit of Patriotic Irish Girl," *Irish World*, 19 Aug. 1916, 2; "Friends of Irish Freedom Meet in Faneuil Hall, Boston," *Irish World*, 26 Aug. 1916, 3.

86. Eichacker, *Irish Republican Women*, 63.

87. In 1916 Cumann na mBan, First American Auxiliary, passed resolutions, stating, "We claim, therefore, that Ireland has fully established her right to be regarded as an ally of Germany" and "We call emphatically for an official statement from the German Government of its intention with regard to Ireland, and we ask that this statement be made in the face of the world." "Irish Women's Council," *Irish World*, 23 Dec. 1916, 2. The Boston FOIF adopted Cumann na mBan's resolutions as well as their own, asking for Ireland to be recognized as a belligerent nation because of the Easter Rising. "Boston Friends of Irish Freedom," *Irish World*, 30 Dec. 1916, 2.

88. Patrick McCartan, *With De Valera in America*, 39. Patrick McCartan arrived in the United States in 1917 to work on behalf of recognition of the Irish Republic. He pointed out that the AOH postponed its national convention and suspended the *National Hibernian* during the war. However, he credited Mary McWhorter and the LAAOH as a "conspicuous exception."

89. Hanna Sheehy Skeffington, *Impressions of Sinn Fein in America: An Account of Eighteen Months' Irish Propaganda in the United States*, 19.

90. "Savage Attack on Friends of Irish Freedom," *Irish World*, 8 Sept. 1917, 2.

91. "Cumann na mBan, Inc.," *Irish World*, 17 Nov. 1917, 7.

92. Eichacker, *Irish Republican Women*, 82, 85.

93. Carroll, *American Opinion*, 106.

94. O'Reilly to Frank Walsh, 17 June 1920, Walsh Papers, New York Public Library, box 28.

95. Francis Carroll, "Irish Progressive League," in *Irish American Voluntary Organizations*, edited by Funchion, 207; Eichacker, *Irish Republican Women*, 81.

96. Katherine Hughes to Daniel Cohalan, 28 Mar. (no year), Daniel Cohalan Papers, box 7, folder 7, American Irish Historical Society, New York.

97. Pádraig Ó Siadhail, *Dictionary of Canadian Biography*, vol. 15, s.v. "Hughes, Katherine (Catherine) Angelina," http://www.biographi.ca/en/bio/hughes_katherine_angelina_15E.html.

98. Padraig Ó Siadhail, *Katherine Hughes: A Life and a Journey*, 169, 181, 196.

99. Catherine Burns, "American Identity and the Transatlantic Irish Nationalist Movement, 1912—1925"; "Irish Progressive League," *Irish World*, 20 Oct. 1917, 7; "Irish Progressive League," *Irish World*, 8 Dec. 1917, 7; "Urges Votes for Hillquit as President's Opponent," *New York Times*, 2 Nov. 1917, 1.

100. Gertrude B. Kelly, "The Irish Progressive League," *Irish World*, 3 Nov. 1917, 12.

101. Carroll, "Irish Progressive League," in *Irish American Voluntary Organizations*, edited by Funchion, 207, 208.

102. "The Irish Race Convention," *Irish World*, 25 May 1918, 3.

103. "Plea to President by Irish Mothers," *Irish World*, 31 July 1918, 12. Another appeal, by the president of the Pennsylvania LAAOH, asked Wilson to intercede with the British Ministry to prevent conscription in Ireland.

104. "Appeal by National President," *Irish World*, 18 May 1918, 3; "Irish Self-Determination," *Irish World*, 4 Jan. 1919; "Woman Upholds Critic of Her Sex," *Chicago Daily Tribune*, 22 May 1910, 3.

105. M. Ward, *Unmanageable Revolutionaries*, 172.

106. Carroll, *American Opinion*, 122, 139.

107. Ibid., 156; Dennis Sullivan, "Eamon De Valera and the Forces of Opposition in America, 1919–1920," 98; A. Ward, *Ireland and Anglo-American Relations*, 214.

108. P. Foner, *Women and the American Labor Movement*, 40, 66–68, 339, 175, 345.

109. Ibid., 256; Elizabeth Faue, *Community of Suffering & Struggle: Women, Men, and the Labor Movement in Minneapolis, 1915–1945*, 55.

110. Before US entry into World War I, Irish American labor leaders parted from the official policy of Samuel Gompers and the AFL when they resisted preparedness efforts, but most muted their criticism of President Wilson once the United States entered the war. David Brundage, "American Labour and the Irish Question, 1916–1923," 59–61.

111. Elizabeth McKillen, "American Labor, the Irish Revolution, and the Campaign for a Boycott of British Goods, 1916–1924," 36, 42; Elizabeth McKillen, "Ethnicity, Class, and Wilsonian Internationalism Reconsidered: The Mexican-American and Irish-American Immigrant Left and U.S. Foreign Relations, 1914–1922," 554.

112. San Francisco was also the site of a controversial wartime arrest. Tom Mooney, an Irish American labor sympathizer, allegedly set off a bomb during a preparedness parade in 1916, killing ten people. Eichacker, *Irish Republican Women*, 33–35.

113. See also Lisa Rubens, "The Patrician Radical: Charlotte Anita Whitney."

114. Al Richmond, *Native Daughter: The Story of Anita Whitney*, 71.

115. Eichacker, *Irish Republican Women*, 36. For an example of the stationery, see Florence Mullen to Frank Walsh, 6 May 1920, Walsh Papers, New York Public Library, box 28.

116. "Women's Education League," *Irish World*, 27 Sept. 1919, 12; "Woman's Educational League of San Francisco," *Irish World*, 18 Sept. 1920, 7; "San Francisco Ladies Work for Ireland," *Irish World*, 13 Mar. 1920, 3; Eichacker, *Irish Republican Women*, 36–37.

117. Hughes to Cohalan, 11 Sept. 1919, Cohalan Papers, American Irish Historical Society, New York.

118. Eichacker, *Irish Republican Women*, 36.

119. This picketing campaign was not the first such protest. Gertrude Kelly was arrested in December 1919, while demonstrating for the release of political prisoners. Cumann na mBan, First American Auxiliary, had discussed a plan to hold a mass meeting "to demand the release of Irish political prisoners at home and abroad" months earlier. "Amnesty Parade on Fifth Avenue Halted by Police," *New York Times*, 26 Dec. 1919, 1; "Cumann na mBan," *Irish World*, 22 Feb. 1919, 10.

120. McCartan, *With De Valera in America*, 53. The articles were republished in pamphlet form as *The Irish Issue* by American editor Father Tierney, SJ, and distributed by the FOIF.

121. Gertrude Kelly and Cumann na mBan, First American Auxiliary, sided with Maloney. Kelly informed Maloney of a resolution supporting him, McCartan, and President de Valera. Kelly to Maloney, 5 Mar. 1920, Maloney Collection of Irish Historical Papers, New York Public Library, box 8. However, Cumann na mBan, Inc., led by Sarah McKelvey, remained loyal to Devoy throughout the feud and continued to support him in the 1920s. "John Devoy Congratulated by Cumman [*sic*] na m-ban, Inc.," *Gaelic American*, 30 June 1923, 4.

122. Joe Doyle, "Striking for Ireland on the New York Docks," in *The New York Irish*, edited by Bayor and Meagher, 360–61; McCartan, *With De Valera in America*, 173.

123. Burns, "American Identity," 181–82, 179.

124. Catherine M. Burns, "Kathleen O'Brennan and American Identity in the Transatlantic Irish Republican Movement," in *Irish in the Atlantic World*, edited by Gleeson, 194.

125. McCartan, *With De Valera in America*, 178; "The Lady Pickets at Washington, D.C.," *Irish World*, 7 Apr. 1920, 12. According to the article, three of the women arrested were not Irish but English and Scottish. The two women in the picture were Miss Mary Galvin of Philadelphia and Miss Maura Quinn of Boston. "Lady Pickets in Washington," *Irish World*, 10 Apr. 1920, 12. Maura Quinn was probably an early member of the Friends of Irish Freedom as well. "Friends of Irish Freedom, Boston," *Irish World*, 23 July 1916, 3.

126. "American-Irish Women Picket John Bull's 'American Citadel,'" *Citizen*, 9 Apr. 1920, 1. The article pointed out that one of the "vigilant sentinels" was Ruth Russell, daughter of the late editor in chief of the *Chicago Chronicle*. Also a journalist, Ruth Russell became a supporter of Sinn Fein while working as a correspondent in Ireland in 1919.

127. Among the women arrested were Elaine Barrie (an actress), Kathleen O'Brien, Katherine McKeon, Mary Walsh, Mrs. Thomas Currin, and Mrs. Honor Walsh (all of Philadelphia); Helen O'Brien (St. Louis); Maura Quinn (Boston); and Mrs. James Walsh and Mrs. Katherine Columbine (New York). "Women Picket Churches," *New York Times*, 12 Apr. 1920, 4. One picket was scratched by

an unidentified woman outside St. Matthew's Catholic Church. According to Rossa Downing of the Washington, DC, FOIF, his branch helped bail out the women who were arrested. A. Ward, *Ireland and Anglo-American Relations*, 238; Francis M. Carroll, "Frank P. Walsh," in *American National Biography*, edited by John Garraty and Mark Carnes, 22:568.

128. Harriette Hifton worked at the Library of Congress, and O'Reilly ran into her while she was in Washington. In 1915 Hifton married Edward King. Harriet Hifton to O'Reilly, 25 Apr. 1920, O'Reilly Papers, reel 8, frames 118–23. Hifton included his words in quotation marks in the letter.

129. "Women Fly over British Embassy," *New York Times*, 7 Apr. 1920, 1; "Miss Carroll, in Aeroplane, Dropped the Irish 'Bombs,'" *Washington Post*, 7 Apr. 1920, 1.

130. McCartan, *With De Valera in America*, 178; Doyle, "Striking for Ireland," in *The New York Irish*, edited by Bayor and Meagher, 362, 662n30. Joseph McGarrity hired the airplane. "Lady Pickets in Washington," 12.

131. "Women Picketers Meet Geddes Boat," *Irish World*, 24 Apr. 1920, 12.

132. McCartan, *With De Valera in America*, 180–81.

133. Burns, "Kathleen O'Brennan," in *Irish in the Atlantic World*, edited by Gleeson, 180.

134. "Minute Women Arrive in Boston," *Irish World*, 22 May 1920, 12.

135. "American Pickets," *Irish World*, 29 May 1920, 12; "Are the Pickets Politicians?," *Irish World*, 5 June 1920, 12.

136. "Mr. Colby Embarrassed—No Wonder," *Irish World*, 19 June 1920, 12.

137. "The American Pickets," *Irish World*, 26 June 1920, 12.

138. "Arrest Irish Pickets," *New York Times*, 10 July 1920, 3.

139. "Shameless Criticism of Noble Women," *Irish World*, 17 Apr. 1920, 4.

140. "So-Called 'Women Friends' of Ireland Repudiated," *Citizen*, 11 June 1920, 4; "British Flag Burning to Be Investigated," *New York Times*, 4 June 1920, 15. In spite of this announcement, the Pickets had to deny that they received pay for their work from the FOIF during the longshoremen's strike in August and September. "Denies Pickets Are Paid," *New York Times*, 12 Sept. 1920, W14.

141. "Captain Maloney's Pickets Invade Congress," *Gaelic American*, 12 June 1920, 1, 5.

142. "Defense of the Pickets," *Gaelic American*, 10 July 1920, 5.

143. Mary McWhorter, "Pickets Create Great Interest in Europe," *Irish World*, 31 July 1920, 12.

144. Kathleen M. O'Brennan, "Mrs. Laurence Ginnell," *Irish World*, 14 Aug. 1920, 12. O'Brennan was the publicity agent of the Pickets. When arrested during a protest, O'Brennan denied taking part, arguing that she was following only to get the story. "Arrest Irish Pickets," 3; "Reception to the Ginnells," *Irish World*, 21 Aug. 1920, 12.

145. Doyle, "Striking for Ireland," in *The New York Irish*, edited by Bayor and Meagher, 363–64.

146. "Fist Fights Mark Adieus to Mannix," *New York Times*, 1 Aug. 1920, 1. The estimates are from the *New York Times*, but reports vary, with the *New York Times* numbers falling on the low side for the crowd but on the high side for the number of Pickets. "Women Pickets Denounce British Tyranny," *Irish World*, 7 Aug. 1920, 12.

147. The American Commission on Irish Independence was created as a result of the Irish Race Convention of 1919. It appointed three men, Frank Walsh, Edward Dunne, and Michael Ryan, to represent the interests of Ireland at the Peace Convention in Paris. Following their failure to secure permission for an Irish delegation, Walsh and Dunne met with members of the American delegation, including President Wilson. After returning to the United States, they headed a bond drive for de Valera and the Irish Republican government.

148. McKillen, "American Labor," 47; Brundage, "American Labour," 63. Gompers opposed the boycott and moved against the boycott resolution before the AFL convention. Despite the efforts of John Fitzpatrick and Frank Walsh, the boycott resolution never made it past the resolutions committee, which proposed a substitute resolution, endorsing Irish independence without mentioning a boycott.

149. McKillen argues that the Labor Bureau of the American Commission on Irish Independence relied on municipal labor organizations, newspapers, and progressive Irish organizations to implement campaigns at the local level, while also attempting to win support through the traditional channels of the AFL. McKillen, "American Labor."

150. Doyle, "Striking for Ireland," in *The New York Irish*, edited by Bayor and Meagher, 365. An employee in the building above dumped water on the women as they picketed on Whitehall Street. "Women Here Picket British Consulate," *New York Times*, 24 Aug. 1920, 2. When asked, Kelly declined to associate the picketing with a particular group, referring the reporter to telegrams in the paper signed by the Irish Women's Council, the Irish Progressive League, and the Irish Liberal Society.

151. Burns, "Kathleen O'Brennan," in *Irish in the Atlantic World*, edited by Gleeson, 186.

152. Czira, *The Years Flew By*, 88.

153. "Irish Crews Tie Up New York Liners," *Washington Post*, 28 Aug. 1920, 1.

154. Doyle, "Striking for Ireland," in *The New York Irish*, edited by Bayor and Meagher, 357, 362.

155. "Women Fail to See Colby in Behalf of Cork Mayor," *Washington Post*, 28 Aug. 1920, 3; "Take Irish Plea to Colby," *New York Times*, 28 Aug. 1920, 3. The Reverend Sister MacSwiney lived in the United States and had appealed to Secretary Colby on her brother's behalf. "Women's Appeal to Colby," *New York Times*, 29 Aug. 1920, 3. With the letter, Corless included the flyer *Nine Things You Do When You*

Trade with England. She claimed to have circulated one million flyers already. The flyer was signed, "Women's Irish Education League."

156. "Picketing at the State Department," *Irish World*, 11 Sept. 1920.

157. "Irish Crews Tie Up New York Liners," 1. Two rallies had to be held to accommodate the overflow crowd. Although the *Washington Post* estimated the crowd at four thousand, Joe Doyle estimated closer to seven thousand people in and outside the theater. Meanwhile, the Friends of Irish Freedom held their own meeting. Doyle, "Striking for Ireland," in *The New York Irish*, edited by Bayor and Meagher, 368; "Irish Fail to Halt British Steamers," *Washington Post*, 29 Aug. 1920, 1.

158. "Protest against English Barbarism," *Irish World*, 4 Sept. 1920, 12.

159. "3,000 Strike Here to Humble Britain," *New York Times*, 3 Sept. 1920, 1. This quote was attributed to Helen O'Reilly of the women Pickets at the British Embassy. However, in her diary, Leonora O'Reilly recorded speaking to longshoremen at "St. V-Hall" on 1 September 1920. O'Reilly, diary, 1 Sept. 1920, O'Reilly Papers, reel 2; "3,000 Strike Here to Humble Britain," 1. Dudley Field Malone, candidate for governor of New York on the Farm-Labor Party ticket, spoke at meetings during the strike and led negotiations between Irish strikers and the United Negro Improvement Association. Doyle, "Striking for Ireland," in *The New York Irish*, edited by Bayor and Meagher, 370.

160. "Boston Pier Strike Grows," *New York Times*, 4 Sept. 1920, 3; "Extend Boston Ship Strike," *New York Times*, 9 Sept. 1920, 4. A much smaller number of workers struck in Boston than in the New York area. "Labor Revolts against English," *Irish World*, 11 Sept. 1920, 12. This issue carried a picture of the Boston Pickets. Longshoremen also struck in San Francisco. Eichacker, *Irish Republican Women*, 37.

161. Doyle, "Striking for Ireland," in *The New York Irish*, edited by Bayor and Meagher, 372–73; "Mass Meeting in Bayonne," *Gaelic American*, 25 Sept. 1920, 8. Collections were taken at other meetings as well. Minute Women of America (Mary O'Malley, secretary) to Frank Walsh, 18 Jan. 1921, Walsh Papers, New York Public Library, box 29. The *New York Times* charged the longshoremen of New York with taking a "vacation at the expense of the Friends of Irish Freedom." "Replace Irish Pier Men," *New York Times*, 11 Sept. 1920, 7.

162. Doyle, "Striking for Ireland," in *The New York Irish*, edited by Bayor and Meagher, 372.

163. O'Reilly, diary, 12 Sept. 1920, O'Reilly Papers, reel 2.

164. "Irish Women's Purchasing League," *Irish World*, 6 May 1922, 10.

165. This letter thanks the Irish Women's Educational League for answering her request concerning which teas to buy. O'Reilly to Irish Women's Educational League, 1 Dec. 1920, O'Reilly Papers, reel 8, frames 353–54; O'Reilly to Walsh, 19 Jan. 1921, Walsh Papers, New York Public Library, box 29.

166. Joyce Milton, "Arthur Brisbane," in *American National Biography*, edited by Garraty and Carnes, 3:565.

167. O'Reilly to Arthur Brisbane, 23 Nov. 1920, O'Reilly Papers, reel 8, frames 335–36.

168. O'Reilly to Frank Walsh, 19 Jan. 1921, Walsh Papers, New York Public Library, box 29 (irregular punctuation in the original). O'Reilly also sold Irish lace directly to American consumers. Walsh to O'Reilly, 27 Jan. 1921, ibid.

169. "Irish Women's Purchasing League," *Irish World*, 5 Feb. 1921, 10. O'Reilly asked Walsh to secure de Valera's permission to name one tea "Irish Republic Tea De V—Brand." O'Reilly to Walsh, n.d., Walsh Papers, New York Public Library, box 28.

170. O'Reilly to Walsh, 13 Feb. 1921, Walsh Papers, New York Public Library, box 29.

171. "Irish Hold '1921' Tea Party," *New York Times*, 25 Feb. 1921, 17.

172. Carroll, *American Opinion*, 162.

173. Obituary of Leonora O'Reilly, *Life and Labor*, May 1927, in O'Reilly Papers, reel 3, frame 41; O'Reilly to Walsh, 28 May 1921, Walsh Papers, New York Public Library, box 29.

174. O'Reilly to Walsh, 14 May 1921, and Walsh to O'Reilly, 16 May 1921, Walsh Papers, New York Public Library, box 29.

175. Burns, "Kathleen O'Brennan," in *Irish in the Atlantic World*, edited by Gleeson, 189–90.

176. Women's Irish Education League to members, 15 Apr. 1921, Walsh Papers, New York Public Library, box 29. The letter lists officers and directors. Charlotte Anita Whitney's name does not appear. "American Irish Liberty League of San Francisco," *Irish World*, 22 July 1922, 10. This article describes the work, mostly of women, in boycotting British goods. Minnie McCarthy, the other woman who presided at the first meeting of the WIEL, became the secretary of the American Irish Liberty League.

177. David Montgomery, *Fall of the House of Labor: The Workplace, the State, and American Labor Activism, 1865–1925*, 6–7, 332; David Montgomery, "Nationalism, American Patriotism, and Class Consciousness among Immigrant Workers in the United States in the Epoch of World War I," in *"Struggle a Hard Battle": Essays on Working-Class Immigrants*, edited by Dick Hoerder.

178. The AARIR had broad appeal. Among the women elected national directors were Adelia Christy of the LAAOH and Mrs. Frank (Evelyn) Scanlan, president of the Margaret Brent Suffrage Guild. Mary McWhorter was also active in the AARIR. "New Organization to Hasten Ireland's Triumph," *Irish World*, 17 Nov. 1920, 3; Mary McWhorter, "A Band of Brave Irishwomen," *Irish World*, 14 Apr. 1923, 5. Mary McWhorter remained active during the civil war. In 1923 the Illinois state chair of the AOH wrote to Daniel Cohalan, "There is still a small element of

radical Bolshevists here in Chicago, shouting for him [de Valera]. They are led by Mrs. McWhorter." Eichacker, *Irish Republican Women*, 40. McWhorter was not the only LAAOH woman criticized for continuing to support de Valera. John Devoy attacked Adelia Christy (then national president of the LAAOH) in the pages of the *Gaelic American* in 1923. "Mrs. Christy Issues Circular with a Bundle of Fibs," *Gaelic American*, 28 Apr. 1923. The LAAOH broke with the men of the AOH over the men's support of the Free State in 1922. "Declare for Free Ireland," *Washington Post*, 28 Jan. 1922, 2.

179. Francis Carroll, "American Association for the Recognition of the Irish Republic," in *Irish American Voluntary Organizations*, edited by Funchion.

180. Doyle, "Striking for Ireland," in *The New York Irish*, edited by Bayor and Meagher, 373; "Plead for Irish Women," *New York Times*, 20 Jan. 1923, 4.

181. "Irish Here Pleased over Monday Truce," *New York Times*, 9 July 1921, 1:7.

5. The Politics of Identity

1. "The Public Rights of Women: A Second Round-Table Conference," 300, 315; Cummings, *New Women of the Old Faith*, 175.

2. Cliona Murphy, *Women's Suffrage Movement and Irish Society in the Early Twentieth Century*, 2, 6. One exception is Owens, *Smashing Times.*

3. Louise Ryan and Margaret Ward, eds., *Irish Women and the Vote: Becoming Citizens.*

4. Owens, *Smashing Times*, 20, 25.

5. Maria Luddy, "From Women and Politics in Nineteenth Century Ireland," in *Irish Women's History Reader*, edited by Alan Hayes and Diane Urquhart, 32–33.

6. Louise Ryan, "Traditions and Double Moral Standards: The Irish Suffragists' Critique of Nationalism," 491–92.

7. Jennifer Naccarelli, "Guided by Their Conscience: Catholic Suffragists in America, 1890–1920," 58–59.

8. "News and Notes," *Woman's Journal*, 7 July 1894, 215.

9. Moloney, *American Catholic Lay Groups*, 1.

10. James J. Kenneally, "Catholicism and Woman Suffrage in Massachusetts," 46.

11. "Woman Suffrage: Cardinal Gibbons Is Opposed to It for the Sake of Womanhood," *Irish World*, 13 Oct. 1894, 6.

12. Quoted in Diner, *Erin's Daughters in America*, 143–45.

13. Cummings, *New Women of the Old Faith*, 160, 164, 171.

14. Robert Ellis Thompson, "Shall Women Vote," *Irish World*, 9 June 1894, 6.

15. Soper, "From Swarthy Ape to Sympathetic Everyman," 263–64.

16. Maureen Murphy, "Bridget and Biddy," in *New Perspectives*, edited by Fanning, 154, 166.

17. "Mrs. Deland Talks on Suffrage," *Washington Post*, 29 Dec. 1909, 6.

18. "Woman Suffrage Workers," *New York Times*, 14 Jan. 1894, 20.

19. S. Sara Monoson, "Lady and the Tiger: Women's Electoral Activism in New York City before Suffrage," 106.

20. "The Women's Conquest of New York," *Harper's Bazaar*, 14 July 1894, 555; "A Jovial Look Ahead," *New York Times*, 22 July 1894, 23.

21. John Kendrick Bangs, "Paradise Club," 9.

22. Corrine M. McConnaughy, *The Woman Suffrage Movement in America: A Reassessment*, 2.

23. Edmund B. Thomas Jr., "School Suffrage and the Campaign for Women's Suffrage in Massachusetts, 1879–1920," 3.

24. McConnaughy, *Woman Suffrage Movement*, 2.

25. Streitmatter, "Nativist Press," 673, 679.

26. Nolan, "Irish-American Teachers," 13, 18.

27. Nolan, *Servants of the Poor*, 3–4.

28. Stephen McIntyre, "'Our Schools Are Not Charitable Institutions,'" 28; Nolan, *Servants of the Poor*, 3; Nolan, "Irish-American Teachers," 13.

29. McIntyre, "'Our Schools Are Not Charitable Institutions,'" 36, 38.

30. Ibid., 28; Nolan, "Irish-American Teachers," 18.

31. Thomas, "School Suffrage," 7.

32. *Boston Pilot*, 19 Sept. 1885, quoted in Lois Bannister Merk, "Boston's Historic Public School Crisis," 178.

33. Thomas, "School Suffrage," 9; Merk, "Boston's Historic Public School Crisis," 180; Polly Welts Kaufmann, "Julia Harrington Duff: An Irish Woman Confronts the Boston Power Structure, 1900–1905," 115.

34. Kenneally, "Catholicism and Woman Suffrage," 49.

35. "Woman Suffrage in Nutmegdom," *New York Sun*, 17 June 1894.

36. "Women Defeat the A.P.A.," *Irish World*, 6 Apr. 1895, 1; "Catholic Women in Bridgeport Were Not Sufficiently Instructed," *Irish World*, 13 Apr. 1895, 6.

37. Several women in Ireland took tentative steps to form leagues after reading Fanny Parnell's letter, and once Anna Parnell issued the official call to join, the response was enthusiastic. Cote, *Fanny and Anna Parnell*, 160.

38. M. Ward, "Gendering the Union," 83, 85.

39. Ibid., 86–87.

40. "Irish Convention," *Columbus Daily Enquirer*, 28 Apr. 1883, 1; "Irish in Convention," *New York Times*, 14 Aug. 1884, 2; "Woman Suffrage to Help Ireland," *Woman's Journal*, 12 Apr. 1884, 119.

41. C. S. L., "Representative Irishmen for Woman Suffrage," *Woman's Journal*, 6 Sept. 1884, 289.

42. "Mrs. Parnell for Woman Suffrage," *Woman's Journal*, 13 Sept. 1884, 300.

43. "Ireland and Women," *Woman's Journal*, 23 Jan. 1886, 32. This letter to the editor was written by "An Irish Suffragist."

44. Diner, *Erin's Daughters in America*, 150.

45. "Ireland and Women," *Woman's Journal*, 13 Mar. 1886, 82.

46. C. S. L., "Representative Irishmen for Woman Suffrage," 289. Willcox and Lozier were active in the Woman Suffrage Party (WSP) in New York. Blake also cooperated with the Woman Suffrage Party until a split with the organization in the mid-1880s. She announced this split in the *Woman's Journal* in 1885 and reminded readers that the WSP was not the same organization as the New York State Suffrage Woman Association. Ann Gordon, ed., *The Selected Papers of Elizabeth Cady Stanton & Susan B. Anthony*, 4:467n1.

47. "Women's Work for Ireland," *Woman's Journal*, 6 Feb. 1886, 48.

48. "Labor's Voice for Home Rule," *New York Times*, 5 July 1886, 8; "Ireland and Women," *Woman's Journal*, 23 Jan. 1886, 32.

49. Lucy Stone, "Irishmen in Ireland Women in America," *Woman's Journal*, 2 Apr. 1892.

50. L. S., "Home Rule and Women's Rights," *Woman's Journal*, 9 July 1892, 222. Beginning in the early 1880s, Stone's daughter, Alice Blackwell, took over primary responsibility for publishing the journal.

51. "Political Progress," *Women's Herald* (London), 7 May 1892, 3; *Women's Herald*, 26 Mar. 1892, 7.

52. Interview, *Women's Herald*, 17 Dec. 1892, 8.

53. Elizabeth Cady Stanton, "Greatest Question Ever before the British Parliament," *Women's Herald*, 7 Mar. 1891, 307.

54. Elizabeth Cady Stanton, *Eighty Years & More*, 90; Jacqueline Van Voris, "Daniel O'Connell and Women's Rights: One Letter."

55. Stanton, *Eighty Years & More*, 90.

56. "A Grand Demonstration: The Masses of New York Celebrate Independence Day and Declare for Ireland," *Irish World*, 10 July 1886, 5; "A Speaker's Stand Collapses," *Washington Post*, 6 July 1886, 1.

57. Marguerite Moore, "My Experience in a New York Campaign," *Woman's Journal*, 19 Nov. 1887, 376. Moore spoke on behalf of the United Labor Party but also claimed that Democrats and Republicans came to listen to her. Lillie Devereux Blake, "Our New York Letter," *Woman's Journal*, 24 Feb. 1894, 61.

58. Blake, "Our New York Letter," 61.

59. "She'll Speak for Bryan," *Baltimore Sun*, 22 Aug. 1900, 10.

60. For more accounts of Moore's activities, see Lillie Devereux Blake's column, "Our New York Letter," *Woman's Journal*, 29 Oct. 1887, 349; 7 Apr. 1894, 109; 14 Jan. 1888, 13; 17 Mar. 1894, 84; 17 Feb. 1894, 53.

61. "New York City Woman Suffrage League," *Woman's Journal*, 22 May 1886, 168; "Women Who Want the Vote: They Held a Mass Convention Yesterday Afternoon in Two Halls," *New York Times*, 27 Feb. 1894, 3.

62. "New York Convention," *Woman's Journal*, 3 Apr. 1886, 112. Suffragists from the New York City League also spoke to branches of the Irish National League in the 1880s. "Irish Suffragists," *Woman's Journal*, 16 Jan. 1886, 18; "Ireland and Women," *Woman's Journal*, 23 Jan. 1886, 32; "Mrs. Parnell for Woman Suffrage," *Woman's Journal*, 13 Sept. 1884, 300.

63. "Woman Suffragists Are Undaunted: They Will Work Harder than Ever to Gain the Right to Vote," *New York Times*, 5 Oct. 1894, 8; "Our New York Letter," *Woman's Journal*, 13 Oct. 1894, 325.

64. Grace Farrell, "Lillie Devereux Blake (1833–1913)," 46, 149.

65. Grace Farrell, *Lillie Devereux Blake: Retracing a Life Erased*, 152, 155; Grace Farrell, "Beneath the Suffrage Narrative."

66. Farrell, *Lillie Devereux Blake*, 154.

67. Katherine Blake and Margaret Louise Wallace, *Champion of Women: The Life of Lillie Devereux Blake*, 147; Lillie Devereux Blake, diary, 8 Oct. 1882, Lillie Devereux Blake Papers, Missouri History Museum.

68. *Irish World*, 10 July 1886, 5; "Day in New York," *Boston Daily Advertiser*, 6 July 1886, 8; "For Erin's Cause," *Los Angeles Daily Times*, 6 July 1886.

69. Janis, *A Greater Ireland*, 141.

70. Advertisement for the Woman Suffrage Party Convention, *Buffalo Express*, 8 Oct. 1884; "Woman Suffrage Advocates," *New York Times*, 9 Oct. 1884, 1; *Amsterdam Daily Democrat*, 20 Oct. 1885, 1.

71. Blake, diary, 12 Feb. 1885, Blake Papers, Missouri History Museum.

72. "Memorial Exercises for Mrs. Parnell," *New York Times*, 9 Apr. 1898, 7; "In Memory of Delia Parnell," *New York Tribune*, 9 Apr. 1898, 5.

73. "Irish Women's Council," *Irish World*, 23 Dec. 1916, 2; Mary J. O'Donovan Rossa to M. W. Chapman (president of the Brooklyn Suffrage League), 10 May 1896, Mariana W. Chapman Family Papers, Friends Historical Library.

74. Mrs. O'Donovan Rossa to John Devoy (n.d., [autumn 1915]), in *Devoy's Post Bag, 1871–1928*, by John Devoy, 482.

75. Oates, *Catholic Philanthropic Tradition*, 81; Deirdre Moloney, *American Catholic Lay Groups*, 139.

76. O'Grady, *Catholic Charities*, 319, 327; Tentler, *Seasons of Grace*, 213.

77. Oates, *Catholic Philanthropic Tradition*, 55.

78. Moloney, *American Catholic Lay Groups*, 4–6.

79. J. Dolan, *American Catholic Experience*, 205; O'Grady, *Catholic Charities*, 327; Mary V. Toomy, "The Work and Aims of the Queen's Daughters," *Catholic World* 67 (1898): 611.

80. "Catholic Women in Session: A Brilliant Gathering of Scholarly Catholic Ladies at the Columbian Exposition," *Irish World*, 3 June 1893, 1; Alice Timmons Toomy, "There Is a Public Sphere for Catholic Women," in "The Woman Question among Catholics: A Roundtable Conference," special issue, *Catholic World* 57 (1893): 675. Catholic women did join the Catholic Total Abstinence Union by the 1890s, but men dominated the movement. Moloney, *American Catholic Lay Groups*, 44, 62.

81. Moloney, *American Catholic Lay Groups*, 44, 46–48, 62, 66.

82. Lois Bannister Merk, "Massachusetts and the Woman Suffrage Movement," 341–42.

83. *Philadelphia Times*, 9 Mar. 1898, 8.

84. Orr, "Mary Elizabeth Lease," 141–43.

85. Moloney, *American Catholic Lay Groups*, 65–67.

86. "Mrs. Barry's Lecture," *New Orleans Daily Picayune*, 21 Nov. 1887, 2.

87. "Mrs. Leonora M. Barry," *New Orleans Daily Picayune*, 21 Feb. 1889, 6; "Leonora M. Barry," *New Orleans Daily Picayune*, 22 Feb. 1889, 3.

88. "Closer Fellowship," *Boston Daily Globe*, 2 Dec. 1895, 12.

89. "Demands the Vote," *Rocky Mountain News* (Denver), 30 Aug. 1890, 7; "A Woman on Whiskey," *Rocky Mountain News*, 13 May 1889.

90. Mari Jo Buhl and Paul Buhl, eds., *Concise History of Woman Suffrage*, 334.

91. R. Edwards, *Angels in the Machinery*, 102, 104.

92. Ellen Carol DuBois, *Woman Suffrage & Women's Rights*, 74–75.

93. Mary Kenney O'Sullivan, unpublished autobiography, 95.

94. "Mary Kenney O'Sullivan," in *Notable American Women*, 655–56.

95. "Delegate Lennon in the Chair," *Daily Inter Ocean* (Chicago), 14 Dec. 1893, 7.

96. "Susan B. Anthony Well-Known Reformer Is Visiting in Detroit," *Detroit Free Press*, 13 Dec. 1899, 1; "Applause When A.F.L. President's Ruling Was Sustained," *Detroit Free Press*, 13 Dec. 1899, 1; Peter J. Albert, ed., *Samuel Gompers Papers*, 140.

97. P. Foner, *Women and the American Labor Movement*, 294.

98. "Worker and the Chance to Work," *Boston Daily Globe*, 8 May 1910, 46.

6. Twentieth-Century Connections

1. "Militant Maud Malone," 1191; "Pickets in Solitary," *Washington Post*, 23 Oct. 1917, 14.

2. "Militant Maud Malone," 1191; "Maud Malone Comes of Fighting Stock," *Woman's Journal*, 11 May 1912, 151.

3. "Maud Malone Quits the Suffragettes: Not Because She No Longer Believes, but Because Social Leanings Hinder the Cause," *New York Times*, 27 Mar. 1908, 4.

4. Catherine Shanley, "The Library Employees' Union of Greater New York, 1917–1929," 239.

5. For example, in a 1905 letter Gompers apologizes to Anthony for not being available to meet with her, but assures her that he has had messages from suffrage organizations across the country expressing support for the AFL's position on woman suffrage. Gordon, *Selected Papers*, 6:282.

6. DuBois, *Harriot Stanton Blatch*, 91.

7. Ibid., 94.

8. Ibid., 95, 99. Leonora O'Reilly served as vice president, but did not remain active for very long.

9. Anna Howard Shaw to O'Reilly, 28 Sept. 1908, O'Reilly Papers, reel 4, frame 1002; O'Reilly to Shaw, 14 Oct. 1908, ibid., frames 1003–8. O'Reilly told Shaw to select from her remarks, but to let O'Reilly know what she chose.

10. By 1913 New York also had a Wage Earner's Anti-Suffrage Association. "Do Not Want the Ballot: Antisuffragists Will Appear before the House," *Washington Post*, 4 Dec. 1913, 2; "'Antis' Now Lead: House Committee Turns from Suffragists, Says Reports," *Washington Post*, 5 Dec. 1913, 2.

11. Susan Englander, *Class Conflict and Coalition in the California Woman Suffrage Movement, 1907–1912*, 96.

12. Ibid. The president, Minna O'Donnell, was a German American who worked as a printer in Wisconsin before her marriage to E. H. O'Donnell. After the couple moved to San Francisco, she joined the women's auxiliary to her husband's union, the International Typographical Union Local 21, and became its president.

13. O'Reilly, diary, 15 Sept. 1911, O'Reilly Papers, reel 2.

14. Leonora O'Reilly, "The Incentive to Motherhood," handwritten draft, ibid., reel 9, frames 591–605.

15. O'Reilly to Miss Lornbern [?], n.d., ibid., reel 6, frame 724.

16. O'Reilly to Mrs. Brown, 22 Apr. 1913, ibid., frames 802–3.

17. O'Reilly to Miss Brody, 23 Jan. 1914, ibid., reel 7, frames 31–35.

18. Robert Wesser, *A Response to Progressivism: The Democratic Party and New York Politics, 1902–1918*, 225.

19. DuBois, *Harriot Stanton Blatch*, 133, 137; Wesser, *Response to Progressivism*, 225. The *New York Times* criticized Sullivan's position in 1912, declaring, "We have not understood that the women in his district have had much leisure to consider the suffrage, or have been very eager supporters of the 'votes for women' movement." The article claimed that his fellow senators did not take him seriously. "Woman Suffrage at Albany," *New York Times*, 20 Mar. 1912, 12.

20. John Buenker, "Urban Political Machine and Woman Suffrage: A Study in Political Adaptability."

21. Margaret Finn to O'Reilly, 16 Aug. 1916, O'Reilly Papers, reel 7, frames 690–93 (emphasis in the original).

22. James Gimpel, "Reform-Resistant and Reform-Adopting Machines: The Electoral Foundations of Urban Politics, 1910–1930"; Buenker, "Urban Political Machine," 264–65.

23. Buenker, "Urban Political Machine," 265, 273.

24. Ibid., 279.

25. DuBois, *Harriot Stanton Blatch*, 100–101.

26. Owens, *Smashing Times*, 40–42.

27. DuBois, *Harriot Stanton Blatch*, 100–101.

28. Ibid., 101.

29. Diner, *Erin's Daughters in America*, 99.

30. The same argument has been made for Jewish women, who also played a very important role in the labor and suffrage movements. Annelise Orleck, *Common Sense and a Little Fire: Women and Working-Class Politics in the United States, 1900–1965*.

31. "500 Women Cheer for Mother Jones," *New York Times*, 23 May 1914, 3.

32. "Maud Malone Comes of Fighting Stock," 151.

33. Nolan, *Servants of the Poor*, 89; Flynn, *Rebel Girl*, 23.

34. "Why Women of Trade League Joined the Union," *Chicago Daily Tribune*, 3 Oct. 1909, E10; *Cleveland Federationist*, 12 Nov. 1914, O'Reilly Papers, reel 9, frame 836; *New Canaan (CT) Advertiser*, Jan. 1912, ibid., frames 561–62.

35. DuBois, *Harriot Stanton Blatch*, 113n114.

36. *Tributes to the Life, Character, and Services of Dr. Edward Malone* (Brooklyn: privately printed, 1891), 14–15, Virginia Historical Society, Richmond.

37. "Honoring Dr. Malone," *New York Times*, 19 June 1890, 2; "Rome Nonpluse," *Christian Advocate*, 17 July 1890, 456.

38. General Federation of Women's Clubs, *Club Women of New York* (New York, 1906–7), 35, books.google.com; "Mere Man Couldn't Stop 500 Women 'Voting,'" *New York Times*, 7 Nov. 1906, 9.

39. "Women in Unofficial March," *New York Sun*, 17 Feb. 1908, 1; "March Despite Police," *New York Times*, 17 Feb. 1908, 3.

40. "Amazons Bluff New York Police," *Washington Times*, 17 Feb. 1908, 9; "American Suffragists," *Hawaiian Star*, 28 Mar. 1908, 3. This article lists the members of the executive committee, including Marguerite Moore, possibly the same Marguerite Moore who had been active in New York suffrage campaigns in the nineteenth century.

41. "Men She Can't Reason With," *Idaho Statesman*, 10 Jan. 1909, 2.

42. "Miss Malone on Her Rights," *New York Times*, 22 June 1909, 6.

43. "Militant Woman Causes Trouble for Roosevelt," *Atlanta Constitution*, 26 Mar. 1912, 1. This story was widely covered.

44. "Bull Moose Part Has Woman Leader," *New York Times*, 11 Aug. 1912, 6; "Maud Malone Held; Court Rebukes Her," *New York Times*, 24 Oct. 1912, 11; "Kempner Places Maud Malone under Bond," *New York Tribune*, 24 Oct. 1912, 7.

45. "Maud Malone Asks in Vain to Be Fined," *New York Times*, 13 Nov. 1912, 24; "Ignore Maud Malone," *New York Tribune*, 14 Nov. 1912, 7.

46. Tim Cresswell, "Mobilising the Movement: The Role of Mobility in the Suffrage Politics of Florence Luscomb and Margaret Foley, 1911–1915," 451.

47. Walter Leon Sawyer, "Our First Suffragette—Miss Margaret Foley Who Heckles," *Boston Evening Transcript*, 30 Sept. 1911, Margaret Foley Papers, reel 6, series 1, Woman Suffrage, pt. D: New England; "M'Inerney Is Heckled Again," *Boston Herald*, 22 Sept. 1911, scrapbook, ibid., series 3, frame 59.

48. "M'Inerney Is Heckled Again." See also John D. Buenker, "The Mahatma and Progressive Reform: Martin Lomasney as Lawmaker, 1911–1917."

49. Caroline I. R. to Foley, n.d., Foley Papers, reel 7. In 1913 Foley targeted Levi Greenwood, president of the Massachusetts Senate. Greenwood later acknowledged Foley's activities as one cause of his defeat. Kenneally, "Catholicism and Woman Suffrage," 54.

50. "Trailed All Day," *Boston Daily Globe*, 10 Oct. 1911, 1.

51. "'Votes for Women' Converts Newton: Representative Surrenders as Miss Foley Appears at Rally Ready to 'Heckle,'" *Boston American*, 24 Sept. 1911, Foley Papers, reel 6.

52. Sawyer, "Our First Suffragette."

53. "Misses Luscomb and Foley Speak at Interesting Woman Suffrage Meeting," *Worcester Telegram*, 10 Apr. 1913, Foley Papers, reel 6.

54. Margaret L. Foley, "A Reason a Day Why Women Should Vote," *Boston Daily Globe*, 27 Feb. 1913, 13. See also "Democracy of the West," *Boston Daily Globe*, 5 Jan. 1913, 40.

55. Janet Buell, "Alva Belmont: From Socialite to Feminist."

56. Pete Geidel, "Alva E. Belmont: A Forgotten Feminist," 207.

57. Eleanor Booth Simmons, "Names of Suffrage Pioneers Not Forgotten in Victory," *New York Sun*, 9 Dec. 1917, sec. 5, p. 10.

58. "Jail Is the Worst Kind of Dive," *Salem (OR) Daily Capital Journal*, 17 Sept. 1910, 3; "Woman Refuses to Leave Jail," *New York Tribune*, 29 Oct. 1907, 5.

59. "Lunchroom Queen Quits Mrs. Belmont," *New York Times*, 30 Jan. 1912, 20; Geidel, "Alva E. Belmont," 207.

60. Geidel, "Alva E. Belmont," 265.

61. "Lunchroom Queen Quits Mrs. Belmont," 20.

62. "Maud Malone Asks in Vain to Be Fined," 24; "Stands by Militant Maud," *New York Tribune*, 22 Oct. 1912; "Maud Malone Gets Suspended Sentence," *New York Sun*, 13 Nov. 1912, 3.

63. "Women to Police Suffrage Parade," *Christian Science Monitor*, 10 May 1912, 2; "Will Ask Devery to Drill Policewomen," *New York Times*, 10 May 1912, 22; "Youthful Suffragists Invade Wall Street," *Boston Journal*, 10 Apr. 1913, 4.

64. "Women Delegates Take Their Babies," *New York Times*, 5 Sept. 1912, 3. Donnelly supported Wilson in 1916.

65. "Will Ask Devery to Drill Policewomen," 22.

66. Sidney R. Bland, "'Never Quite as Committed as We'd Like': The Suffrage Militancy of Lucy Burns," 5–8.

67. Ibid., 14; Anita Danker, "Grassroots Suffragists: Josephine Collins and Louise Mayo, a Study in Contrast," 55.

68. Neil Hogan, "Hartford Irishwoman Was Heroine of Suffrage Drive" and "Suffragist Heroine Took Up Cause of Irish Freedom," Connecticut Irish-American Historical Society, East Haven, CT. Thank you to Neil Hogan for sending these articles to me.

69. Crista DeLuzio, ed., *Women's Rights: People and Perspectives*, 110.

70. Naccarelli, "Guided by Their Conscience," 67, 72–73.

71. Ida Husted Harper, *History of Woman Suffrage, 1900–1920*, 282.

72. Carrie Chapman Catt, *Woman Suffrage and Politics*, 281, 283.

73. Harper, *History of Woman Suffrage*, 462–63; Catt, *Woman Suffrage and Politics*, 286.

74. "Winning the 'Foreign' Voter," *Woman Voter*, June 1915, 23.

75. Introduction to "Thirty Days," *Life and Labor*, Sept. 1913, 264–65, copy from O'Reilly Papers, reel 3, frames 256–57. In May 1913, Hinchey served thirty days in jail for her participation in the panama-hat strike.

76. Wage Earners Suffrage League, *Senators vs. Working Women*" (New York, 1913?), O'Reilly Papers, reel 12, frames 55–70.

77. Jeannette Rankin to Foley, 29 Jan. 1914, Foley Papers, reel 8; Rankin to Foley, 27 Jan. 1914, ibid., reel 7.

78. "Margaret Foley Tells of Work for Suffrage," *Christian Science Monitor*, 17 Mar. 1914, 5; "Campaigner Tells How Suffragists Won in Nevada," *Christian Science Monitor*, 17 Nov. 1914, 9.

79. Mary O'Neill [Montana Equal Suffrage Assoc.] to O'Reilly, 20 June 1914, O'Reilly Papers, reel 7, frames 107–8.

80. Ida Porter-Boyer [Ohio Woman's Suffrage Association] to Foley, 7 Aug. 1912, Foley Papers, reel 7. Irish Day fell through when they left Foley's name off the program.

81. Ibid., 9 Aug. 1912. When the Ohio campaign failed, Margaret Dreier Robins told O'Reilly that she believed that defeat was the lack of a suffrage movement among working women and the failure to reach working men. Robins to O'Reilly, 14 Sept. 1912, O'Reilly Papers, reel 6, frames 412–13; Robins to O'Reilly, 19 July 1914, ibid., reel 7, frames 122–31.

82. Harriet Taylor Upton to Foley, 13 Aug. 1912, Foley Papers, reel 7.

83. "Maggie and Maggie to Shake for Votes," *New York Times*, 8 Sept. 1915, 8; "Missing Girl Alarm for Maggie Hinchey," *New York Times*, 9 Sept. 1915, 12.

84. "Margaret Hinchey Tells of Wilson," *New York Times*, 5 Feb. 1914.

85. Clipping of "Suffrage in Bowery Hotel," *New York Times*, 5 May 1915, O'Reilly Papers, reel 7, frame 314.

86. "Suffragists Form Trench Brigade: Women Will Visit Workmen in Subway Excavations to Enlist Them in the Cause," *New York Times*, 27 June 1915. Hinchey apparently used this strategy earlier as well. After a chilly reception from a group of firemen, she reported asking the chairmen to "give some Irish leaflets to any Irishmen." Hinchey to O'Reilly, 29 May 1913 [?], O'Reilly Papers, reel 6, frames 946–49.

87. Kenneally, "Catholicism and Woman Suffrage," 46.

88. Eileen McDonagh and H. Douglas Price, "Woman Suffrage in the Progressive Era: Patterns of Opposition and Support in Referenda Voting, 1910–1918," 430.

89. Kenneally, "Catholicism and Woman Suffrage," 52; "Home Is the Place for Women Says Cardinal Gibbons," *Irish World*, 3 Dec. 1910, 3.

90. "Cardinal Gibbons on Suffrage," *Irish World*, 26 Apr. 1913, 2.

91. "Catholics and Suffrage," *Woman's Journal*, 21 Sept. 1912, 300.

92. Foley Papers, reel 8, frames 116–17.

93. O'Reilly Papers, reel 12, frames 255–56.

94. Finn to O'Reilly, 2 Apr. 1912, ibid., reel 6, frames 178–80. The flyer listed Catholic periodicals, societies, politicians, and clergy supporting woman suffrage and also listed two Catholic women suffragists, Jane Campbell, president of the Philadelphia Woman Suffrage Association, and Sara McPike, chair of the Catholic Committee of the Woman Suffrage Party. "The Catholic Church Not Opposed to Woman Suffrage," ibid., reel 12, frame 256.

95. Finn to O'Reilly, 28 Apr. 1913, ibid., reel 6, frames 831–32; ibid., 18 Aug. 1915 [?], reel 7, frames 485–87. Finn also used the flyers among Catholics in New York's 1915 suffrage campaign.

96. Margaret Hayden Rorke, *Letters and Addresses on Woman Suffrage by Catholic Ecclesiastics.* Rorke was the mother of actor Hayden Rourke and also did some acting herself. She is best known as the head of the Textile Color Card Association. According to the 1910 US Census, her parents were both born in the United States, so her ethnicity is unclear. However, her maiden name was Monahan. "Margaret Rorke, Color Authority," *New York Times*, 3 Mar. 1969, 35; "Sister M. Bernadette," *New York Times*, 9 Apr. 1932, 15.

97. "Bath and a Meal Best Part of Trip," *Evening Star* (Washington, DC), 24 June 1915, 4; "Suffragist Pioneers Returning from 1000 Mile Tour through Maryland," *Washington Times*, 21 June 1915, 3.

98. "Woman Immigrant Became a Judge," *Brooklyn Eagle Magazine*, 17 May 1931, 84, http://bklyn.newspapers.com/image/57581572.

99. "For Equality in Jury Service," *Equal Rights* 13, no. 38 (1926): 306, Gerritsen Collection Online.

100. J. O. Miller to O'Reilly, 17 June 1915, and O'Reilly to Miller, 22 June 1915, O'Reilly Papers, reel 7, frame 370.

101. Minutes of the WTUL committee to secure votes for women, n.d., ibid., reel 12, frames 133–34.

102. "Margaret Hinchey Speaks Again Tonight," *Missoulian*, 7 Aug. 1914, 2.

103. Margaret Hinchey, "Votes for Women: Appeal to Irish Citizens to Support the Woman Suffrage Amendment," *Gaelic American*, 27 Oct. 1917, 3.

104. Sawyer, "Our First Suffragette."

105. Mayor Farrell to Foley, 29 May 1912, Foley Papers, reel 5. The Amherst Knights of Columbus also asked her to speak in 1913. The Catholic Club of Dorchester invited Foley to be a judge at their annual Barn Party in 1914. Thomas Casey to Foley, 14 Nov. 1914, ibid., reel 7.

106. Lucy Kennedy Miller [Equal Franchise Federation of Pittsburgh] to Foley, 23 June 1914, ibid., reel 8.

107. Kenneally suggests growing support for suffrage among middle-class Catholics between 1910 and 1920. James J. Kenneally, *The History of American Catholic Women*, 92, 96, 119, 134.

108. Elizabeth Cullen [Daughters of Isabella, Court Santa Maria, no. 150] to Foley, 25 Mar. 1912, Foley Papers, reel 7.

109. Evelyn Beverly Coe to Foley, 28 Oct. 1914, ibid.

110. James Connolly, *The Triumph of Ethnic Progressivism: Urban Political Culture in Boston, 1900–1925*, 148, 180. In 1921, when the League of Women Voters endorsed Curley's opponent, several Irish American members, led by Carrie F. Sheehan, a self-described suffragist, left in protest, citing Curley's support of women's suffrage as a reason for loyalty and criticizing the class composition of the league. Curley appealed directly to Irish American women to register and vote.

111. The MWSA dismissed its speakers, including Foley, after the campaign. Foley to Anna Bird, 9 Aug. 1918, Foley Papers, reel 5.

112. Alice Stone Blackwell to Foley, 6 Aug. 1918, ibid.

113. O'Reilly to Mary Hay, 3 Dec. 1917, O'Reilly Papers, reel 7, frames 843–45.

114. O'Reilly to Hay, 29 Dec. 1917, ibid., frames 862–63.

115. Hinchey to O'Reilly, 24 (or 29) Jan. 1918, ibid., reel 7. When Hinchey wrote this letter, she was looking for work. O'Reilly to Hay, 3 Dec. 1917, ibid., frames 843–45.

116. J. Dolan, *American Catholic Experience*, 329, 335; David Noel Doyle, "Catholicism, Politics, and Irish America since 1890: Some Critical Considerations," 206–7.

117. Moloney, *American Catholic Lay Groups*, 168.

118. Helen Haines, "Catholic Womanhood and the Suffrage," *Catholic World* 102 (Oct. 1915): 59.

119. Francis Mason, "The Newer Eve: The Catholic Women's Suffrage Society in England, 1911–1923," 621; Naccarelli, "Guided by Their Conscience," 147.

120. Maria Luddy, ed., *Women in Ireland, 1800–1918: A Documentary History*, 283–84.

121. "Catholic Committee," *Woman Voter*, Sept. 1912; "Suffrage Meeting at the Catholic Summer School of America, Cliff Haven, N.Y.," *Woman Voter*, Oct. 1912, 9.

122. Naccarelli, "Guided by Their Conscience," 148, 143.

123. "Debt of Suffrage to Catholic Women," *New York Times*, 19 Nov. 1917, 11; Sara McPike, "St. Catherine's Welfare Association," *Woman Voter*, Sept. 1915, 26; *New York Times*, "For Catholic Suffragists," 12 Mar. 1916, 16.

124. "Miss Sara M'Pike, Suffrage Leader," *New York Times*, 27 Feb. 1943, 13; "Catholic Suffrage," *New York Tribune*, 26 Apr. 1914, 12.

125. "Priest for Suffrage," *New York Times*, 30 Apr. 1914, 7; "Catholic Women Work for Cause," *Woman's Journal*, 6 June 1914, 182.

126. "Catholics Say Ballot Needed," *Woman's Journal*, 24 May 1913, 163; "Bad Bills Swell Suffrage Ranks," *Woman's Journal*, 17 Apr. 1915, 119–20. The association passed a resolution in favor of a national suffrage amendment in 1914. "Catholic Women Work for Cause," 182.

127. Sara H. McPike, "St. Catherine Welfare Association," *Woman Voter*, Sept. 1915, 26.

128. Sara McPike to William Bourke Cockran, n.d., Cockran Papers, New York Public Library.

129. "Cardinal Gibbons May Shift Views," *Woman's Journal*, 24 Feb. 1917, 44.

130. New York State Woman Suffrage Party Records, slipcase 1, New York Public Library.

131. "Catholic Women Carried No Banners in Suffrage Parade," *Idaho Statesman*, 27 Oct. 1915, 5.

132. "Priests Oppose Suffrage," *Philadelphia Inquirer*, 10 July 1915, 7.

133. "Suffrage Parader Loses Teaching Job," *New York Times*, 22 May 1912, 1.

134. "Courses for Women Voters," *Irish World*, 28 Sept. 1918, 2; "Debt of Suffrage to Catholic Women," *New York Times*, 19 Nov. 1917, 1.

135. Sara McPike, "Democratic Women: Why New Voters Should Support the Administration," *New York Times*, 18 May 1918, 14; "Republicans Guess Whitman's Vote," *New York Times*, 4 Oct. 1918, 11.

136. Fund-raising letter from the Margaret Brent Suffrage Guild, Apr. 1919, Foley Papers, reel 7.

137. Foley to Scanlan, 21 July 1919, ibid.

138. Mary Healy to Foley, 22 June 1919, ibid.; M. Louise Murray to Foley, 17 June 1919, ibid.

139. "Mrs. Frank C. Scanlan Honored at Banquet," *Boston Daily Globe*, 18 Mar. 1923, 12.

140. May O'Conor Hickey to Foley, 13 June [no year], and two letters, Hickey to Foley, n.d., ibid.

141. Foley to members of the executive board of the Margaret Brent Suffrage Guild, 25 Sept. 1919, ibid.

142. "Suffs Guild Changes Name: Now Margaret Brent Civic League," unidentified newspaper clipping, ibid. Although there is no definitive evidence of her ethnicity, Mrs. Frank (Evelyn) Scanlan was chairwoman of the reception committee for the wife of Eamon de Valera when she arrived in Boston. Scanlan reportedly spoke at some length. See "Boston Women Greet the President's Wife," *Irish World*, 25 Sept. 1920, 11. She was also active in the AARIR.

143. "Warns Women Voters against Radicalism," *Boston Daily Globe*, 13 June 1919, 2.

144. Evelyn Savidge Sterne, *Ballots and Bibles: Ethnic Politics and the Catholic Church in Providence*, 201.

145. Edward W. Quinn to Daniel Cohalan, 1 June 1920, Cockran Papers, New York Public Library, box 3, folder 3.

146. Cliona Murphy, "'The Tune of the States and Stripes': The American Influence on the Irish Suffrage Movement," in *Women Surviving: Studies in Irish Women's History in the 19th and 20th Centuries*, edited by Maria Luddy and Cliona Murphy, 181.

147. Quoted in James McConnel, "Franchise Factor in the Defeat of the Irish Parliamentary Party," 362.

148. C. Murphy, *Women's Suffrage Movement*, 176. Murphy does not include the names of these women. David Brundage, "'In Time of Peace, Prepare for War': Key Themes in the Social Thought of New York's Irish Nationalists, 1890–1916," in *The New York Irish*, edited by Bayor and Meagher, 330.

149. Murphy, "'Tune of the Stars and Stripes,'" 194.

150. Louie Bennett to Foley, 2 July 1914, Foley Papers, reel 8 (emphasis in the original).

151. Skeffington, *Impressions of Sinn Fein*, 10. As reported in "English Militarism in Ireland," *Irish World*, 13 Jan. 1917, 1–2.

152. "Irish Women's Council," *Irish World*, 25 Sept. 1915, 6.

153. Katherine Hughes to Daniel Cohalan, Cohalan Papers, American Irish Historical Society, box 7, folder 7.

154. Harry Boland to Cohalan, ibid., box 2, folder 5.

155. Eichacker, *Irish Republican Women*, xxi; Eleanor Brennan [headquarters secretary, National Woman's Party] to John Finerty, 3 Oct. 1922, and Finerty to

Brennan, 17 Oct. 1922, John Finerty Papers, box 5. Finerty also shared Harry Boland's letters with Alice Paul after Boland's death. This John Finerty is not the same John Finerty who headed the United Irish League of America but may be his son.

Conclusion

1. "Mayor Eulogizes Woman Surgeon," *New York Times*, 17 May 1936, N10.

2. Carroll, *American Opinion*, 177; Funchion, *Irish American Voluntary Organization*, 9–12.

3. Meagher, *Inventing Irish America*, 371.

Bibliography

Newspapers and Periodicals

Alarm
Baltimore Sun
Boston Daily Globe
Boston Journal
Boston Morning Journal
Boston Pilot
Catholic Mirror
Catholic World
Chicago Daily Tribune
Christian Science Monitor
Citizen (Chicago)
Detroit Free Press
Gaelic American (New York)
Inter Ocean (Chicago)
Irish Nation (New York)
Irish World (New York)
Liberty (Boston)
Los Angeles Daily Times
National Hibernian: Monthly Publication of the Ancient Order of Hibernians
New World (Chicago)
New York Times
New York Tribune
San Francisco Call
Standard (New York)
Washington Post
Woman's Journal (Boston)
Woman Voter (New York)
Women's Herald (London)

Manuscript Collections

American Irish Historical Society, New York
Cohalan, Daniel. Papers.
Devoy, John. Papers.

Burns Library, Boston College
Collins, Patrick. Papers.

Friends Historical Library, Swarthmore College, Swarthmore, PA
Chapman, Mariana W. Family Papers.

Missouri History Museum, St. Louis
Blake, Lillie Devereux. Papers.

New York Public Library, Manuscripts and Archives Division, Astor, Lenox, and Tilden Foundations
Cockran, William Bourke. Papers.
George, Henry. Papers.
Maloney Collection of Irish Historical Papers.
New York State Woman Suffrage Party Records.
Walsh, Frank P. Papers.

Schlesinger Library, Radcliffe Institute, Harvard Univ., Cambridge, MA
Allen, Annie Ware Winsor. Papers.
O'Sullivan, Mary Kenney. Papers.

Special Collections Library, University of Michigan, Ann Arbor
Finerty, John. Papers.

Collections on Microfilm

Foley, Margaret. Papers. Research Collections in Women's Studies—Women's Studies Manuscript Collections from the Schlesinger Library, Radcliffe College. Series 1, Woman Suffrage, Part D: New England.

O'Reilly, Leonora. Papers. Microfilm edition of the Papers of the Women's Trade Union League and Its Principal Leaders.

O'Sullivan, Mary Kenney. Unpublished autobiography. Microfilm edition of the Papers of the Women's Trade Union League and Its Principal Leaders.

Other Sources

Abell, Aaron. "The Reception of Leo XIII's Labor Encyclical in America, 1891–1919." *Review of Politics* 7 (1945): 464–95.

Albert, Peter J., ed. *Samuel Gompers Papers.* Urbana: Univ. of Illinois Press, 1995.

Anbinder, Tyler, and Hope McCaffrey. "Which Irish Men and Women Immigrated to the United States during the Great Famine Migration of 1846–54." *Irish Historical Studies* 39 (2015). doi:10.1017/his.205.22.

Andreassi, Anthony D. "'The Cunning Leader of a Dangerous Clique'? The Burtsell Affair and Archbishop Michael Augustine Corrigan." *Catholic Historical Review* 86, no. 4 (2000): 620–39.

Bangs, John Kendrick. "Paradise Club." *Ladies' Home Journal*, Dec. 1894.

Bayor, Ronald H., and Timothy J. Meagher, eds. *The New York Irish*. Baltimore: Johns Hopkins Univ. Press, 1996.

Becker, Penny Edgell. "'Rational Amusement and Sound Instruction': Constructing the True Catholic Woman in the *Ave Maria*, 1865–1889." *Religion and American Culture* 8 (1998): 55–90.

Bell, Stephen. *Rebel, Priest, and Prophet: A Biography of Dr. Edward McGlynn*. New York: Devin-Adair, 1937.

Blake, Katherine, and Margaret Louise Wallace. *Champion of Women: The Life of Lillie Devereux Blake*. New York: Fleming H. Revell, 1943.

Bland, Sidney R. "'Never Quite as Committed as We'd Like': The Suffrage Militancy of Lucy Burns." *Journal of Long Island History* 17, no. 2 (1981): 4–23.

Blewett, Mary. *Men, Women, and Work: Class, Gender, and Protest in the New England Shoe Industry, 1780–1910*. Urbana: Univ. of Illinois Press, 1988.

Boone, Gladys. *The Women's Trade Union Leagues in Great Britain and the United States of America*. New York: Columbia Univ. Press, 1942.

Boyce, D. George. *Nationalism in Ireland*. 3rd ed. London: Routledge, 1995.

Brooks, Frank H., ed. *The Individualist Anarchists: An Anthology of Liberty (1881–1908)*. New Brunswick, NJ: Transaction, 1994.

Brown, Dorothy, and Elizabeth McKeown. *The Poor Belong to Us: Catholic Charities and American Welfare*. Cambridge, MA: Harvard Univ. Press, 1997.

Brown, Thomas. *Irish-American Nationalism, 1870–1890*. Philadelphia: J. B. Lippincott, 1966.

Brown, Victoria Bissell, ed. *Twenty Years at Hull-House*. Boston: Bedfords/St. Martin's, 1999.

Brundage, David. "After the Land League: Persistence of Irish-American Labor Radicalism in Denver, 1897–1905." *Journal of American Ethnic History* 11, no. 3 (1992): 3–26.

———. "American Labour and the Irish Question, 1916–1923." *Saothar* 24 (1999): 59–66.

———. *Irish Nationalists in America: The Politics of Exile, 1798–1998*. New York: Oxford Univ. Press, 2016.

———. *The Making of Western Labor Radicalism: Denver's Organized Workers, 1878–1905*. Urbana: Univ. of Illinois Press, 1994.

Buell, Janet. "Alva Belmont: From Socialite to Feminist." *Historian* 52, no. 2 (1990): 219–41.

Buenker, John D. "The Mahatma and Progressive Reform: Martin Lomasney as Lawmaker, 1911–1917." *New England Quarterly* 44, no. 3 (1971): 397–419.

———. "The Urban Political Machine and Woman Suffrage: A Study in Political Adaptability." *Historian* 33 (1971): 264–79.

Buhl, Mari Jo, and Paul Buhl, eds. *Concise History of Woman Suffrage*. Urbana: Univ. of Illinois Press, 2005.

Bularzik, Mary J. "The Bonds of Belonging: Leonora O'Reilly and Social Reform." *Labor History* 24 (1983): 60–83.

Burns, Catherine. "American Identity and the Transatlantic Irish Nationalist Movement, 1912–1925." PhD diss., Univ. of Wisconsin, 2011.

Campbell, Malcolm. *Ireland's New Worlds: Immigrants, Politics, and Society in the United States and Australia, 1815–1922*. Madison: Univ. of Wisconsin Press, 2008.

Carroll, Francis M. *American Opinion and the Irish Question, 1910–1923: A Study in Opinion and Policy*. Dublin: Gill and Macmillan, 1978.

Carter, Patricia A. *"Everybody's Paid but the Teacher": The Teaching Profession and the Women's Movement*. New York: Teacher's College Press, 2002.

Catt, Carrie Chapman. *Woman Suffrage and Politics*. Seattle: Univ. of Washington Press, 1969.

Coburn, Carol, and Martha Smith. *Spirited Lives: How Nuns Shaped Catholic Culture and American Life, 1836–1920*. Chapel Hill: Univ. of North Carolina Press, 2005.

Connolly, James J. *The Triumph of Ethnic Progressivism: Urban Political Culture in Boston, 1900–1925*. Cambridge, MA: Harvard Univ. Press, 1998.

Cote, Jane McL. *Fanny and Anna Parnell: Ireland's Patriot Sisters*. New York: St. Martin's Press, 1991.

Cresswell, Tim. "Mobilising the Movement: The Role of Mobility in the Suffrage Politics of Florence Luscomb and Margaret Foley, 1911–1915." *Gender, Place & Culture: A Journal of Feminist Geography* 12, no. 4 (2005): 447–61.

Cummings, Kathleen Sprows. *New Women of the Old Faith: Gender and American Catholicism in the Progressive Era*. Chapel Hill: Univ. of North Carolina Press, 2009.

Curran, Robert Emmett. "The McGlynn Affair and the Shaping of the New Conservatism in American Catholicism, 1886–1894." *Catholic Historical Review* 66, no. 2 (1980): 184–204.

———. "Prelude to 'Americanism': The New York Academia and Clerical Radicalism in the Late Nineteenth Century." *Church History* 47, no. 1 (1978): 48–65.

Curtis, Georgina Pell. *The American Catholic Who's Who.* St. Louis: B. Herder, 1911.

Czira, Sidney Gifford. *The Years Flew By.* Rev. ed. Galway: Arlen House, 2000.

Danker, Anita. "Grassroots Suffragists: Josephine Collins and Louise Mayo, a Study in Contrast." *New England Journal of History* 67, no. 2 (2011): 54–72.

DeLuzio Crista, ed. *Women's Rights: People and Perspectives.* Westport, CT: Greenwood, 2010.

Deutsch, Sarah. *Women and the City: Gender, Space, and Power in Boston, 1870–1940.* Oxford: Oxford Univ. Press, 2000.

Devoy, John. *Devoy's Post Bag, 1871–1928.* Vol. 2. Dublin: C. J. Fallon, 1953.

Diner, Hasia. *Erin's Daughters in America: Irish Immigrant Women in the Nineteenth Century.* Baltimore: Johns Hopkins Univ. Press, 1983.

Doherty, Robert. "Tempest on the Hudson: The Struggle for 'Equal Pay for Equal Work' in New York City Public Schools, 1907–1911." *History of Education Quarterly* 19, no. 4 (1979). http://www.jstor.org/stable/368052.

Dolan, Jay P. *The American Catholic Experience: A History from Colonial Times to the Present.* Notre Dame, IN: Univ. of Notre Dame Press, 1992.

———. *In Search of an American Catholicism: A History of Religion and Culture in Tension.* New York: Oxford Univ. Press, 2002. https://ebookcentral.proquest.com/lib/cmich-ebooks/detail.action?docID=3051839.

Doorley, Michael. *Irish-American Diaspora Nationalism: The Friends of Irish Freedom, 1916–1935.* Dublin: Four Courts Press, 2005.

Doyle, David Noel. "Catholicism, Politics, and Irish America since 1890: Some Critical Considerations." *Irish Studies* 4 (1985): 191–230.

Doyle, David Noel, and Owen Dudley Edwards, eds. *America and Ireland, 1776–1976: The American Identity and the Irish Connection.* Westport, CT: Greenwood Press, 1976.

Drury, P. J., ed. *Irish in America: Emigration, Assimilation and Impact.* Irish Studies 4. London: Cambridge Univ. Press, 1985.

DuBois, Ellen Carol. *Harriot Stanton Blatch and the Winning of Woman Suffrage.* New Haven, CT: Yale Univ. Press, 1997.

———. *Woman Suffrage & Women's Rights.* New York: New York Univ. Press, 1998.

Dye, Nancy Schrom. *As Equals and as Sisters: Feminism, the Labor Movement, and the Women's Trade Union League of New York.* Columbia: Univ. of Missouri Press, 1980.

Edwards, Rebecca. *Angels in the Machinery: Gender in American Party Politics from the Civil War to the Progressive Era.* New York: Oxford Univ. Press, 1997.

———. *New Spirits: Americans in the Gilded Age, 1865–1905.* 2nd ed. New York: Oxford Univ. Press, 2011.

Edwards, Wendy Deichmann, and Carolyn De Swarte Gifford, eds. *Gender and the Social Gospel.* Urbana: Univ. of Illinois Press, 2003.

Eichacker, Joanne Mooney. *Irish Republican Women in America: Lecture Tours, 1916–1925.* Dublin: Irish Academic Press, 2003.

Englander, Susan. *Class Conflict and Coalition in the California Woman Suffrage Movement, 1907–1912.* Lewiston, NY: Edwin Mellen Press, 1992.

Fanning, Charles. *The Irish Voice in America: 250 Years of Irish-American Fiction.* Lexington: Univ. Press of Kentucky, 1990.

———, ed. *New Perspectives on the Irish Diaspora.* Carbondale: Southern Illinois Univ. Press, 2000.

Farbman, David. "Developing an Esprit de Corps." *Rhode Island History* 56, no. 2 (1998): 35–51.

Farrell, Grace. "Beneath the Suffrage Narrative." *Canadian Review of American Studies* 36, no. 1 (2006): 49.

———. *Lillie Devereux Blake: Retracing a Life Erased.* Amherst: Univ. of Massachusetts Press, 2002.

———. "Lillie Devereux Blake (1833–1913)." *Legacy* 14, no. 2 (1997): 146–53.

Faue, Elizabeth. *Community of Suffering & Struggle: Women, Men, and the Labor Movement in Minneapolis, 1915–1945.* Chapel Hill: Univ. of North Carolina Press, 1991.

Fitzgerald, Maureen. *Habits of Compassion: Irish Catholic Nuns and the Origins of New York's Welfare System, 1830–1920*. Urbana: Univ. of Illinois Press, 2006.

Flynn, Elizabeth Gurley. *The Rebel Girl: An Autobiography*. New York: International, 1955.

Foner, Eric. "Class, Ethnicity, and Radicalism in the Gilded Age: The Land League & Irish America." *Marxist Perspectives* 1, no. 2 (1978): 1–55.

Foner, Philip. *Women and the American Labor Movement: From Colonial Times to the Eve of World War I*. New York: Free Press, 1979.

Funchion, Michael F., ed. *Irish American Voluntary Organizations*. Westport, CT: Greenwood Press, 1983.

Garraty, John, and Mark Carnes, eds. *American National Biography*. New York: Oxford Univ. Press, 1999.

Geidel, Pete. "Alva E. Belmont: A Forgotten Feminist." PhD diss., Columbia Univ., 1993.

Gimpel, James. "Reform-Resistant and Reform-Adopting Machines: The Electoral Foundations of Urban Politics, 1910–1930." *Political Research Quarterly* 46 (1993): 371–82.

Glazier, Michael, ed. *Encyclopedia of the Irish in America*. Notre Dame, IN: Univ. of Notre Dame Press, 1999.

Gleeson, David, ed. *The Irish in the Atlantic World*. Columbia: Univ. of South Carolina Press, 2012. https://ebookcentral.proquest.com/lib/cmich-ebooks/reader.action?docID=2054740.

Gordon, Ann, ed., *The Selected Papers of Elizabeth Cady Stanton & Susan B. Anthony*. Vol. 4. New Brunswick, NJ: Rutgers Univ. Press, 2006.

Harper, Ida Husted. *History of Woman Suffrage, 1900–1920*. Vol. 6. New York: Arno Press, 1969.

Harrington, John P., ed. *Irish Theater in America: Essays on Irish Theatrical Diaspora*. Syracuse, NY: Syracuse Univ. Press, 2009.

Hayes, Alan, and Diane Urquhart, eds. *Irish Women's History Reader*. London: Routledge, 2001.

Hennesey, James. *American Catholics: A History of the Roman Catholic Community in the United States*. Oxford: Oxford Univ. Press, 1981.

Hoerder, Dirk, ed. *American Labor and Immigration History, 1877–1920s: Recent European Research*. Urbana: Univ. of Illinois Press, 1983.

———, ed. *"Struggle a Hard Battle": Essays on Working-Class Immigrants.* Dekalb: Northern Illinois Univ. Press, 1986.

Hogan, David John. *Class and Reform: School and Society in Chicago, 1880–1930.* Philadelphia: Univ. of Pennsylvania Press, 1985.

Hogan, Neil. "Hartford Irishwoman Was Heroine of Suffrage Drive." *Shanachie* 18, no. 1 (2006): 1–2.

———. "Suffragist Heroine Took Up Cause of Irish Freedom." *Shanachie* 19, no. 1 (2007): 4–5.

Hoy, Suellen. "Chicago Working Women's Struggle for a Shorter Day, 1908–1911." *Journal of the Illinois State Historical Society* 107, no. 1 (2014): 9–44.

———. "The Irish Girls Rising." *Labor: Studies in Working-Class History of the Americas* 9, no. 1 (2012): 77–100. doi:10.1215/15476715-1461131.

———. "The Journey Out: The Recruitment and Emigration of Irish Religious Women to the United States." *Journal of Women's History* 6, no. 4 (1995): 64–98.

Hoy, Suellen, and Margaret MacCurtain, eds. *From Dublin to New Orleans: Nora and Alice's Journey to America, 1889.* Dublin: Attic Press, 1994.

Jacobson, Matthew Frye. *Special Sorrows: The Diasporic Imagination of Irish, Polish, and Jewish Immigrants in the United States.* Cambridge, MA: Harvard Univ. Press, 1995.

Janis, Ely. *A Greater Ireland: The Land League and Transatlantic Nationalism in Gilded Age America.* Madison: Univ. of Wisconsin Press, 2015.

———. "Land League in the United States and Ireland: Nationalism, Gender, and Ethnicity in the Gilded Age." PhD diss., Boston College, 2008.

Kane, Paula. *Separatism and Subculture: Boston Catholicism, 1900–1920.* Chapel Hill: Univ. of North Carolina Press, 1994.

Kaufmann, Polly Welts. "Julia Harrington Duff: An Irish Woman Confronts the Boston Power Structure, 1900–1905." *Historical Journal of Massachusetts* 18 (1990).

Kelly, Mary C. "'Forty Shades of Green': Conflict over Community among New York's Irish, 1860–1920." PhD diss., Syracuse Univ., 1997.

———. *The Shamrock and the Lily: The New York Irish and the Creation of a Transatlantic Identity, 1845–1921.* New York: Peter Lang, 2005.

Kenneally, James J. "Catholicism and Woman Suffrage in Massachusetts." *Catholic Historical Review* 53 (1967): 43–57.

———. *The History of American Catholic Women.* New York: Crossroads, 1990.

———. "Sexism, the Church, Irish Women." *Eire-Ireland* 21 (1986): 3–16.

Kennelly, Karen, ed. *American Catholic Women: A Historical Exploration.* New York: Macmillan, 1989.

Kenny, Kevin. *The American Irish: A History.* Harlow, England: Longman Press, 2000.

———, ed. *New Directions in Irish-American History.* Madison: Univ. of Wisconsin Press, 2003.

Kibler, M. Alison. "Pigs, Green Whiskers, and Drunken Widows: Irish Nationalists and the 'Practical Censorship' of *McFadden's Row of Flats* in 1902 and 1903." *Journal of American Studies* 42 (2008): 489–514.

———. "Rank Ladies, Ladies of Rank: The Elinore Sisters in Vaudeville." *American Studies* 38, no. 1 (1997): 97–115.

Lagemann, Ellen Condliffe. *A Generation of Women: Education in the Lives of Progressive Reformers.* Cambridge, MA: Harvard Univ. Press, 1979.

Lamoureux, Patricia A. "Irish Catholic Women and the Labor Movement." *U.S. Catholic Historian* 16, no. 3 (1998): 24–44.

Leroux, Karen. "'Lady Teachers' and the Genteel Roots of Teacher Organization in Gilded Age Cities." *History of Education Quarterly* 46, no. 2 (2006): 164–91.

———. "'Unpensioned Veterans': Women Teachers and the Politics of Public Service in the Late-Nineteenth-Century United States." *Journal of Women's History* 21, no. 1 (2009): 34–62. doi:https://doi.org/10.1353/jowh.0.0066.

Levine, Susan. *Labor's True Woman: Carpet Weavers, Industrialization, and Labor Reform in the Gilded Age.* Philadelphia: Temple Univ. Press, 1984.

———. "Labor's True Woman: Domesticity and Equal Rights in the Knights of Labor." *Journal of American History* 70, no. 2 (1983): 323–39.

Lindner, Eileen Williams. "Redemptive Politics of Henry George: Legacy to the Social Gospel." PhD diss., Union Theological Seminary, 1985.

Luddy, Maria. *Women in Ireland, 1800–1918: A Documentary History.* Cork: Cork Univ. Press, 1995.

Luddy, Maria, and Cliona Murphy, eds. *Women Surviving: Studies in Irish Women's History in the 19th and 20th Centuries.* Dublin: Poolbeg Press, 1989.

Lynch-Brennan, Margaret. *The Irish Bridget*. Syracuse, NY: Syracuse Univ. Press, 2009.

MacPherson, D. A. J. *Women and the Irish Nation: Gender, Culture and Irish Identity, 1890–1914*. New York: Palgrave Macmillan, 2012.

Manfra, Jo Ann, and Robert Kolesar. "Irishmen, Elites, and Reformers: Behavioral Continuities in Nineteenth Century Anti-Catholicism." *Mid-America* 76, no 1 (1994): 27–52.

Marsh, Margaret. *Anarchist Women, 1870–1920*. Philadelphia: Temple Univ. Press, 1981.

Marston, Sallie A. "Neighborhood and Politics: Irish Ethnicity in Nineteenth Century Lowell, Massachusetts." *Annals of the American Association of Geographers* 73, no. 3 (1988): 414–32.

Martens, Allison. "Working Women or Women Workers? The Woman's Trade Union League and the Transformation of the American Constitutional Order." *Studies in American Political Development* 23 (Oct. 2009): 143–70. doi:1017/S0898588X0990034.

Maschio, Geraldine. "Ethnic Humor and the Demise of the Russell Brothers." *Journal of Popular Culture* 26 (1992): 81–92.

Mason, Francis. "The Newer Eve: The Catholic Women's Suffrage Society in England, 1911–1923." *Catholic Historical Review* 72 (1986): 620–38.

Mattina, Anne F. "'Yours for Industrial Freedom': Women of the IWW, 1905–1930." *Women's Studies* 43 (2014): 170–201. doi:10.1080/00497878.2014.863105.

McCartan, Patrick. *With De Valera in America*. New York: Brentano, 1932.

McCarthy, Tara M. "'Progress and Poverty': Marguerite Moore, an Irish Woman in the American Reform Tradition." *Recorder: Journal of the American Irish Historical Society* 19, no. 2 (2007).

———. "Woman Suffrage and Irish Nationalism: Ethnic Appeals and Alliances in America." *Women's History Review* 23 (2014): 188–203. http://www.tandfonline.com/doi/abs/10.1080/09612025.2013.849143.

McConnaughy, Corrine M. *The Woman Suffrage Movement in America: A Reassessment*. New York: Cambridge Univ. Press, 2013.

McConnel, James. "Franchise Factor in the Defeat of the Irish Parliamentary Party." *Historical Journal* 47, no. 2 (2004): 355–77.

McCoole, Sinead. *No Ordinary Women: Irish Female Activists in the Revolutionary Years, 1900–1923*. Madison: Univ. of Wisconsin Press, 2003.

McDannell, Colleen. *The Christian Home in Victorian America, 1840–1900.* Bloomington: Indiana Univ. Press, 1986.

———. "'True Men as We Need Them': Catholicism and the Irish-American Male." *American Studies* 27 (1986): 19–36.

McDonagh, Eileen, and H. Douglas Price. "Woman Suffrage in the Progressive Era: Patterns of Opposition and Support in Referenda Voting, 1910–1918." *American Political Science Review* 79, no. 2 (1985).

McElroy, Wendy. *Individualist Feminism of the Nineteenth Century.* Jefferson, NC: McFarland, 2001.

McGreevy, John T. *Catholicism and American Freedom.* New York: W. W. Norton, 2003.

McIntyre, Stephen L. "'Our Schools Are Not Charitable Institutions': Class, Gender, Ethnicity, and the Teaching Profession in Nineteenth-Century St. Louis." *Missouri Historical Review* 92, no. 1 (1997): 27–44.

McKillen, Beth [Elizabeth]. "The Corporatist Model, World War I, and the Public Debate over the League of Nations." *Diplomatic History* 15, no. 2 (1991): 171–97.

———. "Irish Feminism and Nationalist Separatism, 1914–1923." *Eire-Ireland* 17, no. 3 (1981): 52–67.

McKillen, Elizabeth. "American Labor, the Irish Revolution, and the Campaign for a Boycott of British Goods, 1916–1924." *Radical History Review* 61 (Winter 1995): 35–61.

———. "Ethnicity, Class, and Wilsonian Internationalism Reconsidered: The Mexican-American and Irish-American Immigrant Left and U.S. Foreign Relations, 1914–1922." *Diplomatic History* 24, no. 4 (2001): 553–87.

Meagher, Timothy J. *The Columbia Guide to Irish American History.* New York: Columbia Univ. Press, 2005.

———. *Inventing Irish America: Generation, Class, and Ethnic Identity in a New England City, 1880–1928.* Notre Dame, IN: Univ. of Notre Dame Press, 2001.

Merk, Lois Bannister. "Boston's Historic Public School Crisis." *New England Quarterly* 31 (1958): 172–99.

———. "Massachusetts and the Woman Suffrage Movement." PhD diss., Radcliffe College, 1956.

"Militant Maud Malone." *Literary Digest*, 21 Dec. 1912.

Miller, Kerby. *Emigrants and Exiles: Ireland and the Irish Exodus to North America.* New York: Oxford Univ. Press, 1985.

Moloney, Deirdre. *American Catholic Lay Groups and Transatlantic Social Reform in the Progressive Era.* Chapel Hill: Univ. of North Carolina Press, 2002.

———. "Land League Activism in Transnational Perspective." *U.S. Catholic Historian* 22, no. 3 (2004): 61–74.

Monoson, S. Sara. "Lady and the Tiger: Women's Electoral Activism in New York City before Suffrage." *Journal of Women's History* 2, no. 2 (1990).

Montgomery, David. *Fall of the House of Labor: The Workplace, the State, and American Labor Activism, 1865–1925.* Cambridge: Cambridge Univ. Press, 1987.

———. "Workers' Movements in the United States Confront Imperialism: The Progressive Era Experience." *Journal of the Gilded Age and Progressive Era* 7, no. 1 (2008): 7–42.

Murphy, Cliona. *Women's Suffrage Movement and Irish Society in the Early Twentieth Century.* Philadelphia: Temple Univ. Press, 1989.

Murphy, Marjorie. *Blackboard Unions: The AFT and the NEA, 1900–1980.* Ithaca, NY: Cornell Univ. Press, 1990.

Naccarelli, Jennifer. "Guided by Their Conscience: Catholic Suffragists in America, 1890–1920." PhD diss., Claremont Graduate Univ., 2011.

Nestor, Agnes. *Woman's Labor Leader: An Autobiography of Agnes Nestor.* Rockford, IL: Bellevue Books, 1954.

Ni Bhroimeil, Una. "The American Mission: The Gaelic Revival and America, 1870–1915." PhD diss., Lehigh Univ., 1998.

———. *Building Irish Identity in America, 1870–1915.* Dublin: Four Courts Press, 2003.

Nicklason, Fred. "Henry George: Social Gospeller." *American Quarterly* 22, no. 3 (1970): 649–64.

Nolan, Janet. "Irish-American Teachers and the Struggle over American Urban Public Education, 1890–1920: A Preliminary Look." *Records of the Catholic Historical Society of Philadelphia* 103, nos. 3–4 (1992): 13–22.

———. "A Patrick Henry in the Classroom: Margaret Haley and the Chicago Teachers' Federation." *Eire-Ireland* 30 (1995): 104–17.

———. *Servants of the Poor: Teachers and Mobility in Ireland and Irish America.* Notre Dame, IN: Univ. of Notre Dame Press, 2004.

———. "Women's Place in the History of the Irish Diaspora: A Snapshot." *Journal of American Ethnic History* 28, no. 4 (2009): 76–81.

Notable American Women. Cambridge, MA: Belknap Press of Harvard Univ. Press, 1971.

Nutter, Kathleen Banks. "'The Necessity of Organization': Mary Kenney O'Sullivan, the American Federation of Labor, and the Boston Women's Trade Union League, 1892–1919." PhD diss., Univ. of Massachusetts–Amherst, 1998.

Oates, Mary J. *The Catholic Philanthropic Tradition in America.* Bloomington: Indiana Univ. Press, 1995.

O'Connor, Emmet. "James Larkin in the United States, 1914–23." *Journal of Contemporary History* 37, no. 2 (2002): 183–96.

O'Dea, John. *History of the Ancient Order of Hibernians and Ladies' Auxiliary.* Philadelphia: Keystone, 1923.

O'Donnell, Edward Thomas. "Henry George and the 'New Political Forces': Ethnic Nationalism, Labor Radicalism, and Politics in Gilded Age New York City." PhD diss., Columbia Univ., 1995.

———. "'Though Not an Irishman': Henry George and the American Irish." *American Journal of Economics and Sociology* 56, no. 4 (1997): 407–19.

O'Grady, John. *Catholic Charities in the United States.* 1930. Reprint, New York: Arno Press, 1971.

Orleck, Annelise. *Common Sense and a Little Fire: Women and Working-Class Politics in the United States, 1900–1965.* Chapel Hill: Univ. of North Carolina Press, 1995.

Orr, Brooke Speer. "Mary Elizabeth Lease: Nineteenth-Century Populist and Twentieth-Century Progressive." PhD diss., George Washington Univ., 2002.

Ó Siadhail, Padraig. *Katherine Hughes: A Life and a Journey.* Newcastle, Ontario: Penumbra Press, 2014.

Owens, Rosemary Cullen. *Smashing Times: History of the Irish Women's Suffrage Movement, 1889–1922.* Dublin: Attic Press, 1984.

Parnell, Anna. *Tale of a Great Sham.* Edited by Dana Hearne. Dublin: Arlen House, 1986.

Paseta, Senia. *Irish Nationalist Women, 1900–1918.* Cambridge: Cambridge Univ. Press, 2013. http://www.myilibrary.com?ID=568904.

"Persons in the Foreground: The Indomitable Spirit of Mother Jones." *Current Opinion* 55 (July 1913).

Pfalzgraf, Taryn Benbow. *A Critical Reference Guide from Colonial Times to the Present.* Detroit: St. James Press, 2000.

"The Public Rights of Women: A Second Round-Table Conference." *Catholic World* 59 (1894).

Reeve, Carl, and Ann Barton Reeve. *James Connolly and the United States: The Road to the 1916 Irish Rebellion.* Atlantic Highlands, NJ: Humanities Press, 1978.

Reid, Robert, ed. *Battleground: The Autobiography of Margaret A. Haley.* Urbana: Univ. of Illinois Press, 1982.

Richmond, Al. *Native Daughter: The Story of Anita Whitney.* San Francisco: Anita Whitney Anniversary Committee, 1942. https://archive.org/stream/nativedaughterst00richrich#page/70/mode/2up.

Ridarsky, Christine, and Mary Huth, eds. *Susan B. Anthony and the Struggle for Equal Rights.* Rochester, NY: Univ. of Rochester Press, 2012.

Ridge, John T. *The History of the Ancient Order of Hibernians and Ladies' Auxiliary of Brooklyn.* New York: AOH, 1985.

Rorke, Margaret Hayden. *Letters and Addresses on Woman Suffrage by Catholic Ecclesiastics.* New York: Devin Adair, n.d.

Rousmaniere, Kate. *Citizen Teacher: The Life and Leadership of Margaret Haley.* New York: State Univ. of New York Press, 2005.

Rubens, Lisa. "The Patrician Radical: Charlotte Anita Whitney." *California History* 65 (1986): 158–71.

Ryan, Louise. "Traditions and Double Moral Standards: The Irish Suffragists' Critique of Nationalism." *Women's History Review* 4, no. 4 (1995): 487–503.

Ryan, Louise, and Margaret Ward, eds. *Irish Women and the Vote: Becoming Citizens.* Dublin: Irish Academic Press, 2007.

Schmuhl, Robert. *Ireland's Exiled Children: America and the Easter Rising.* New York: Oxford Univ. Press, 2016.

Scibilia, Dominic. "Edward McGlynn: American Social Catholic." *Records of the American Catholic Historical Society* 101, nos. 3–4 (1990): 1–16.

Shanaberger, Manuel Scott. "Reverend Dr. Edward McGlynn: An Early Advocate of the Social Gospel in the American Catholic Church, an Intellectual History." PhD diss., Univ. of Virginia, 1993.

Shanley, Catherine. "The Library Employees' Union of Greater New York, 1917–1929." *Libraries and Culture* 30, no. 3 (1995).

Shea, Ann M., and Marion R. Casey. *The Irish Experience in New York City: A Select Bibliography.* New York: New York Irish History Roundtable, 1995.

Skeffington, Hanna Sheehy. *Impressions of Sinn Fein in America: An Account of Eighteen Months' Irish Propaganda in the United States.* Dublin: Davis, 1919.

Sklar, Kathryn Kish. *Florence Kelley and the Nation's Work.* New Haven, CT: Yale Univ. Press, 1995.

Soper, Kerry. "From Swarthy Ape to Sympathetic Everyman and Subversive Trickster: The Development of Irish Caricature in American Comic Strips between 1890 and 1920." *Journal of American Studies* 39 (2005): 257–96. doi:10.1017/S0021875805009710.

Sprows, Kathleen. "New Footsteps in Well-Trodden Ways: Gender, Religion and Ethnicity in Irish-America." PhD diss., Notre Dame Univ., 1999.

Stanton, Elizabeth Cady. *Eighty Years & More.* Edited by Ellen Carol Dubois. Boston: Northeastern Univ. Press, 1993.

Sterne, Evelyn Savidge. *Ballots and Bibles: Ethnic Politics and the Catholic Church in Providence.* Ithaca, NY: Cornell Univ. Press, 2004.

———. "Bringing Religion into Working-Class History: Parish, Public, and Politics in Providence, 1890–1930." *Social Science History* 24 (2000): 149–82.

Streitmatter, Rodger. "The Nativist Press: Demonizing the American Immigrant." *Journalism and Mass Communication Quarterly* 46, no. 4 (1999): 673–83.

Strom, Sharon Hartman. "Leadership and Tactics in the American Woman Suffrage Movement: A New Perspective from Massachusetts." *Journal of American History* 62, no. 2 (1975): 296–315.

Sullivan, Dennis. "Eamon de Valera and the Forces of Opposition in America, 1919–1920." *Eire-Ireland* 19 (1984).

Tarpey, Marie. "Joseph McGarrity, Fighter for Irish Freedom." *Studia Hibernica* 11 (1971): 164–80.

Tax, Meredith. *Rising of the Women.* New York: Monthly Review Press, 1980.

Tentler, Leslie Woodcock. *Seasons of Grace: A History of the Catholic Archdiocese of Detroit.* Detroit: Wayne State Univ. Press, 1990.

Thomas, Edmund B., Jr. "School Suffrage and the Campaign for Women's Suffrage in Massachusetts, 1879–1920." *Historical Journal of Massachusetts* 25, no. 1 (1997): 1–17.

Thomas, Samuel J. "Catholic Journalists and the Ideal Woman in Late Victorian America." *International Journal of Women's Studies* 4 (1981): 89–100.

———. "Portraits of a 'Rebel' Priest: Edward McGlynn in Caricature, 1886–1893." *Journal of American Culture* 7, no. 4 (1984): 19–32.

Van Ingen, Linda. "'One Can't Live on Air': Sarah McComb and the Problem of Old-Age Income for Single Women Teachers, 1870s–1930s." *History of Education Quarterly* 54, no. 2 (2014): 172–96.

Van Voris, Jacqueline. "Daniel O'Connell and Women's Rights: One Letter." *Eire-Ireland* 17, no. 3 (1982): 37.

Vapnek, Lara. *Breadwinners: Working Women and Economic Independence, 1865–1920.* Urbana: Univ. of Illinois Press, 2009.

———. *Elizabeth Gurley Flynn: Modern American Revolutionary.* Boulder, CO: Westview Press, 2015. http://ebookcentral.proquest.com/lib/cmich-ebooks/detail.action?docID=1771947.

Voss, Kim. *The Making of American Exceptionalism: The Knights of Labor and Class Formation in the Nineteenth Century.* Ithaca, NY: Cornell Univ. Press, 1993.

Walsh, Victor. "'A Fanatic Heart': The Cause of Irish-American Nationalism in Pittsburgh during the Gilded Age." *Journal of Social History* 15 (Winter 1981): 187–204.

Ward, Alan J. *Ireland and Anglo-American Relations, 1899–1921.* Toronto: Univ. of Toronto Press, 1969.

Ward, Margaret. "Gendering the Union: Imperial Feminism and the Ladies' Land League." *Women's History Review* 10 (2001): 71–92.

———. *Unmanageable Revolutionaries: Women and Irish Nationalism.* London: Pluto Press, 1983.

Weir, Robert E. "A Fragile Alliance: Henry George and the Knights of Labor." *American Journal of Economics and Sociology* 56, no. 4 (1997): 421–39.

Wesser, Robert F. *A Response to Progressivism: The Democratic Party and New York Politics, 1902–1918.* New York: New York Univ. Press, 1986.

Whelan, Bernadette. "Women on the Move: A Review of the Historiography of Irish Emigration to the USA, 1750–1900." *Women's History Review* 24, no. 6 (2015): 900–916. doi:10.1080/09612025.1013305.

Willard, Frances, and Mary Livermore, eds. *American Women.* 1897. Reprint, New York: Mast, Crowell, and Kirkpatrick, 1973.

Woloch, Nancy. *"Muller v. Oregon": A Brief History with Documents.* Boston: Bedford/St. Martin's, 1996.

Index

Italic page number denotes illustration

Tara M. McCarthy is an associate professor of history at Central Michigan University.